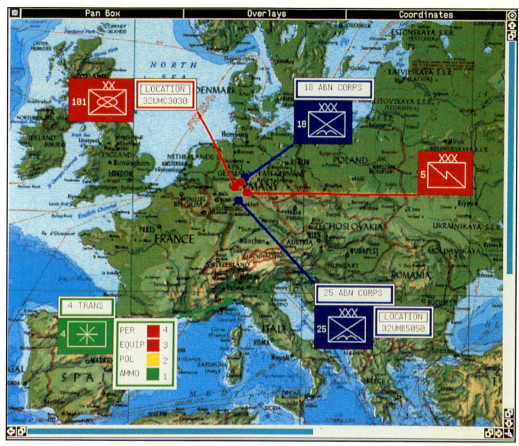

Color Plate 2.2 SITMAP Unit Overlays.

SITMAP monitors combat units that are players in a wargame or simulation. Unit overlays display interactive icons that show various levels of detail, such as a unit's location, symbol, name, and equipment status. These overlays are updated in real-time as new information is available.

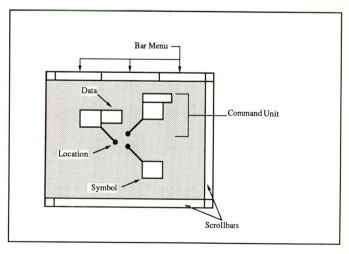

Applications of
Object-Oriented Programming

Applications of
Object-Oriented Programming

Edited by

LEWIS J. PINSON

RICHARD S. WIENER

University of Colorado at Colorado Springs

ADDISON-WESLEY PUBLISHING COMPANY
Reading, Massachusetts • Menlo Park, California • New York
Don Mills, Ontario • Wokingham, England • Amsterdam • Bonn
Sydney • Singapore • Tokyo • Madrid • San Juan

Many of the designations used by manufacturers and sellers to distinguish their products are claimed as trademarks. Where those designations appear in this book, and Addison-Wesley was aware of a trademark claim, the designations have been printed in initial caps or all caps.

The programs and applications presented in this book have been included for their instructional value. They have been tested with care, but are not guaranteed for any particular purpose. The publisher does not offer any warranties or representations, nor does it accept any liabilities with respect to the program or applications.

Library of Congress Cataloging-in-Publication Data

Pinson, Lewis J.
    Applications of object-oriented programming / by Lewis J. Pinson, Richard S. Wiener.
        p. cm.
    Includes bibliographical references.
    ISBN 0-201-50369-7
    1. Object-oriented programming.   I. Wiener, Richard, 1941-
II. Title.
QA76.64.P56 1990   89-77781
005.1—dc20   CIP

ABCDEFGHIJ–DO–943210

CONTENTS

Preface   _ix_

Chapter 3

Building Interactive Graphical Applications Using C++   66
Raghunath Raghavan

Chapter 4

Development of a Visual Database Interface: An Object-Oriented
Approach   101
  C. Thomas Wu

Chapter 5 _____

DoubleVision: A Foundation for Scientific Visualization   139
Mary Mock

Chapter 6 _____

Object-Oriented Design of a Branch Path Analyzer for C-Language Software Systems   164
Lewis J. Pinson and Richard S. Wiener

This book presents a set of case studies implemented in several object-oriented programming languages including C++, Smalltalk, Objective-C, Actor, and Object Pascal. Each case study represents a system that has actually been designed and implemented. The focus in each case study is on the object-oriented design, its implementation, and the lessons learned.

The book is aimed at software engineers and programmers who wish to see OOP in action and to learn more about C++, Smalltalk, Objective-C, Actor, or Object Pascal or who wish to compare these languages. Since the emphasis in each case study is on design, this book may be read without concern about any particular OOP language. It is hoped that we may all learn from the experiences of others and in particular the experience and opinions of the authors of the chapters in this book.

Chapter 1 describes a library of reusable software objects and uses them to model the operations of a typical wafer fabrication shop in a semiconductor manufacturing facility. BLOCS (Berkeley Library of Objects for Control and Simulation) is implemented in the language Objective-C. BLOCS has been used to design and test different strategies for real-time resource allocation decisions, including short-term scheduling and personnel assignment in semiconductor manufacturing. This chapter discusses the design rationale and the experience obtained from implementing the system.

Chapter 2 describes the object-oriented design and Objective-C implementation of SITMAP, a military situation assessment tool that monitors a combat situation by presenting map backgrounds and real-time tactical overlays. An object-oriented design is used because it offers better extensibility, reusability, and maintainability than other software development techniques. SITMAP's highly interactive graphical user interface, implemented in Objective-C, was modelled after the Smalltalk-80 Model-View-Controller paradigm.

Chapter 3 describes an object-oriented framework used for developing interactive graphical applications. While no one particular application is described, the common architecture underlying all Mentor Graphics applications is presented. The foundation libraries for the framework are written in C++. A number of applications using the framework have been written in C++, C, and Pascal. This chapter deals primarily with the architectures of the user interface management system and the graphics subsystem.

Chapter 4 presents a visual interface, called GLAD (Graphics Language for Accessing Database), that supports an object-oriented data model and operates under a windowing environment. The implementation is in Actor. This chapter provides a brief description of Actor and discusses the design and implementation of GLAD.

Chapter 5 presents DoubleVision, a general-purpose visualization program to display two-dimensional data. DoubleVision was written in Object Pascal for the Apple Macintosh, using MacApp, a class library for the Macintosh.

Chapter 6 describes the object-oriented design and Smalltalk-80 implementation of a branch path analysis software system for the C language. A specific approach to completion of an object-oriented design is presented and used in developing the branch path analyzer. The system was designed and prototyped using Smalltalk-80 on the Sun 3/50 workstation.

Colorado Springs

L. J. P.
R. S. W.

CHAPTER 1

Berkeley Library of Objects for Control and Simulation of Manufacturing (BLOCS/M)

C.R. Glassey and S. Adiga
Department of Industrial Engineering & Operations Research,
University of California at Berkeley

1.1 NATURE OF THE APPLICATION

1.1.1 Introduction

Production control in a manufacturing system is defined [21] as the function of directing or regulating the orderly movement of goods (and services) through the entire manufacturing cycle from the requisitioning of raw materials to the delivery of finished product to meet the objectives of customer service. The term *shop-floor control* is used synonymously with the term *production control* in the literature. Most production shops operate in an environment constrained by availability of resources. Some of the important resources are materials, equipment, and labor. In our opinion, one of the most important problems in shop-floor control is that of real-time resource allocation. Most of our work is focused on developing decision strategies for real-time resource allocation. Examples of such decisions include (1) which lot to select from a queue when a machine becomes idle (the traditional dispatching decision), (2) when new lots should be released into the factory, and (3) which machine to repair next.

The study of such decisions requires constructing simulations of complex production systems incorporating different decision rules. We had to resort to writing our own software, as the traditional approaches did not meet these needs.

1.1.2 Background

As a part of our earlier research [8] in this area, a special-purpose simulation of wafer fabrications called FABSIM [18] was written. This program contained about 6000 lines of

C source code, but it represented only the small set of real-world phenomena that were important for that particular research. A second version of FABSIM was written to expand its scope slightly; this simulation required an additional 2000 lines of source code and considerable effort by a second student in understanding the original program. At this point it became obvious that FABSIM was threatening to become a monster that would be difficult to document and maintain, particularly since our software was not supported by a professional crew of programmers but by graduate students with a high turnover rate (they finish their degrees).

After a careful examination of the software options available to us, we decided to use an object-oriented approach to software design to build our simulation library. Details of our deliberations can be found in Adiga and Glassey [2]. Considerations of system portability, computer resource requirements, developmental and run-time efficiency, support for numerical computation, and so forth, made us decide in favor of a C implementation over Smalltalk and Lisp implementations of OOP. Finally, we selected Objective-C (a product of Stepstone Corp., Sandy Hook, CT) as our implementation language. Objective-C offers the option of having an interpreter to facilitate interactive development and a compiler to achieve faster run times. A library of software objects known as ICpak 201 is available for use with Objective-C. This library allows us to design specialized user interfaces. Another advantage offered by Objective-C is that method binding can be done in either compile time or run time.

1.1.3 Project Objectives

Reuse, extension, and maintenance of software objects are the main productivity benefits we sought from our adoption of object-oriented programming technology. Software reusability is a goal of great promise; however, it is also a goal whose promise has been largely unfulfilled [3]. Readers are referred to the September 1984 issue of *IEEE Transactions on Software Engineering* [11] for more detailed discussion and different perspectives on the topic of software reuse.

According to Meyer [4], simply being organized will not help one design reusable software; the issues are technical, not managerial. Designing types (or classes) for reusability gives one leverage when program functionality is included [9]. Designing for reusability includes identification of object behaviors that are useful in more than one context. Designing for maintenance involves designing objects to be independent of others. We formulated a set of important design goals for the library of software objects that we set out to build.

We had no intention of developing yet another general-purpose simulation language; nor did we attempt to build a monolithic general-purpose factory simulator that could be used for all situations. Instead, our plan was to design and build a library of software modules or "software-ICs" [6]. Based on these considerations, we established several design goals for this library.

The first goal was to make it easy to assemble special-purpose simulation models, customized for individual research questions. Effective research is largely asking the right question, which is often simple but abstract. Consequently, a research simulation model should contain no more detail than is required to explore the particular question at hand. Our strategy was to design a library of reusable software objects. With the right library of software objects, we expected that the work of designing simulations would be one of choosing and interconnecting objects of interest and linking those objects with code of one's own research strategy related to the problem one is trying to solve.

The second goal was that the library should be easily modified and extended and that parts of it could be reused in other contexts. Since we could not anticipate in detail all possible future research questions, we could be sure that added functionality would be required. The inheritance of methods and variables in the hierarchy of object classes allowed the programming of customized simulation models with economy of effort. Achievement of this objective depended to a large extent on identifying the proper conceptual framework for the library of objects and on the use of design principles that capitalized on the strengths of the object-oriented programming paradigm.

The third, and the least important, goal was that simulation models assembled from the library run reasonably efficiently.

Finally, the overall goal was that the library must be easy to understand, both the individual objects and the way they work together.

1.1.4 Design Principles

Several design principles are deduced from the goals for the library. These principles are as follows.

Objects should be simple, which implies that each object performs only one major function. For example, objects in the class WorkStation maintain the status of machines in a workstation but do not keep track of which lots are in queues at the workstation. We are willing to increase the number of different classes of objects in order to keep individual objects simple.

The interactions among objects should be simple, logical, consistent, and unambiguous. Since objects interact only by sending messages and receiving replies, it is easy to observe this principle, provided one observes a related principle of object-oriented programming, namely, that messages between objects should not rely on the internal data structure of objects. For example, the initial position of the WorkStation state vector happens to contain the number of idle machines. However, the format for the state query to a workstation is machinesIdle not machinesInState: 0. The location of the idle machine counter in the state vector is an internal WorkStation matter, a fact that no other object uses.

The library should impose as few restrictions as possible on the way different objects are "mixed and matched" in assembling a simulation, much as a stereo music system can be readily assembled by choosing speakers, amplifiers, tuners, and turntables. We strive for "plug compatibility." Fortunately, the inheritance mechanism facilitates this objective.

All communication between objects and humans should be in the form of natural language text strings, for example, "Lithography workstation" instead of "WS 5." However, communication among objects can be designed for execution efficiency.

The preceding principles guided our design of the software objects named as BLOCS (Berkeley Library of Objects for Control and Simulation)/M (Manufacturing).

1.2 CONCEPTUAL DESIGN AND IMPLEMENTATION

This section describes our approach to the design of the software object library BLOCS/M (Berkeley Library of Objects for Control and Simulation of Manufacturing), its structure, and some of the techniques used to enforce our design guidelines in implementing the objects.

1.2.1 Relating to Object-Oriented Concepts

The domain of object-oriented programming offers many attractive features to model a manufacturing system (which might be a factory). Some of the obvious correspondences between the two domains follow.

In our view, a manufacturing system (which might be a factory) consists of objects like machines, workers, and lots (batches of piece parts). The state variables of these objects change in response to events, such as the completion of a machining operation on a lot; these events occur at discrete points in time. There is a natural one-to-one correspondence between physical objects in a factory and instances of software objects that represent them. The encapsulation within software objects of local data (instance variables) representing the state of the physical object and procedures (methods) for updating the state variables provides modularity of software.

The use of the object-oriented programming paradigm of "send messages to objects" in place of "procedure calls with parameters" is a convenient way to represent a real-world event. For example, when the message endProductionOperation is sent to the object representing a workstation, that object increments its count of idle machines and decrements its count of busy machines. The same message can be sent to a lot, which will change its status variable from "busy" to "waiting" and will also increment another instance variable: nextOperation. This use of polymorphism emphasizes the fact that the same event is experienced by several objects of different classes, which react in ways appropriate to their individual natures.

Finally, the inheritance of methods and instance variables by use of a hierarchical class structure permits the addition of complexity and functionality to simple objects as necessary by creating subclasses of existing classes. The objects in the new (sub)class will recognize all the messages of the original parent class as well as new messages to implement new functions, so that other objects that work with the original simple versions will still work with the new complex objects. This feature is particularly useful in constructing special-purpose simulations for research purposes because it avoids unnecessary complexity, permitting run-time efficiency, and also avoids confusing the researcher.

1.2.2 Overall Approach

An examination of the contemporary literature on related topics did not reveal any specific guidelines useful in our application. Hence we decided to avoid a narrow focus on the requirements specification and instead to rely more on the use of our knowledge base. This approach was consistent with the recent practices aimed at improved systems life-cycle management [19].

We began by designing several simple, special-purpose factory simulations, using the object/message paradigm and a new design tool—the message flow diagram described in Section 1.2.6. These initial designs were then used to identify the common structure for a generalized design for the simulation library. The design principles and the subsequent design of the library described here are the result of experience gained both in these object-oriented designs and the background investigations and data collection that resulted in FABSIM.

The development approach we followed falls into the category of "incremental development" described by Boehm [4]. The objects in the library are being developed in increments of functional capability as required by applications. The advantages of this approach allow us to incorporate our end users' experience in refining the product.

1.2.3 The Conceptual Framework: Discrete Event Simulation of Manufacturing Systems

This section describes briefly the conceptual framework we have used for the discrete event simulation of manufacturing systems. We have underlined words representing objects that have corresponding classes in the BLOCS system.

In a discrete event simulation, the time sequence of real-world events is reproduced by the simulation; the state of the simulated system changes only at the discrete times when events occur. After the state update has been computed, the simulation clock is advanced to the time of the next event.

A manufacturing system (a factory, for example) is composed of machines, production workers, maintenance workers, work-in-progress inventory, materials-handling equipment, and so on. Machines are often grouped together in workstations. Work-in-progress inventory typically moves from workstation to workstation in lots (batches of identical piece parts or subassemblies). At a workstation, an operation (an elemental step in the manufacturing process) is performed on (the piece parts of) a lot. The sequence of operations is determined by the technology of the manufacturing process. If each operation can be performed at only one workstation, the operation sequence determines the route (the sequence of workstation visits) a lot must follow. Events that cause changes in the state of the components of the manufacturing system include the arrival of a lot at a workstation, the beginning (and completion) of an operation on a lot, failure or repair of a machine, and so forth. Some events are exogenous (machine failures, for example), while others are the result of resource allocation decisions such as the beginning of an operation or the repair of a machine.

Resource allocation decisions are associated with the beginning of a task. For the duration of the task, the allocated resources are busy and cannot be assigned to another task. For example, a simple production task occupies a single machine and a single lot (and perhaps a production worker) until it is finished. A repair task likewise occupies a machine and a maintenance worker. The events that mark the beginning and end of a task generally change the state of several resources simultaneously.

Since much of our research is supported by firms in the semiconductor industry, we have concentrated our efforts on developing objects that represent wafer fabrication. We have extended and modified these classes to model other kinds of manufacturing processes discussed later, but we have not developed extensions to represent assembly lines or automatic storage and retrieval systems.

Implementation. The update of the simulation clock in response to discrete events results in the interaction of objects in two classes: Timer and FutureEvent. A simulation will contain only one instance of the class Timer. This global timer is a sorted collection of instances of the class FutureEvent, kept in order of increasing wake-up time. It also contains the simulation clock. The timer drives the simulation by repeating the simple three-step cycle: Remove the next event (of earliest wake-up time), advance the simulation clock to the wake-up time, and send the message wakeUp to the event.

Future events may be permanent or temporary objects. Only objects in this class or its subclasses can be stored on the timer's event calendar. Each future event contains its wake-up time and a method of comparing itself with other future events on the basis of wake-up time. When an instance of this class is created, the duration of the event must be specified. This duration is added to the current simulation clock time, and the sum is stored as the wake-up time instance variable. The event is then added to the timer automatically. When an event receives a wake-up message from the timer, it sends a message to a particular object (its owner). FutureEvent was designed as an abstract superclass and was not much used directly.

Factory State. The state of the factory is actually the union of the state vectors of all of its component resources: machines, workers, and workpieces. However, many resource allocation decisions are indifferent to the identity of these low-level objects. For example, if machines in a workstation are really identical, it makes no difference which one is assigned to a particular production task. The identity of the lower-level objects should not be explicitly introduced into a simulation unless really needed. In our design, access to lower-level objects (for example, machines) is only by way of the aggregate object (workstation). For this reason, the level of detail need not be uniform across all objects in a simulation.

Resource objects change their states when events occur; often several objects are involved in a single event. For example, the start or end of a production operation will change the state of a workstation, a lot, and perhaps a skill group (of workers).

Resource. BLOCS includes an abstract superclass Resource. This class implements several utility methods for maintaining a state vector and cumulative data for analyzing simulation results that are used by its subclasses: Lot, WorkStation, and SkillGroup.

BasicLot. A basic lot has only three possible states: waiting, in-process (at a WorkStation), and in-transit (between workstations). It also has several instance variables: number of pieces, next step number, workstation (of next operation), route, and entry time (into the factory). The methods that change the state of the lot are startTransport, endTransport, startProduction, and endProduction. This last method also increments the next step number and updates the WorkStation variable from information obtained from its route.

WorkStation. Instances of this class represent collections of identical machines and maintain aggregate information about machine states. The state vector of a workstation is just a vector of counters that keep track of the number of machines in each state. The state vectors of the simple WorkStation have only two elements: the number of idle machines and the number of busy machines. These vectors are updated by the startProduction and endProduction methods. The startProduction method decrements the count of idle machines and increments the count of busy machines by 1, and endProduction does the reverse.

UnreliableWorkStation. As the name suggests, the machines in an unreliable workstation can fail. Hence the state vector contains two additional elements to count the number of machines waiting repair and the number undergoing repair. The methods that alter these state variables are fail and startRepair and endRepair.

SkillGroup. The SkillGroup class was designed to represent a collection of workers with identical skills. We have had very little experience using this class in simulations because we have generally studied factories in which workers were not a bottleneck resource, so we will not discuss it here.

Tasks. An important subclass of FutureEvent is Task, also an abstract superclass, not expected to be used itself. Task represents a temporary association of resources required to accomplish a production operation or other elementary job in the factory. Pointers to these resource objects are instance variables that must be specified when a task is created. A task has a fixed duration, determined when it is created. When it is created, and again when it receives the wakeUp message from the timer at the end of its duration, Task sends a suitable start (or end) message to all of its resources. The actual message is different in each subclass.

The last thing a task does, on receiving the wakeUp message, is to free itself. Thus a task is designed to be a transient object, created for a particular purpose and then destroyed.

ProductionTask. When an instance of the ProductionTask class is created, its resources (workstation, lot, and possibly skill group) must be specified. The create method will calculate the duration of the task, which may be deterministic or random. This method assumes that lots can be queried for route and that route will return a distribution type, which may be deterministic.

As soon as it is created, ProductionTask sends the startProduction message to all its resources and (like all future events) adds itself to the timer. It also removes the lot from the queue associated with its workstation. When it receives the wakeUp message from the timer, it sends the endProduction to its resources and frees itself.

TransportTask. TransportTask only has two resources: a lot and a destination workstation. The duration may depend on both the origin and the destination if they are specified at creation (in which case the time is obtained from a global object called travelTimeTable). Alternatively, the duration may be specified as an argument of the create method.

TransportTask sends to lot the message startTransport when it is created and sends endTransport when it is awakened by the timer. It also adds the lot to the queue associated with the destination workstation.

RepairTask. RepairTask always has a workstation, and possibly a skill group, as a resource. When created, the repair task obtains its duration from the workstation and sends startRepair to all its resources. When awakened by the timer, it sends endRepair.

Queues. A queue is a dynamic collection of objects that are waiting for a particular service, for example, lots waiting to be processed at a workstation or workstations waiting for repair. In our simulations of manufacturing, we usually have a queue associated with each workstation. This association is maintained by the use of a parallel array structure, discussed in Section 1.2.7.

Data Collection. Simulation results must be written to files for subsequent statistical analysis and graph plotting. The analysis of simulation results is treated extensively in Law and Kelton [13], for example. Typical quantities of interest are the estimated average number of busy machines at each workstation and the average size of each queue. It is also useful to calculate the variance of each such estimate; such a technique is described in Law and Kelton. The idea is to partition the simulation time line into blocks. A subclass of FutureEvent called BlockEnd sends a reInitialize message to selected resource objects periodically (at the end of each simulation block). Each object that is a subclass of Resource maintains not only a state vector but also a history vector that is the time integral of the state vector. For example, one element of the state vector of WorkStation is the number of busy machines. Let $n(t)$ be the value of this element at time t. Let $N(t)$ be the corresponding element in the history vector,

$$N(t) \;=\; \int_{t_0}^{t} n(x)dx$$

where t_0 is the beginning of the current simulation block. Then $N(t)/t$ is the average number of machines busy during that interval. Since $N(t)$ is a step function, its integral is calculated by adding a rectangular area each time $n(t)$ changes. This rectangular area is $(t-t_1)n(t)$, where t_1 is the time of last change and $n(t)$ is the value of the state variable prior to the step change. When a resource object receives the reInitialize message, it writes its history vector to a file and resets the history vector to zero. The block duration and the number of blocks in the simulation are fixed when the BlockEnd object is created.

In addition, the instantaneous value of the state vector of any resource object can be sampled and written to a file when it receives the message sampleStatus. This message is sent periodically by an object called a Sampler. The operation of Sampler is very similar to the operation of BlockEnd.

Decision Making. We strive for a strict separation between those objects that represent physical states and those that implement decision heuristics. This distinction is consistent with that between "plant" and "control" in control theory and follows from the "one object– one function" principle. Our resource objects contain no decision-making ability, not even implicitly.

In our first design, all resource allocation decisions were, in principle, made by a software object called Manager. Although different decision strategies would require different versions of Manager, they could use the same resource objects. Different decision strategies rely on different information. In our first design, we separated the functions of decision making from those of data collection, to be done by an object called a data summarizer. Experience convinced us that this distinction was not as clear as it first appeared, and we have written many simulations without a Manager object. We adopted the convention that every event, when it is completed, would inform the data summarizer, a single global object.

We have found it desirable to decentralize decision support functions as much as possible. For example, a very large class of decision rules for picking the next lot from a queue (the dispatching decision) can be implemented by calculating a priority index of each lot and then picking the lot with the largest index. We provide for each lot (and, indeed, for each resource object) a companion decision information object, abbreviated dInfo, and a method priorityIndex. When a lot receives this message, it transmits it to its dInfo object and returns the result. While this procedure requires an extra message sequence, its advantage is that different schemes for calculating a priority index can be programmed into different versions of the lot dInfo object without altering the code in lot. We have carried the idea of decentralized decision making one step further by providing Queue with a method max-PriorityIndex. When a queue receives this message, it sends the priorityIndex message to all its lots and returns the lot that reported the maximum value. Thus not only is the data support for decision making highly decentralized but so is the actual decision itself. There is no need for a Manager object. Constructing simulation to explore new heuristics for dispatching often requires nothing more than providing a new method in a lot dInfo object for calculating the lot priority index.

Utility Objects. Utility objects are designed to enhance the features of applications. An example is NameArray, which allows users to use an English name that they understand to address the physical objects. It implements the method findByName: aName that returns the object that has an instance variable, name, that contains the value aName. A NameArray is designed to be a permanent collection of objects, which are added as they are created. Examples are the standard globals workStationList and queueList. When an object is added to an instance of NameArray, it assigns to the object a number, its location in the NameArray. This number is used mainly to reduce external referencing between objects, as discussed in Section 1.2.7. So, this object enables users a friendly interface while maintaining the number for internal referencing. Most simulations have a queue associated with each workstation. The existence of the workStationList and the queueList in parallel represents this association.

```
queueList: Q0 Q1 Q2 Q3 . . .
workStationList: W0 W1 W2 W3 . . .
```

Thus W2, the workstation in position 2 of the workstation list, is associated with Q2, the queue in position 2 of the queue list. In order to utilize this structure, all resource objects, queues, and many others implement the name and number messages. The following code fragment shows how to access the queue corresponding to the ion implant workstation:

```
extern id queueList, workStationList
id aWks; // a work station
aWks = [workStationList findByName:"Ion Implant"];
return [queueList at:[aWks number]];
```

Several other utility objects have been implemented as extensions of Stepstone's Foundation Library. These include

— IntVector, which extends IntArray to implement methods for vector arithmetic

— IntTable, which allows access to integers by a row and a column index

— PerfOrdCltn, which extends OrdCltn to implement search and extract methods.

This last utility object can return individual objects (or subcollections) from a collection.

The inheritance tree for the major objects in BLOCS/M is shown in Fig. 1.1. Note that the root objects in the subtrees are subclasses of the Stepstone Foundation Library.

1.2.4 Objects/Assumptions Design Table

Table 1.1 is a representation of the way the design of object classes is driven by the physical assumptions of the simulation. It is quite useful for communicating the overall structure of the library from an application point of view. Simulation event-related objects are not listed in this table because they are used in all simulations independent of the model; decision support objects are also not listed because, in general, their design depends on all physical assumptions as well as on the particular decision algorithms under investigation.

Table 1.1 indicates whether a particular assumption requires the presence of the generic object in the simulation or a special version of the object. Because we have restricted each object to a single function, each assumption affects the design of only a few objects. Blanks in the table indicate objects that are independent of the assumption.

1.2.5 Design of the Object Hierarchy

As discussed earlier, we identified the objects of interest by relating software objects to the domain of semiconductor manufacturing and discrete event simulation. Our first priority was to focus on the functional specifications of individual objects. That is, we did not define any inheritance hierarchy to start with. We then examined the objects for common instance variables and methods. This allowed us to abstract superclasses. For example, the common need to maintain and update state vectors and history vectors in the objects WorkStation, SkillGroup, and BasicLot gave rise to the superclass Resource. The main function of this abstract class is to propagate the facilities to maintain history and status to any object that needs it.

The inheritance linkage with the Objective-C foundation library was decided on the basis of matching what we wanted our objects to perform with the functionality offered by the objects in the foundation library. For example, two of the basic functions that object Queue is expected to perform are (1) to add a Lot and (2) to remove a Lot from the list maintained by Queue. It follows that the object Queue that implements these two methods should be a subclass of either OrdCltn or SortedCltn. Since the size of the Queue (or the number of items to be maintained) is not generally predetermined and is subject to variation during the program, Queue had to be declared as a subclass of OrdCltn. SortedCltn does not allow dynamic resizing of the collection of objects.

Timer is an object essential in any implementation of discrete event simulation. Readers are referred to a book on simulation by Law and Kelton [13] for details on implementation of time-handling procedures in discrete event simulation. Timer's main function is to maintain a list of future events and to send a message to the corresponding object when it is time for an event to take place. To perform its function, it is necessary for Timer to maintain

Figure 1.1 —————————————————————————————————

Inheritance Tree for Major Objects in BLOCS/M.

```
FutureEvent
├──Task
│    ├─ProductionTask
│    │   ├─MultiPhaseTask
│    │   ├─RepairTask
│    │   ├─TransportTask
│    │   ├─MoveTask
│    │   └─SetUpTask
├──FailureEvent
├──BlockEnd

Resource
├──WorkStation
│    ├─UnreliableWorkStation
│    │   ├─SetUpWorkStation
│    │   └─MultiPhWorkStation
├──SkillGroup
├─BasicLot
│    ├─Lot
├──OrdClt
├──PerfOrdCltn
│    ├─Queue
│    │   ├─NestedQueue
│    ├─Route
│    │   ├─OpnSeq
```

Subclasses of Object:

IntVector
IntTable
DataSummarizer
Display
File
InvByRoute
NameArray
Operation
Product
RandGen
SetUp
Timer

a collection of future events sorted by the time of their expected activation. Hence, we had two options: to implement Timer as a subclass of SortedCltn or to let Timer contain a sorted collection. We chose the earlier option because we wanted any object to be able to add itself to the group of objects waiting for action at some point in the future. An object can do this by sending an add message to Timer.

Table 1.1 Object/Assumption Design Table

Assumptions	Objects								
	WkS	Lot	SkG	Tsk Rcp¹	Opn	SU	Tabl²	Genr	Queue
1. Production operators are limiting				Prod	V				
(a) Multiphase tasks: wait for unload			G	Multi					
(b) Operator move time — fixed random			G	Move					
(c) Operator move time depends on source and destination			G						
2. Setups: queue by opn; individual machine	M			SetUp		G			Nested
(a) Wait for set up operator: queue	M		G						Nested
(b) Time depends on old/new operation							SetUpTime		
3. Machines fail	G			Fail				Failure	
(a) Wait for maintenance technician: queue	G		G	Rep				Repair	
4. Processing batch size > 1: batch queuing	G			Prod					Nested
5. Transport time — fixed random				Transp			Move		
(a) Transport time depends on source and destination				Prod					
(b) Wait for transport: queue³									
(c) Transport batch size > 1³									
6. Routing is not fixed				Prod G	M				
7. Lot due dates		G							
8. Due dates for customer orders of lots		G							
9. Wafer count within lot: random yield		G		Prod (M)	V				

Objects: WorkStation, Lot, SkillGroup, Task, Recipe, Operation, SetUp, Table, Event, Generators, Queue

Key: G = Generic version of this object can be used if this assumption applies
M = Modified version (subclass) is needed
V = Minor modification of Generic class (include another instance variable)

Notes: [1]Names of individual Task classes are listed where needed
[2]Names of individual Event Generator classes are listed where needed
[3]Not designed yet; we need a new Resource object to represent Transport

Our initial design resulted in a library that was used to build and test a couple of new applications. Our approach then was to add methods and instance variables as and when needed. When a new member (a new graduate student) who joined the research group after the library was designed complained that the objects were too complicated, we did some restructuring of the levels of the objects. We introduced more levels in our hierarchy. For example, our original object was Lot. A simpler version of Lot, BasicLot, was introduced as a superclass. The rationale is that simple simulations should be designed using simple objects; they should not be forced to use more complicated objects than needed.

Even after a careful structuring of the library, we realized that we had to retain some duplication of instance variables/methods, as Objective-C does not have any built-in feature to handle multiple inheritance. Hence we had to devise our own ways to implement situations when an object needed features already provided in multiple objects.

All the resource objects such as WorkStation and SkillGroup, as well as objects such as Queues, have both names and numbers to identify them. Provision for referencing by name is considered an important feature by our users. This method was achieved by putting these objects on the object NameArray (described earlier). Though Queues and WorkStations need to be on a NameArray, they cannot be descendants of a common superclass. For the reasons discussed earlier, Queue needs to be a subclass of OrdCltn, whereas WorkStation does not need to inherit any feature of OrdCltn. The same is true for Lot. We included the necessary features to qualify the objects to be on the NameArray through "include" statements in the superclass of Lot and WorkStation (i.e., Resource). The relevant segment of code is shown in Listing 1.1.

Listing 1.1 _____

```
/****************************************************************
 *
 *
 * Object Name : Resource
 *
 * November 16, 1987 written by Woo-Tsong Lin
 *
 ****************************************************************/

#include "simu.h"
@requires        IntVector, String, File, IdArray;
extern           id timer;

//Resource is the superclass for WorkStation, SkillGroup, and Lot. Contains status
vector, history vector, and methods for updating history. Also contains name and number
of the resource and pointer to the decision data object owned by the resource.

= Resource:Object(Simulation,Primitive)
{
/*********** Instance variables ****************/

unsigned  number; //an unsigned variable to record the
                  //identifier of the resource.
```
                                                                                   (continues)

```
id          statusVector,  //the id of an integer array
                            //records the status of resource.
            historyVector,  //the id of an integer array to
                            //record the cumulative history
                            //information of the resource.

            dInfo;  //pointer to the decision information
                    //object.
long        timeLastChange,  //an array to record the time
                            //of last change in status of
                            //resource.
            seed;  //stores the value of seed required
                   //for random proc time generation.
char        name[50];  // a string variable to record the
                       //description of the resource.
id          statusFile,  //The id of an instance of File to
                         //record the status of resource.
            historyFile;  //The id of an instance of File to
                          //record the history of Resource.
}
```

/********************* Factory Methods *********************/
// This factory method creates a new instance with two arrays
//with variable dimensions; initializes to 0 each element in
//statusVector, historyVector, identifier, and timeLastChange.

```
+ createSize: (unsigned) maxSize
{
    unsigned i;

    self = [self new];
    statusVector = [IntVector new: maxSize];
    historyVector = [IntVector new:maxSize];
    for (i = 0; i < maxSize; ++i)
    {
    [statusVector intAt: i put: 0];
    [historyVector intAt: i put: 0];
    }
    number = 0;
    timeLastChange = [timer currentTime];
    return self;
}
```
/************ Instance Methods ********************/

// Using methods in Name.h to set and to access number and
// name of the resource
#include "Name.h"

```
/****** Methods to set and return instance variables ******/

- dInfo: (id) aDecisionInfoObject
{
    dInfo = aDecisionInfoObject;
    return self;
}

//This instance method is used to create the status file for
// the resource. The file name is resource's name.status
// (ex: wks1.status)
- openStatusFile
{

    statusFile = [File openName: name type: "status"];
    [statusFile writeString: " STATUS FILE FOR"];
    [self writeHeaders: statusFile];
    return self;

}
//This instance method is used to write the header into
//aFile according to its resource type (ex: IDLE BUSY
//in WorkStation).
- writeHeaders: aFile
{
    id fullString, aString, strings;
    unsigned i, size;

    [aFile writeString: name];
    [aFile skipOneLine];
    fullString = [IdArray new: 5];
    strings = [IdArray new: 5];
    aString = [String str: "IDLE"];
    [fullString at: 0 put: aString];

}
:=
```

An alternate method for achieving multiple inheritance shown in Listing 1.1 is by declaring the object that qualifies as a secondary superclass as an instance object. We have not used this option much in our designs.

1.2.6 Message Flow Diagram to Show Interactions Between Objects

The message flow diagram has proven to be a useful design aid, both for conceptual understanding of the relationship among objects and also for detecting inefficiencies and omissions in the conceptual design. A message flow diagram is simply a network in which the nodes represent objects and the arcs connecting them represent messages. (See Figs. 1.2, 1.3, and 1.4.) The arcs are numbered sequentially to show the order in which messages are sent. We construct such diagrams for significant simulation events, such as the start and the end of a production operation. Such an event triggers a cascade of messages that flow

Figure 1.2

Message Flow Diagram Showing the Generation of a New Lot.

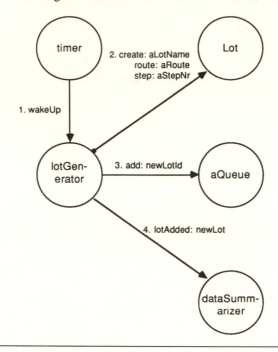

simultaneously from the view of the simulation (the simulation clock time does not change).

Message flow diagrams reveal requirements for the design of objects by showing the information content of messages. In order to send a message, the sending object must know the identity of the receiving object. Furthermore, all parameters of the message must likewise be known to the sending object; that is, they must be an instance variable, a parameter of a received message, or computable from these. For example, the diagram of Fig. 1.3 shows that message 9, sent by ProductionTask to aQueue (an instance of Queue), contains the identity of aLot. It can be verified from message 1 that ProductionTask has already received the id of aLot.

In considering alternative designs, the message flow diagram enables one to trace information flows, ensure that required information is present in senders when the message is sent, and compare designs based on the number of messages and the complexity of the message flows.

We shall use the message flow diagrams shown in Fig. 1.2, 1.3, and 1.4 to describe the interactions among some important objects in our library when they are used to simulate a production operation. The three important events shown here are generation of a new lot (which is a collection of wafers), start of a production operation, and end of the production operation. These message flow diagrams show only exchange of messages between objects

Figure 1.3 _____

Message Flow Diagram for the Event startProduction.

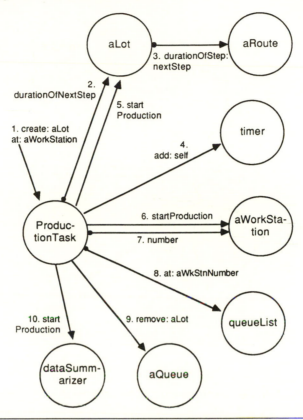

at the level of objects. We have not shown the internal activity that takes place inside the objects.

Generation of a New Lot. Figure 1.2 is the message flow diagram for the generation of a new lot in simulation of a typical semiconductor manufacturing system. The diagram assumes that the event that triggers the generation is already placed in Timer. When it is time to generate aLot, Timer sends a wakeUp message to the object lotGenerator. The message wakeUp is a standard message that is implemented by all the objects that need to be placed on the list of future events maintained by Timer. Each object implements the method wakeUp in its own unique way depending on the message sequencing requirements of the respective object.

The main function of a LotGenerator is to introduce new lots into the system at the appropriate place and time. LotGenerator does three things upon receiving a wakeUp message. First, it creates the object aLot. We know from functional specification for the Lot (derived on the basis of other message flow diagrams shown in Figs. 1.3 and 1.4) that aLot

Figure 1.4 _____

Message Flow Diagram for the Event endProduction.

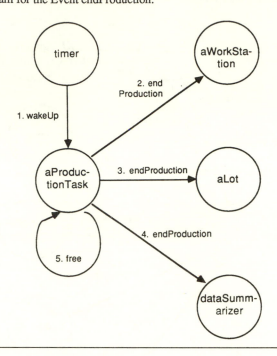

should have the id of aRoute (which contains information needed to support the processing requirements of the lot), and a step number (implications of the step number have been discussed earlier). According to one of our design principles, we have to allow users to address objects by name, if needed. Hence, the create message sent to create a lot has three arguments: a name for the lot, the route that has the relevant processing information, and a step number. This message returns with the id of the newly created lot. Then lotGenerator adds this new lot to aQueue (to be processed by a workstation whenever it is time to do so). Next, a message is sent to the object dataSummarizer informing it of the addition of a new lot to the system.

StartProduction Event. Figure 1.3 shows the message flows between objects involved when a production event begins. As discussed in an earlier section, the production process involves allocation of multiple resources. Such an allocation is generally done through the creation of an instance of the class, ProductionTask, and making it control the sequence of messages required to accomplish the task. It is important to note in this context that the object productionTask will be created only if it is found that a resource allocation is feasible—that is, the resources are free and need for a production operation has been established.

    The responsibility of productionTask is to keep the required resources busy for the duration of the production process by removing aLot from the appropriate queue. It does not know the duration of the task, as the duration depends on the lot being processed, the step in the overall process, and the number of pieces in the lot. Since all this information is related to the lot, productionTask has to ask aLot for it. It is represented by message 2 durationOfNextStep.

The information requested by productionTask is not permanently stored in aLot. The reason is that duration depends on the Route assigned to the lot, which is subject to change. Early in our design we had discovered that one of the ways of promoting plug compatibility in design is to separate the static from the variable information storage. Hence, aLot has to get the duration from aRoute. A black dot at the sending end of message 3 indicates that the message returns a value of interest to the object (the default convention followed by Objective-C is to return the receiving object's id). This value is returned by aLot to productionTask (indicated by the dot at the sending end of productionTask).

Next, productionTask requests the object timer to add the task on the list of future events that require waking up. This is indicated by the message 4 add: self duration. Timer will send a wakeUp message to end the task at time = timeNow + duration (discussed in the event endProduction). It sends the message startProduction to the resources associated with the production assignment, that is, to aLot (message 5) and to aWorkStation (message 6). The resources will then update their respective state and history vectors.

ProductionTask has to account for a lot from the queue associated with aWorkStation (message 9). Since the mapping between workstations and queues is done through a parallel array structure, it has to query aWorkStation and queueList before removal of a lot from the queue can be regularized. We have paid the price for achieving independence in design of objects in the form of two extra messages (messages 7 and 8). Details of the design of parallel array is discussed in the next subsection. The last action of productionTask in the startProduction event is to inform the dataSummarizer about the start of this activity so that it can update its summary information.

EndProduction Event. The beginning of the end production event is triggered by a wakeUp message from the timer to productionTask (message 1). This event will prompt productionTask to send endProduction message to the resources involved and the da-taSummarizer to update respective state and history vectors. The last action of this object is to free itself by sending itself a free message (message 5). It also marks the end of the temporary association of resources to accomplish a particular step in the production of a lot in the manufacturing system.

1.2.7 Approach to Reduce External References to Other Objects

Being able to design and test objects independently is an important step toward achieving plug compatibility among objects. Hence we wanted to minimize external referencing in our programs. One of the techniques we devised to achieve this goal is through the concept of parallel arrays. The following example illustrates this concept of parallel arrays.

Most production facilities provide buffers between workstations to decouple worksta-tions in order to reduce dependencies between them. This phenomenon is represented as a queue before each workstation. Each workstation is to be associated with a queue. At the factory level, a list of workstations has to be associated with a list of queues. Instead of using external referencing, we provided the link between the two sets of objects by a number that is an offset in the workstation list and queue list.

```
queueList: Q0 Q1 Q2 Q3 . . .
workStationList: W0 W1 W2 W3 . . .
```

This procedure forms what we referred to as "parallel array" structure. Thus it follows that workstation 3 will have queue 3. If an object wants to find a queue corresponding to a particular workstation, the following section of code will do it:

```
id aWorkStation, aQueue; aQueue = [queueList at:[aWorkStation number]];
```

where, number is an instance variable implemented in each workstation and queue.

A minor disadvantage of this procedure is that it has introduced an additional constraint to be followed during initialization. The sequence of creating workstations and that of creating queues should be the same. Another expense paid is through increased exchange of messages in the system.

This scheme of referencing is expected to help us minimize the problems when we extend the library, for example, if, at a later date, we decide to attach a "failure generator" to each workstation object. FailureGenerator is a class designed to help simulate the breakdown mode of each workstation. We can extend the functionality of the library without modifying the code of the objects created earlier and without adding any external references. The array structure will then look like the following:

```
queueList: Q0 Q1 Q2 Q3
workStationList: W0 W1 W2 W3
failGenList: F0 F1 F2 F3
```

Another example of parallel array structure is the implementation of the class Route. Parallel arrays are indexed by the step number (step number in a Route indicates the processing step aLot is supposed to go through in order to be turned into a product that meets customer specifications). In this case, three arrays are indexed by step number. The first array contains pointers to WorkStations, the second array is an integer vector containing pieces per lot, and the third is an integer vector containing duration per piece:

```
workStationList: W0 W1 W2 W3 W4
piecesPerLot: P0 P1 P2 P3 P4
durnPerPiece: D0 D1 D2 D3 D4
```

When any object requires duration for a step such as step 2, Route returns a value obtained by a multiplication of p2 and d2.

1.3 APPLICATIONS AND EXPERIENCE WITH THE PROJECT

In this section, we describe three different applications developed using BLOCS.

1.3.1 An Example of Using the Library

To use BLOCS in a particular instance, several objects must be written especially for the problem at hand. Most important are the data summarizer and any supporting decentralized decision-making objects. Next is an initialization routine that may be included in the main program or may be a separately compiled object. Finally, a main program must drive the simulation.

In this example, we wish to study how the efficiency of a factory depends upon the total amount of in-process inventory. We consider a very simple and abstract factory in which all workstations are identical, there is a single product that visits each workstation once in sequential order, and all lots are identical. Machines never fail; the only randomness is the variations in processing time. Inventory is maintained at a constant level, meaning that a new lot is introduced whenever a lot is completed. We are interested in how the steady state average output rate depends upon the inventory level. Inventory serves as a buffer against uncertainty; higher inventory levels mean lower probability of machines starving for lack of work. An equivalent measure of system effectiveness is the fraction of time that the bottleneck workstation is nonproductive due to lack of work. Since all machines are identical with respect to the parameters of the processing time distribution, the bottleneck machine is (after the simulation) the one with the minimum amount of starvation downtime.

The data summarizer contains the logic for starting a new lot when one is completed and for starting a new production task (if possible) when one is completed. It also maintains some summary performance statistics and writes them to files.

1.3.2 Setting Targets and Planning Shift Moves in a Semiconductor Facility

BLOCS served as the basic building block to implementing a system to assist production supervisors in scheduling flow of parts in a wafer fabrication shop belonging to a major electronics manufacturing company [16]. The scheduling system, known as SMARTS (Shift Moves and Routing Targets Scheduler), uses an object-oriented system model of the fabrication shop as the basis to predict the movement of parts through different workstations in order to determine feasible targets to be followed by the shop personnel every shift.

BLOCS provided the infrastructure for this industrial application. But many more objects were designed to provide interfaces to existing databases and desired user-interface features.

1.3.3 Modeling of a Flexible Manufacturing System

BLOCS was designed, primarily, with applications in semiconductor manufacturing systems in view. We were interested in finding out if the library could be used to model other manufacturing systems, such as Flexible Manufacturing Systems currently popular in the metal-forming industry. Hence when an opportunity arose, BLOCS was put to the test.

Flexible Manufacturing Systems (FMS) are computer-controlled integrated systems of two or more production equipment schemes linked by automated material-handling systems. An FMS is capable of producing a variety of discrete parts with minimal human intervention.

The most common example of FMS production equipment is the numerically controlled (NC) machine. The concept of FMS evolved in response to the changing needs of industry with respect to increased variety, lower volumes, and shorter life cycles of products. Readers are referred to Kusiak [12] and Talavage and Hannam [20] for more information on FMS.

The target FMS was analyzed with respect to data requirements, entities or objects in the system, and events they participated in (using message flow diagrams) to arrive at specifications for the objects needed to model the system. Object specifications, expressed in terms of instance variables and functionality required in methods, were compared with those offered by the objects in BLOCS. Identification of the initial set of objects to examine was aided by the OAD table (Table 1.1). The documentation (functional specification sheet) for those objects was examined to select the appropriate set of objects. It was found out that only two objects (WorkStation and Part) needed to be enhanced and that one new object had to be created to model FMS.

Though specific processes, equipment, and routes were different, we found that basic activities were generic enough to permit reuse of many BLOCS objects. Of course, a new dataSummarizer, a main program, and initialization routines had to be written. A couple of new objects were required to handle unique situations in FMS. One of them is described next.

One of the unique features in FMS is the employment of the concept of Group Technology (GT). Group Technology is a concept that encourages one to take advantages of similarities in shape, material, size, and so forth to group parts to optimize overall facility requirements, among other things [10]. Each part has a Group Technology code associated with it. A requirement of this model was that the parts in a queue had to be sorted by groups to determine the setup times.

We found that the object class BasicLot, which represents a group of wafers to be processed in semiconductor manufacturing, can serve the purpose of representing a typical part in FMS. But we did not have the Group Identification concept. There were two choices. One option was to spin off a specialization of BasicLot as GtLot, with the latter having two additional instance variables corresponding to their GT class, and the setup time for each part. We would also need an instance method to return the value of setup time when asked for. The other option was to create a new class named Group with the instance variables and the method mentioned for the first option. Since there is a one:many relationship between a GT class and the parts that belong to it, we decided in favor of the second option.

1.3.4 Our Experience

A summary of our experience in using an object-oriented paradigm is presented next under two categories: design and application.

Design Goals. We feel that we have been able to achieve all the design goals set by us in the beginning of the project. We have been able to reuse and extend objects in our library in both research and industrial environments. One of the reasons for our success is the fact that we tried to adhere to our design guidelines as closely as possible.

We were reasonably successful in achieving our first goal of making it possible to design easy-to-assemble, special-purpose simulations. Designing simulations is quite simple, but we have learned that one must also spend considerable time in knowing the objects in the library and what they are expected to do. To support this process, we have spent considerable time in developing extensive, functional specification documents for each object in the library. Users are expected to learn Objective-C to the extent they can write their own version of the dataSummarizer object. This requirement seems reasonable since our users have individual and sometimes unique research needs. We are in the process of developing support material of a tutorial nature to help new users transition to the OOP library concept of building systems.

Our second design goal was concerned with reusability and extendability of the software. We (and the users) are quite satisfied with the performance of BLOCS in the applications developed so far. Effectiveness, or the degree of reusability, through the library concept is determined mainly by anticipating which objects in the library are likely to change. Our decision to separate the decision-making aspects of the objects (for example, Lot) from their data storage or status-keeping functions was helpful in localizing and reducing the impact of changes. This decision is an implementation of the guideline that each object should have only one major function in the system. Another procedure that we followed was to separate the static aspects of data from the dynamic.

The third goal of run-time efficiency was achieved beyond our expectations. Since we focused more on achieving a clean design even if it meant sending a few more messages, we did not expect to get real-time performance in our early implementations. We were pleasantly surprised when our graduate students were able to design a simulation, as discussed earlier, which is being used in real-time decision-making situations. This accomplishment was probably due to the choice of a C-based language, Objective-C, as the implementation language.

Design Process. It has been documented in the literature that the classical approaches or functional decomposition approaches are inadequate for object-oriented design [5, 6, 15]. But we did not come across any specific approach that appealed to us. The objects were identified based on their correspondence to physical objects and important conceptual events in the factory.

When we started the project, we found that lack of established design guidelines, and absence of documentation of successful case studies, was a clear drawback in pursuing object-oriented design. But as we gained experience with the design process, it was no longer perceived as a problem. It is still a hurdle for newcomers to this project, however. We are now working on a methodology based on a data-modeling approach and message flow diagrams to formalize the design process. This approach should help users to come up with a set of specifications for objects in their respective systems of interest. We feel that it may make the prototyping work easier.

Initially, for some of the team members, the temptation to write code in C to bypass a few messages was almost irresistible. But with some effort, we managed to stay with our design principle of "communication only through messages." It paid off during the revisions we had to make in the initial stages. Strict adherence to an object-oriented paradigm enabled us to develop software in a group setting with relative ease. Once the interface(s) or a message protocol (in the form of message flow diagrams) was agreed upon, different people could work on different objects and we could rely on putting together working programs when needed.

Trade-Offs Involved. Most information systems involve resolution of trade-offs. Common trade-off issues we faced during our design were related to saving of a few messages by allowing violation of design principles versus a cleaner design. For example, you can save many messages by increasing the use of global objects and storing the data (related to other objects) internally. But increased use of global objects will also increase the dependence of objects which will adversely affect plug-compatibility of objects.

Sometimes it is difficult to generalize the design decisions, as they are heavily influenced by the physical process or the domain knowledge. But with the help of the overall design guidelines discussed earlier, we were able to maintain consistency in making such decisions. As discussed earlier, lots which need processing wait in queues before workstations. There is an association between lots, queues, and workstations. At first, two options were obvious. According to the first option, dataSummarizer would maintain all the queues in one place. Since dataSummarizer gets information of all aggregate level state changes, it can do this job without any additional messages. The second option was based on the assumption that most queues are physically located before workstations; hence, assign the responsibility to workstations.

Upon further consideration of some of the important research questions we intended to investigate, we realized that the degree of association among queues, workstations, and lots could change depending on the application. For example, a normal one-to-one association between a queue and a workstation could have become many-to-many when we considered multiple setups. Handling all the queues in one place would have made dataSummarizer a complicated object. We had decided earlier to avoid complicated objects wherever we could. Moreover, queue was not always a physical concept to be used to store parts in front of workstations; we could also have had queues for transporters, conceptual queues of repair jobs waiting for a repair technician, and so forth.

This discussion also reminded us that queue manipulation is a consequence of a resource allocation decision. Hence it was natural that the object responsible for carrying out the decision would inform the queue to adjust its count. This approach would be independent of physical associations of queues. Hence it was decided that those objects such as productionTask that carry out the resource allocation decision would have the responsibility to update queues.

All the preceding deliberations might seem to be too elaborate to people writing programs to be used just once. But a thorough analysis of interactions between objects, and some anticipation of potential changes, is required for designing reusable objects. Another lesson is that the time spent in conceptual design of objects will be rewarded in the form of lesser burden during the implementation stage.

Applications Design Aids. The Object/Assumptions Design (OAD) table (Table 1.1) served as a design aid only for the simpler applications and when the applications were conceptually similar to those investigated earlier. When there was no correct match between the application requirements and the object/assumptions, it could not recommend an object(s) that came closest to meeting one's needs of the application. We are investigating the design of a software system that contains explicit representation of the interrelationships between objects and their applicability in the form of rules. This system will be expected to help users in prototyping their software [1].

We found message flow diagrams very useful as aids to analyze events and to identify method and data requirements to be implemented by different objects. They also proved to be useful in verifying the correctness of program logic, as well as good communication media during our discussions.

Objective-C. Except for the lack of support for multiple inheritance, and the lack of a floating point array class, we were quite satisfied with the foundation library supplied with the Objective-C language by Stepstone Corp. We especially liked the convenience of using the interpreter for quick prototyping and testing, and the compiler for fast execution of programs when needed.

Software Maintenance. Since BLOCS has been in existence for only a short time, we have not had many problems with software maintenance. The question being addressed right now is, which of the new features/functionalities resulting from new applications are to be made part of the library? Our inclination is to add only those enhancements proven to be useful. We also feel the need for efficient configuration control techniques to handle the complexity introduced by updates/changes and for coexistence of different versions of objects in the library.

1.4 SUMMARY AND CONCLUSIONS

We chose the object-oriented programming paradigm to design simulation software because of its potential to improve the productivity of the software design and development team. After our initial investigations, we decided that a good way to achieve reusability is to build a library of software objects. The experience of designing four different-purpose simulators gave us the background for the first set of definitions of the different object classes comprising BLOCS/M. The conceptual design of these objects was based on the objectives of ease of reuse and of extendability. The development of the code since the original conceptual design has been evolutionary; there have been no radical changes in concept, but there have been many additions to functionality and new concepts have been introduced.

BLOCS/M was implemented in the Objective-C language. In its current version, BLOCS/M consists of 33 classes of software objects. Designing a simulation using BLOCS is basically customizing the objects from the library, writing one's own data summarizing object, and tying together all the objects in a main program to produce the desired result. Writing the main program is probably the last activity in the program design process for one building an application using BLOCS/M.

The use of object-oriented programming techniques requires more time and effort in the beginning to become familiar with the design philosophy and the documentation of the software objects. But once that is done, modification and extension of the objects becomes easier than writing code in conventional programming languages.

BLOCS/M has been in use for a short time only, and we are continuing our enhancements to the library. With each additional use, the functionality of our library is growing. Based on this experience, we believe that for a successful object-oriented programming application, it is essential to formulate design guidelines based on the strengths of an object-oriented paradigm and to adhere to them while implementing one's system.

In our experience, the promised productivity gains from using object-oriented programming have actually been realized. In the design phase, the gains arise from two sources. First, the mapping from real-world objects and concepts to software objects is direct and intuitive. By contrast, in the more traditional software engineering approach, deriving specifications of algorithms and data structures of the FABSIM C program was much more difficult. Second, the conceptual design is less dependent on the details of implementation than in traditional approaches. We did not modify any major concepts of our original design because of implementation difficulties.

In the implementation phase of BLOCS, the modularity of objects made coordination of team members relatively easy. Once the interface of each object was specified, users of the object had no need to know its internal workings. This modularity, together with good initial design, explains why the objects from BLOCS/M have been reused and extended in both research and industrial environments. The migration from a university research setting to an industrial environment was done in a relatively short time. Perhaps the greatest benefit, from a researcher's point of view, was that we were able to design our system in an evolutionary manner. That is, we were able to continue our research in seeking answers to interesting research questions in manufacturing systems all the time our library was growing in functionality. The effort invested in the conceptual design and a rigorous enforcement of object-oriented design principles are responsible for its success.

References

[1] Adiga, S. "A Knowledge-Based Framework for Designing Object-Oriented Simulations," *Proceedings of Research Workshop on AI and Simulation*, AAAI–88, August 1988, pp. 161–165.

[2] Adiga, S., and Glassey, C.R. "Object-Oriented Simulation to Support Research in Manufacturing Systems," ESRC 88–20, Engineering Systems Research Center, University of California at Berkeley, 1988.

[3] Biggerstaff, Ted, and Richter, Charles. "Reusability Framework, Assessment, and Directions," *IEEE Software*, March 1987, pp. 41–49.

[4] Boehm, B.W. "Software Life Cycle Factors," in (Eds.) C.R. Vick and C.V. Ramamoorthy, *Handbook of Software Engineering*, Van Nostrand Reinhold, New York, 1984, pp. 494–518.

[5] Booch, Grady. "Object-Oriented Software Development," *IEEE Transactions on Software Engineering*, February 1986, pp. 211–221.

[6] Cox, Brad J. *Object-Oriented Programming*, Addison-Wesley, Reading, MA, 1986.

[7] Glassey, C.R., and Adiga, S. "Conceptual Design of a Software Object Library for Simulation of Semiconductor Manufacturing Systems," ESRC 88–6, Engineering Systems Research Center, University of California at Berkeley, 1988.

[8] Glassey, C.R., and Resende, M.G.C. "Closed-Loop Job Release Control for VLSI Circuit Manufacturing," ORC 87–8a, Engineering Systems Research Center, University of California at Berkeley, 1987.

[9] Halbert, Daniel C., and O'Brien, Patrick D. "Using Types and Inheritance in Object-Oriented Programming," *IEEE Software*, September 1987, pp. 71–79.

[10] Ham, I.; Hitomi, K.; and Yoshida, T. *Group Technology: Applications to Production Management*, Kluwer-Nihoff, Norwell, MA, 1985.

[11] *IEEE Transactions on Software Engineering*, IEEE, September 1984.

[12] Kusiak, A. *Modeling and Design of Flexible Manufacturing Systems*, Elsevier, New York, 1986.

[13] Law, Averill M., and Kelton, W.D. *Simulation Modelling and Analysis*, McGraw-Hill, New York, 1982.

[14] Meyer, Bertrand. "Reusability: The Case for Object-Oriented Design," *IEEE Software*, March 1987, pp. 50–64.

[15] Meyer, Bertrand. *Object-Oriented Software Construction*, Prentice-Hall, Englewood Cliffs, NJ, 1988.

[16] Najmi, Adeel, and Lozinski, C. "Managing Factory Productivity Using Object-Oriented Simulation for Setting Shift Production Targets in VLSI Manufacturing," *Proceedings of AUTOFACT Conference*, Society of Manufacturing Engineers, November 1989.

[17] *Objective-C Reference Manual*, Stepstone Corporation, Sandy Hook, CT, 1987.

[18] Resende, M.G.C. "Computer Simulation of Semiconductor Fabrication," ORC 86–14, Engineering Systems Research Center, University of California at Berkeley, September 1986.

[19] Shemir, Itzhak. "Systems Analysis: A Systemic Analysis of a Conceptual Model," *Communications of ACM*, Vol. 30, No. 6 (1987), pp. 506–517.

[20] Talavage, Joseph, and Hannam, R.G. *Flexible Manufacturing Systems in Practice: Applications, Design and Simulation*, Marcel Dekker, New York, 1988.

[21] Wallace, T.F. (Ed.). *APICS Dictionary*, 4th Ed., American Production and Inventory Control Society, Falls Church, VA, 1980.

CHAPTER 2

SITMAP: A Command and Control Application

Nancy T. Knolle, Martin W. Fong, and Ruth E. Lang _____
SRI International, Menlo Park, California

2.1 INTRODUCTION

SITMAP (SITuation MAP) is a military situation-assessment tool that monitors combat situations by presenting map backgrounds and real-time tactical overlays. It is part of a command and control system, developed at SRI International, that manages, distributes, and presents large volumes of tactical information.

In late 1987 we were given the tasks of running SITMAP on both Sun Microsystems (Sun) and Hewlett Packard (HP) hardware, providing additional functionality, and deploying SITMAP to support a military exercise. Given our experience in designing, implementing, and maintaining the original version of SITMAP (which only ran on Sun hardware), we decided to abandon the procedural language implementation and adopt an object-oriented one. Because of a fixed release date, our task of redesigning and implementing SITMAP had an extremely short time line (eight months total development time).

During SITMAP's development, we spent the first two months defining our technical approach, conducting an industrywide survey on object-oriented programming environments, and training engineers in object-oriented programming. During the next six months, we designed and implemented all the required programming environment extensions (that is, object distribution and interactive graphics), as well as the SITMAP application itself.

The industrywide survey helped us establish an object-oriented programming environment that allowed us to exploit preexisting C software. The conclusions of this survey led us to chose the Objective-C programming language, ICpak 101 foundation class library, and ICpak 201 user interface toolkit, since this combination met most of our requirements, including the ability to run on different hardware platforms and windowing systems without code modification.[1]

---

[1] Objective-C is a registered trademark of The Stepstone Corp. ICpak is a trademark of The Stepstone Corp.

The following sections describe what SITMAP does, how it was designed and implemented, and how object-oriented design and programming were successfully used in this real-world application.

2.2 FUNCTIONAL DESCRIPTION

SITMAP is a military application that automates the labor-intensive process of plotting symbolic graphics on paper maps. Using high-resolution color graphics workstations, SITMAP provides terrain map backgrounds, real-time information overlays, and a graphics editor for creating and storing "grease pencil graphics." This program monitors the combat situation by tracking unit[2] and other status information stored in a tactical database. SITMAP is one application in a large military command and control system called TACTICS III.

2.2.1 The Environment

SITMAP is deployed on military exercises where the hardware consists of a variety of processors, graphics devices, and storage devices accessible through a high-bandwidth communications network. This network is a combination of local area networks (LANs) and wide area networks (WANs), typically allowing over 50 graphics workstations to be connected over distances ranging from a few meters to 500 kilometers. Since units (and their hardware) are continually being relocated, connectivity between nodes is usually poor. Within this environment, the command and control system must distribute and merge data sources, present meaningful displays, and provide real-time notification of new data.

SITMAP obtains its tactical data from TACTICS III. TACTICS III features replicated databases across network nodes, robust data storage, reliable database access, and database consistency. Because database updates can be made from any node and connectivity may be poor, it is difficult to ensure that all databases contain timely and accurate information. SITMAP and other TACTICS III applications also must alert users to critical combat situations. TACTICS III addressed these and other significant problems in information management.[3]

2.2.2 The User

Military users share the same basic need to overlay information on map backgrounds. However, they also have requirements specific to their military functions. For example, logistics personnel want to know how much fuel or ammunition friendly units have, whereas intelligence personnel are more interested in reports of enemy units.[4] Therefore, SITMAP must support many military functions, such as intelligence gathering, logistics, situation assessment, and exercise planning.

---

[2] A *unit* is an army combat unit, such as the 18th Airborne Corps or the 24th Infantry Division.

[3] For more information on TACTICS III, see Davis [4].

[4] *Friendly units* refers to the protagonists during war games, while *enemy units* refers to the antagonists.

2.2.3 System Features

Color Plate 2.1 is a picture of the *SITMAP desktop*, a miniwindow system in which windows can be opened, closed, moved, and resized.* SITMAP actually presents color displays of maps and tactical information. The lower portion of Color Plate 2.1 shows an outline of the SITMAP desktop, with each of its components labeled; each component will now be briefly described, along with any associated terminology.

Users can display a map of a region by selecting from the *map list*, a list of available maps. Several maps can be simultaneously displayed inside *map windows* on the SITMAP desktop. Because each map window is a bird's-eye view of a larger map region, users can scroll using *scrollbars* or a *pan box*. (The pan box is a miniature version of the map containing a rectangular outline. When this outline is moved or resized, the map is scrolled appropriately.) Users can also retrieve attributes of maps, such as the scale (for example, 1:50,000), dimensions, and map coordinates.

Overlays are collections of related objects displayed on top of map backgrounds. Users can select any combination of overlays through a pulldown menu in a map window. There are two types of overlays: real-time information overlays and grease pencil graphics.

Real-time information overlays, such as those displaying friendly and enemy units, are generated from data in a tactical database and are automatically updated as new data become available. If a unit's geographic location is updated, the unit is automatically moved on the map background. In all overlays, color is used to enhance the meaning of displays. For example, friendly objects are colored blue and enemy objects are colored red.

SITMAP provides real-time information overlays for different military functions. For example, army headquarters needs to monitor friendly reinforcements as they travel to the battle area, to ensure that units have enough equipment and supplies for combat. In this case, *unit displays* show the unit's location, symbol, and status information representing its combat readiness. *Unit symbols* are standard army symbols that indicate a unit's designation, size, branch, and duty. The *status displays* contain logistic information (e.g., quantities of fuel, personnel, and ammunition).

Grease pencil graphics are drawings that, before the introduction of SITMAP, had to be made with actual grease pencils on sheets of acetate laid on top of paper maps. By using SITMAP's *graphics editor*, a user can create an electronic version of grease pencil graphics. The user can create overlays corresponding to weather conditions, supply routes, communication equipment, and battle plans. Grease pencil graphics can be saved in a file for redisplay and editing; the saved overlays can also be routed to remote users.

The graphics editor is composed of *palettes* and a *view box*. Items selected from the palettes define the attributes (for example, object type, color, fill pattern, line thickness) of the current object. Users can preview a sample of the current object in the view box.

SITMAP provides specific palettes for different military functions. For example, a palette containing cold-front line styles aids a weather officer in drawing a weather overlay. A line style palette containing FLOT (forward line of troops), FEBA (forward edge of battle area), and barbed-wire line styles aids a planning officer in drawing a combat situation overlay.

---

*Color Plates for this chapter appear inside the front cover of this book.

Figure 2.1 _____
SITMAP Components.

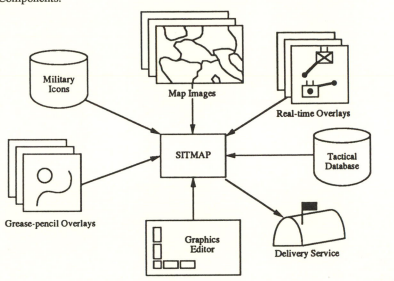

SITMAP's color display of maps and overlays can also be printed and handed out at meetings, and the screen can be projected on a large screen display during briefings. The sharp map image, real-time overlays, and flexible graphics editor thus make SITMAP an invaluable military tool.

2.3 DESIGN

Because SITMAP is a highly interactive graphical application, it easily lends itself to an object-oriented design. One reason is that users interactively manipulate objects on SITMAP's display that correspond to data in a database. As shown in Fig. 2.1, SITMAP brings together a variety of data sources and provides tools for manipulating and sending data. Map images, military icons, and overlays are displayable objects whose data are stored in databases. The graphics editor is a tool for creating new overlays that can be saved and delivered to other users.

Although it is easy to identify these components, it is not obvious how to begin the object-oriented design. Therefore, we used the following rules as guidelines:

- Objects should encapsulate data sources and data structures.
- Objects should provide interfaces to device and operating system services (for example, UNIX[5] domain socket I/O).

_____
[5] UNIX is a registered trademark of AT&T.

Figure 2.2 _____
SITMAP Data Acquisition.

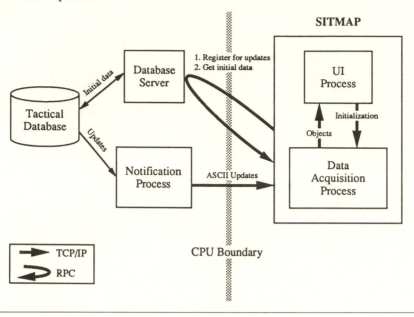

- Objects should correspond to visual objects on the display.
- Related classes should be grouped together as a set.
- Class sets should be separable components that are used to build applications.

Given these guidelines, it is easier to understand SITMAP's design.

In summary, the SITMAP application is built from components that are class sets.[6] Map objects manage the map database and display map images, a military symbol object accesses a database of icons to build unit symbols, real-time overlay objects maintain the displays of military forces, and graphics editor objects interact with the user to create and store grease pencil graphics. Some of these objects encapsulate non-object-oriented software modules, such as geographic projection routines needed to accurately map coordinates to pixel values in map images. The application also makes use of general class sets that support interprocess object distribution, two-dimensional graphics, and graphics editing. The rest of the objects in the design are application-specific: They define the user interface and the relationships between application components.

One interesting aspect of the design is the relationship between real-time overlays and the tactical database. Figure 2.2 illustrates the data flow between processes that are needed

---

[6] We designed a total of 94 classes, of which 16 were direct subclasses of Object and 25 were direct subclasses of other vendor-supplied classes. Half of these classes reside in application-independent libraries and are therefore reusable.

to support real-time overlays. The design separates the SITMAP *data acquisition* component into a different process, so that the *user interface process* is not hindered by delays when querying the database. The *database server* provides an interface to the tactical data, and the *notification daemon* is a service for near real-time notification of database changes. At startup, the data acquisition process retrieves initial data and sends them as objects to the user interface process. Thereafter, changes to the database cause new objects to be sent to the user interface process. The user interface process dispatches these objects to other objects that must propagate updates to the display. Dispatching these objects is difficult because the objects contain only fragments of data needed to generate the display. How these objects are dispatched within the user interface process is described in one of the implementation examples that follow (see Section 2.3.4).

In our SITMAP implementation, we address the difficult problems of managing multiple interactive displays, distributing objects between different processes, and supporting inter- active graphics editing. The following sections provide examples that use object-oriented programming technology to achieve real-world solutions.

2.3.1   The Model-View-Controller (MVC) Paradigm

The Model-View-Controller (MVC) paradigm is a critical design principle used for SITMAP classes and support class libraries. This paradigm separates application-domain (abstract) data, the presentation of these data, and the user's interaction with the presentations, into three components: (1) *models*, which contain application-specific data; (2) *views*, which are the displays presented to users; and (3) *controllers*, which handle user interactions that affect the models and views.

Our approach in handling view and model dependencies differs slightly from Smalltalk-80's [1,7] and significantly from Brad Cox's [2]. Smalltalk-80 manages dependent views in the model objects. Conceptually, every Smalltalk-80 object has its own list of dependents. As shown in Fig. 2.3a, views and controllers enroll themselves in this list to respond to changes in the model (which might result from changes driven by other views that are concurrently changing the model). Smalltalk-80 notifies views of changes by broadcasting a -changed or -changed: message to all dependent views. (-changed: passes an attribute object as its argument.)

In Brad Cox's approach [2], however, models are "slaves" of the user interface. Models never store information about the user interface because views (in Cox's nomenclature, "presentation layers") may be detached and replaced at any time. As shown in Fig. 2.3b, views always reference models, never the reverse. Each view holds a collection of views that have declared they want to be informed about changes in this view's model. Whenever a view changes its model, the *view* (not the model) announces [self changed], which in turn broadcasts -update messages to all objects enrolled as its dependents. Cox states that this approach works well for simple user interfaces, but it is not as general as Smalltalk-80's approach.

Our approach to broadcasting messages differs from Smalltalk-80's, since implement- ing -changed: in Objective-C would not allow simple C types to be differentiated when passed as attribute arguments. Instead, we send an *attribute-specific* broadcast message to the views (for example, -location:, which directly sets the location of the view object) and expect

Figure 2.3 _____

Three MVC Approaches. (a) Smalltalk-80's MVC Approach. (b) Brad Cox's MVC Approach. (c) SRI International's MVC Approach.

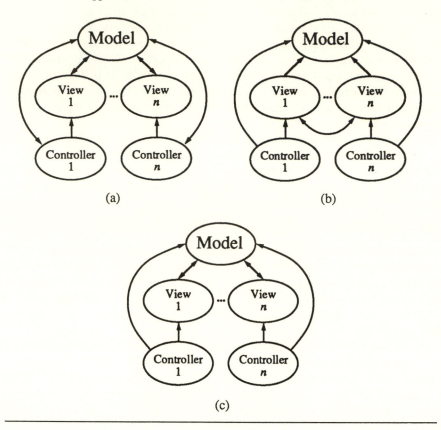

(a)   (b)

(c)

the views to update the display accordingly. As shown in Fig. 2.3c, all our models establish a protocol of specific broadcast messages (which typically consists of a message for each model attribute) to which their dependent views must respond. Although views must respond to all broadcast messages, they need act only on the messages that are germane to their view.

Because SITMAP must also allow its models to be updated from external triggers (namely, updates to tactical databases) as well as from user inputs, SITMAP models are not slaves to the user interface but rather are *gateways* for communications between the database and the user. Therefore, SITMAP models do not contain user interface information, but instead contain pointers to their views. For this reason, we chose the Smalltalk-80-like approach of having models manage a list of their dependent views. Thus, when a model is changed, it broadcasts either a general or specific message to its views to allow views to update their displays.

Because views are inert representations of selected model data, controllers are responsible for filtering user inputs and appropriately updating their views and models. These controllers are view-specific and typically contain pointers to their views and models. For example, in a desktop windowing system, if the user selects a window's close button, the associated controller might send a -collapse message to the window; if, on the other hand, the user selects the delete button, the controller might send a -deleted: message to the model.

We feel strongly that the MVC paradigm was essential in implementing our redesign of SITMAP, which itself is typical of many highly interactive and extensible applications. The following sections present our MVC implemention and SITMAP's use of the MVC paradigm.

2.3.2 MVC Implementation

We used ICpak 201 (Stepstone's user interface toolkit) as a basis for implementing our MVC classes. ICpak 201 is a set of Objective-C classes designed for creating iconic user interfaces composed of windows, icons, menus, and user-dialogue objects (namely, text entry, command buttons, toggles, and choice objects). ICpak 201 supports MVC implementations by providing view and controller classes but does not require that they be used in strict accordance with this paradigm.

From both this user interface toolkit and our own subclasses, we used a combination of the classes Model, Layer, GraphicLayer, OpaqCtlr, and TransCtlr to implement the MVC paradigm. The use and design of model, view, and controller are briefly described next.

Model Classes. In general, each model maintains a list of views and broadcasts changes to these views. We found it useful to define an abstract superclass for application models, called Model. Model is a direct subclass of Object (the fundamental class in any class hierarchy). Model has one instance variable, viewList, which is an ordered collection of view objects, and has methods for manipulating this view list. For example, whenever a view object is created, it is added to the view list via the method -addView:; whenever a view object is deleted, it is removed from the view list via the method -removeView:.

Each model is required to provide a *change method* for each model attribute. Models are changed by user actions, external events, and changes in state; therefore change messages can be sent by views, controllers, or other objects.

When model attributes change, the model broadcasts *update messages* to all views. All views *must* respond to these messages, but they need only act on pertinent ones. Therefore, for each model attribute, views define an update method that takes as an argument the new attribute value.

Necessarily, the change and update messages described here are model-specific and are the responsibility of Model subclasses.

View Classes. ICpak 201's Layer class was used as the abstract superclass for all views. Layers are analogous to sheets of acetate that can be stacked upon one another (e.g., menus and windows). (Figure 2.4 shows a StdSysLayer, a window with scroll bars consisting of many layers.) The collective set of layers forms an internal directed tree structure called the *layer hierarchy*. Each layer has a list of frontLayers, which manage the layer's children in the layer hierarchy, and a backLayer pointer, which indicates the layer's parent (backLayers and frontLayers are equivalent to Smalltalk-80's *superviews* and *subviews*). Each frontLayer in Fig. 2.4 can also be composed of layers. The user interface is modeled with a single layer hierarchy that defines the appearance of the application. The root in the layer hierarchy corresponds to the system window in the native window system and is an instance of ICpak 201's BaseLayer.

Because Layer does not have a model instance variable or creation methods similar to +withModel: (shown in the code sample that follows), we wanted to design a class called View with this instance variable and methods and have all our views inherit both Layer's and View's instance variables and methods. Because we did not want to modify Layer and Objective-C does not support multiple inheritance, we replicated these instance variables and methods in all view class definitions. Since most of SITMAP's views were subclasses of GraphicLayer, we simply added these instance variables and methods to GraphicLayer. (GraphicLayer is a subclass of Layer and is the main class in the 2-D graphics extension to ICpak 201; see Section 2.3.6 for an explanation of this extension.)

Each view has an instance variable model, defined during creation, that is a pointer to its associated model. This pointer allows views to send change messages in response to user actions. As an example, the following view creation method sets model and adds the object to the model's view list.

Figure 2.4 _____
StdSysLayer.

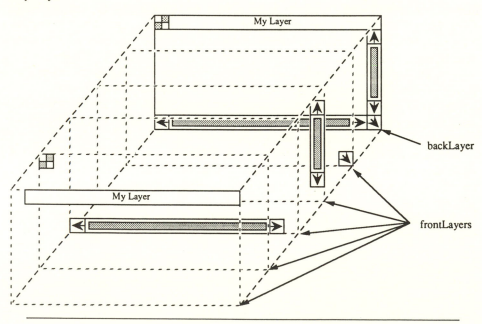

```
// Creates and initializes a new instance with an associated model
+ withModel: (id)aModel
{
    self = [self new];
    [self model: aModel];        // Set the model instance variable
    [model addView: self];       // Add self to the model's view list
    return self;
}
```

Controller Classes. Each layer has a controller that handles all events (e.g., keyboard and mouse input) from the underlying window system occurring within the layer's bounding box. A controller receiving an event can consume the event or pass the event to the associated layer's backLayer. A layer's controller can be swapped at any time simply by sending it a -controller: message.

ICpak 201 provides two controller classes: OpaqCtlr consumes all events reaching its layer, while TransCtlr simply ignores all events (TransCtlr is Layer's default controller). Controllers can be subclasses of either OpaqCtlr or TransCtlr and can consume events by overriding distinct methods for each type of event they wish to consume. For example, the method -rightButtonDown would be overridden to consume the right-mouse-button-down event. All of SITMAP's controllers are subclasses of these two controllers.

2.3.3 SITMAP MVC Examples

Because SITMAP's user interface is highly interactive, it is well suited to the MVC paradigm. It allows SITMAP to maintain only one model of the tactical data while providing multiple views of these data. For example, only one model of a combat unit is needed, although that unit may have multiple views on the display at one time (namely, one view per map window). The MVC paradigm is used throughout the design at various levels of abstraction.

At the highest level is a model of the "world" that contains all tactical data. This model consists of (1) map backgrounds; (2) real-time overlays, generated from database information and updated in near real time; and (3) grease pencil graphics created by users via the graphics editor. Each map window on the SITMAP desktop is simply one view of the tactical world (for example, a view port into a specific geographic region displaying selected overlays).

At the next level of abstraction, there are models and views associated with each map background and overlay (for example, friendly unit or enemy unit overlays). Map windows will display a map view and any combination of overlay views. All views are dynamic and configurable by the user.

At the lowest level of abstraction is a model of each overlay object (for example, units in the friendly unit overlay). Overlay models are collections of model objects, while overlay views are collections of view objects. The portion of the SITMAP desktop in Color Plate 2.2 illustrates a map window with friendly and enemy overlay views that consist of unit view objects.

Following are two examples of SITMAP's MVC implementation. The first example is an abbreviated version of unit model, view, and controller classes used to implement the friendly and enemy unit overlays. It illustrates the flexibility gained by decoupling views from controllers. The second example describes the interrelationship between the SITMAP MVC classes and shows how the MVC paradigm has been used to develop a flexible and maintainable program.

Unit MVC Example

Problem. A unit is a military combat unit, such as the 18th Airborne Corps, that is a player in a war game or simulation. The tactical database contains information on all unit locations and their battle readiness. SITMAP monitors the combat situation by displaying these units on map backgrounds.

A unit displays its information sequentially. In Color Plate 2.2, where unit objects are shown in various stages of display, the unit first presents a colored dot to graphically indicate the unit's location. Next it attaches a military symbol to the dot with a tethered line to indicate the unit's type. Then it displays its name and, finally, its location in geographic coordinates. The military symbol, unit name, and unit location displays are tiled together and form a movable object on the map window (note that dragging only moves the *attributes* of a unit, not the actual unit location, which remains anchored).

Because the tactical database is continually being updated with the latest reports from the battlefield, and because it is essential that a commander see the most current information and be alerted in critical situations, SITMAP displays must be updated in near real time as new information becomes available. For example, when a unit location changes, the unit must move on the map background. In addition, there is a future need to update a unit's location via SITMAP. The action of moving a unit on the SITMAP display might send an update to the tactical database.

Model Classes. UnitModel is the model object for combat units that encapsulates all combat unit information. UnitModel, a subclass of Model, has an instance variable, myData, an instance of UnitData. UnitData encapsulates the unit's name and location data. Since the user can display multiple map windows, many views of the same unit are possible and changes to the model must be propagated to all views.

Figure 2.5 illustrates the message flow between unit model and view objects. Updates to a unit's location in the tactical database or by user interaction with a unitView cause -changeUnitLocation: messages to be sent to a unitModel.

Figure 2.5 _____

Message Flow Between UnitModel and UnitView.

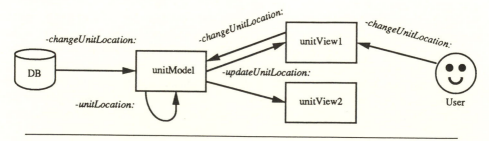

UnitModel's -changeUnitLocation: method broadcasts the -updateUnitLocation: message, with the new location as a parameter, to all of its views. The -changeUnitLocation: method in UnitModel is implemented as follows:

```
-(BOOL)changeUnitLocation: (id)aLocation
{
    // Only update the data if it has changed state
    if (![myData sameUnitLocation:aLocation])
    {
        // Change the model
        [self unitLocation: aLocation];

        // Broadcast the update to all the views
        [viewList elementsPerform:@selector(updateUnitLocation:)
            with:aLocation];
        return (YES);
    }
    return (NO); // If the update was not made return NO
}
```

Although there may be several unit view classes, each must respond to the -updateUnitLocation: message. The -updateUnitLocation: method is responsible for moving the unit to its new location on the map.

View Classes. UnitView presents unit information on a map background. Figure 2.6 shows an outline of UnitView as it appears on the screen. Any combination of the symbol, name, and location frontLayers can be simultaneously displayed. Furthermore, these frontLayers can be moved to unclutter the screen.

When all levels of information are displayed, a unitView layer hierarchy appears, as shown in Fig. 2.7. UnitDot and UnitLine instances are circle and line layers, respectively. The UnitMovable instance is the primary frontLayer that contains instances of UnitName, UnitSym, and UnitLoc as its frontLayers. UnitName, UnitSym, and UnitLoc are composed of rectangle, line, and text layers that define their graphics.

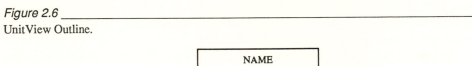

Figure 2.6 _____
UnitView Outline.

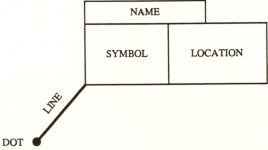

Figure 2.7

UnitView Layer Hierarchy.

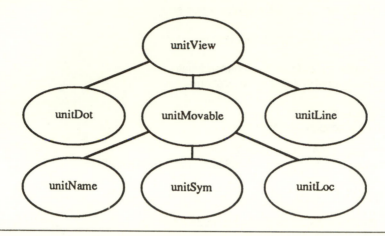

Controller Classes. Two controllers handle user interaction with unit view objects and define the following behavior:

- When the user selects any portion of a unitView with the right mouse button, a pop-up menu appears.
- When the user selects any portion with the left mouse button, the next level of information is displayed.
- When the user holds the middle mouse button down on the movable portion, it becomes draggable. However, if the user holds the middle mouse button down on a *nonmovable* portion (unitDot or unitLine), then no action is taken.

UnitCtlr, a subclass of TransCtlr, handles unitView interactions by overriding the methods -leftButtonDown and -rightButtonDown . -leftButtonDown displays the next level of information, while -rightButtonDown invokes a pop-up menu for selecting attributes to toggle on or off. Since UnitCtlr does not override the -middleButtonDown event, it does not consume this event.

The dragging action is handled by another controller, UnitMovableCtlr. UnitMovableCtlr, also a subclass of TransCtlr, overrides the -middleButtonDown method. This controller is attached to a unitMovable object to allow only the movable portion of a unitView to respond to dragging.

How these controllers work is best illustrated by tracing events as they are processed in the unitView layer hierarchy shown in Fig. 2.9. Events are first passed to frontmost layers (frontmost layers are equivalent to leaf nodes in the layer hierarchy). The associated controller can either consume an event or pass the event to the layer's backLayer. The default controller does not consume any events.

Figure 2.8 _____

Processing UnitView Events.

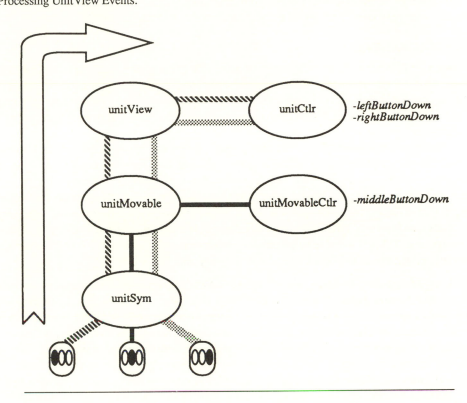

Figure 2.8 illustrates the flow of mouse button events that occur within the bounding box of unitSym. Events that occur on unitSym are handled by unitMovableCtlr. UnitMovableCtlr consumes only middle-button-down events and passes all other events to unitCtlr. UnitCtlr consumes left- and right-button-down events, ignoring all other events.

Discussion. Decoupling views and controllers makes it easy to change the behavior of objects. For example, if we want to enhance unit view objects to allow the user to interactively change a location by dragging it, we simply change the unit view controller using the method -controller:.

We subclass UnitCtlr and create a new class, UnitCtlr2. UnitCtlr2 overrides -middleButtonDown to interactively drag the entire unitView. When an instance of UnitCtlr is swapped with an instance of UnitCtlr2, the behavior of unitView changes. The effect of swapping these controllers is that the dot can be dragged, changing the unit's location but still allowing unitMovable to be dragged. (If the middle-mouse-button-down event occurs on unitMovable, it is consumed by unitMovableCtlr; if the middle-mouse-button-down event occurs on either unitDot or unitLine, it is consumed by unitCtlr2.)

The technique of swapping controllers during run time is very useful when implementing modal user interfaces, where mouse semantics differ from mode to mode. For example, we might employ unitCtlr2 only if the user is authorized to move a unit's location.

Complex MVC Example

Problem. SITMAP addresses the needs of a very large user community whose members have disparate requirements. Additional real-time overlays will be designed for specific military functions. However, we cannot predict what overlays a user might want in the future; since SITMAP will be maintained over a long period of time, it should be easy to define and integrate new overlays into the system.

Another complexity is that overlays applicable to one user group may not be applicable to another (for example, a navy officer would not want to see as much ground force detail as an army officer; a weather officer will not want his or her menus cluttered with options intended for an engineer). Also, the geographic area of interest will change from exercise to exercise, and it is not feasible to provide electronic maps covering the entire world. Therefore we want to tailor the SITMAP user interface for specific user groups and military exercises. Configuring SITMAP will also help run-time performance by trimming the executable image and related databases to make better use of memory and disk space.

SITMAP Model/View Relationship. SITMAP's MVC design uses composite model and view objects throughout. Figure 2.9 illustrates this relationship, in which views have subviews and models have *submodels*. The first level shows the SITMAP display as the user sees it. The next level shows the views and subviews, while the bottom level shows the models and submodels associated with these views. The corresponding component graphs for these objects are shown in Fig. 2.10. A single model component graph is needed to contain all tactical data; multiple views of these data are displayed on the system window or baseLayer.

SITMAP model and view classes also belong to distinct class hierarchies where models are subclasses of Model and views are subclasses of Layer. Figure 2.11 presents a brief description of the model, view, and controller classes that comprise SITMAP.

Model Classes. SitmapModel is the "world" model that encapsulates all tactical and user data. This instance is the supermodel of all other SITMAP models and contains a list of map and overlay submodels whose views may be displayed in map windows. Because the tactical database contains both actual and fictitious tactical information (used for simulations and training), SitmapModel also contains a key used to distinguish between these two types of data. Because of these types of data, different SitmapModel instances can contain entirely different "world" knowledge. (However, in the current SITMAP implementation, there is only one SitmapModel instance per process.)

MapModel encapsulates all of the map data. It is the only SITMAP object that directly accesses the map database and projection routines. The map database contains information about available maps, their attributes, and the actual map images. The projection software is a non-object-oriented C library that implements the conversion algorithms needed to accurately plot units, and other objects, on map backgrounds. MapModel has no submodels.

OverlayModel is an abstract superclass for all overlay models. It has one instance variable, name, used by views for selecting overlays in a pop-up menu.

Figure 2.9 _____
SITMAP Model/View Relationship.

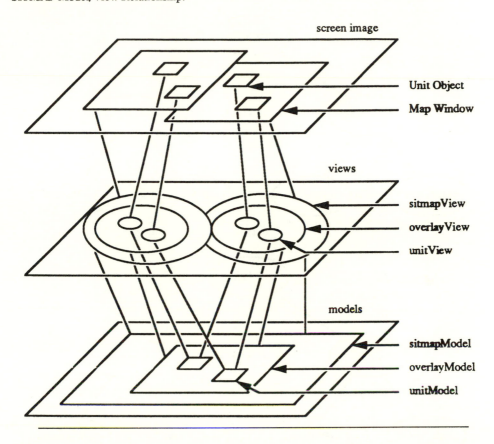

UnitOverlayModel, a subclass of OverlayModel, is an abstract superclass for all overlays that display units. It contains a collection of "players" (a military term denoting units participating in exercises) that are UnitModel instances. (UnitModel encapsulates all of a unit's tactical data; see earlier section, "Unit MVC Example," for further explanation.) UnitModel has no submodels.

FriendlyUnitOverlay and EnemyUnitOverlay, subclasses of UnitOverlayModel, are models of the friendly and enemy unit overlays, respectively.

View Classes. SitmapView is a view of a sitmapModel that manages the map windows that appear on the SITMAP desktop. It is a subclass of ICpak 201's StdSysLayer, which is a layer with a title, close box, stretch box, and scroll bars. SitmapView's instances are windows in a miniwindow system that can be opened, closed, moved, and resized by simple mouse actions. In addition, sitmapViews display a map background and provide a selection of

Figure 2.10
Component Graphs. (a) SITMAP Model. (b) SITMAP View.

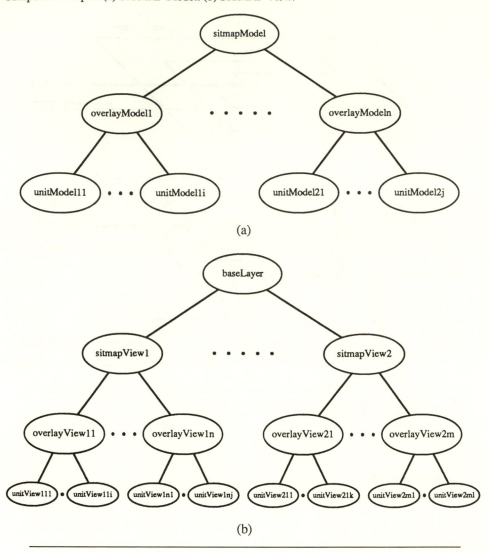

overlays that can be shown and erased by menu selection. SitmapView has a map view and a collection of overlay views as frontLayers. Figure 2.12 shows multiple sitmapViews in which several overlays are displayed on map backgrounds, while Fig. 2.13 shows a sitmapView layer hierarchy.

SitmapView has two instance variables, userLayer and overlayLayer, that are special frontLayers for attaching overlay objects. All grease pencil graphics objects that are created

Figure 2.11 _____

SITMAP Model and View Class Hierarchies. (a) Model Class. (b) View Class.

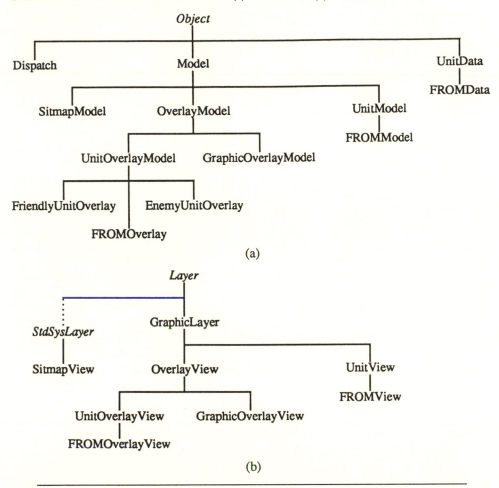

(a)

(b)

with the graphics editor are attached to userLayer, and all real-time overlay objects are attached to overlayLayer. This has the effect of isolating all grease pencil graphics from database objects. The userLayer is always between the displayed map and the overlayLayer.

MapView is a view of a MapModel and is implemented as a subclass of ICpak 201's ImageLayer, a layer that displays an image. MapView is always the lowest layer in sitmapView layer hierarchies; thus overlay objects are always displayed above the map image. Because each map window is a bird's-eye view of a much larger map region, mapView requests a new section of the map image from its model and then displays it whenever the user scrolls the window.

OverlayView is an abstract superclass for all overlay view classes. A subclass of Layer,

Figure 2.12

Multiple SITMAP Views.

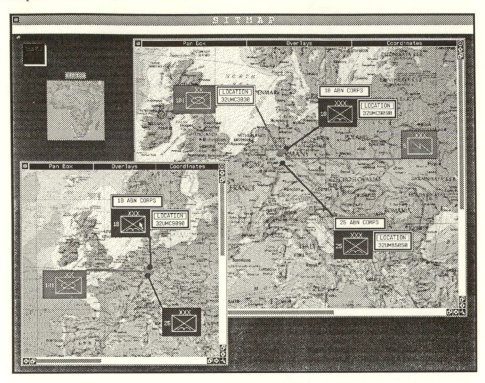

it contains a list of subviews and methods for showing and erasing itself. (We use "subview" here as a general term and "frontLayer" as a layer-specific term.) OverlayViews share subviews with sitmapViews. Notice in Fig. 2.12a that overlayViews do not appear in the sitmapView layer hierarchy. This was done because it is more natural for the user to manage all overlay objects in a single plane. Therefore all overlay subviews are attached directly to the overlayLayer of a sitmapView, while overlayViews are not attached at all. A sitmapView manages the display and distribution of events to its frontLayers, while an overlayView passes show and erase messages to its subviews.

UnitOverlayView is a subclass of OverlayView that implements the friendly and enemy unit overlay views. UnitOverlayView has subviews for each item in the model's playerList. Subviews of UnitOverlayView are instances of UnitView (see preceding "Unit MVC Example" for details).

Controller Classes. Since SitmapView is a subclass of StdSysLayer and uses ICpak 201 menu bars and so forth to implement its user interface, all SitmapView events are handled by ICpak 201 classes. We therefore needed only to implement controllers to handle events

Figure 2.13 _____
SITMAP View Layer Hierarchy.

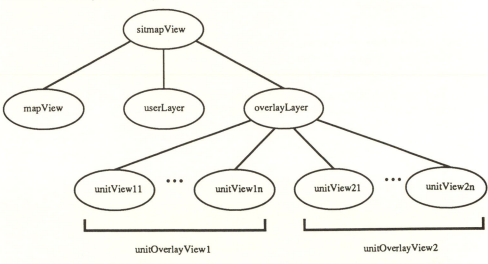

that occur inside the map window, namely, events that occur on overlay subviews and mapViews.

MapView user interaction is handled by MapCtlr. MapCtlr enables the user to retrieve map coordinates in either longitude/latitude or Universal Transverse Mercator (UTM). By using the mouse, the user selects a location and the corresponding coordinate is displayed.

Overlay subview events are handled by view-specific controllers. For example, interaction with a unitView is handled by unitCtlr and unitMovableCtlr. (See preceding "Unit MVC Example" for details.)

Discussion. SITMAP's MVC design might seem complex at first, but in the long run it actually reduces maintenance costs and makes configuration management easier. For example, suppose that we wanted to add a new overlay showing the unit hierarchy (the military chain of command). Figure 2.14 depicts a command overlay and a geographic overlay. To define and integrate this overlay into SITMAP, we follow these simple steps:

1. Implement the new overlay model and view objects. The new overlay model must be a subclass of OverlayModel, while the overlay view must be a subclass of OverlayView.
2. Add an instance of the new overlay model to the supermodel, an instance of SitmapModel.

Step 1 is the implementation of a new overlay class set that must undergo the normal development cycle. However, in this case, the design can use existing unit model, view, and controller classes.

Step 2 is very simple. The following code sample shows how overlay models are added to the overlay list in the SITMAP main routine:

```
main()
{
    id theSitmapModel;

    . . .
    // Create the SitmapModel instance with "operationX", the key
    // used in the tactical database.
    theSitmapModel = [SitmapModel newSitmapModel: "operationX"];

    // Register the friendly/enemy overlay models with theSitmapModel
    [theSitmapModel addOverlay:[FriendlyUnitOverlay new]];
    [theSitmapModel addOverlay:[EnemyUnitOverlay new]];
    . . .
}
```

To add the new unit overlay, we append the following line of code:

```
[theSitmapModel addOverlay:[CommandUnitOverlay new]];
```

where CommandUnitOverlay is the unit hierarchy overlay model.

As shown in the preceding sample code, adding overlays is done in the SITMAP main routine. If an overlay is not added to theSitmapModel, it will not appear as an option in map windows. Similarly, SITMAP will query the map database at startup for available maps and creates an instance of MapModel for each map background. Only those maps contained in the database will appear in the map list for selection by the user. SITMAP is configured by modifying the overlay and map lists.

In fact, all of the overlay objects described thus far are used as tools to build SITMAP;

Figure 2.14 _____

Multiple Unit Overlay Views. (a) CommandUnitOverlay View (b) FriendlyUnitOverlay View.

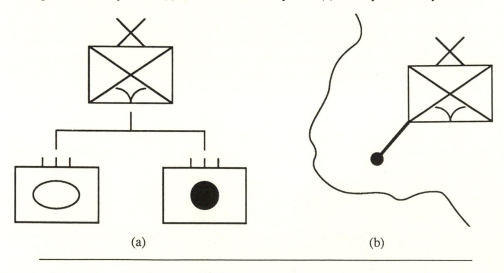

(a)　　　　　　　　　　　　　　　　　(b)

however, it is the main routine that packages these tools to define the overall functionality. The only software component that will differ between configurations is the main routine. This "packaging" approach is used to configure SITMAP for different users and military exercises.

2.3.4 Dispatching Data Objects

Data from the tactical database, used to build real-time overlays, is sent to SITMAP as individual data "objects." Because these objects may be incomplete, their order random, and they contain no links to SITMAP overlays, they must be *incrementally* integrated into the sitmapModel, with appropriate display updates. Thus the user interface process must determine where objects belong and create corresponding models and views when the data objects are *logically complete*. For example, if the user opens map windows and requests the display of real-time overlays when no tactical data are present, new overlay objects appear on the display as data arrive.

The Dispatch class delivers data objects to, and filters data objects for, *data object consumers*. Objects become data object consumers by registering with a Dispatch instance, dispatcher, and indicating the type of data they require.

The following code segment shows how the UnitModel class registers with the dispatcher to receive all UnitData instances:

```
// Create the Dispatch instance
dispatcher = [Dispatch new];

// Register migrant data objects with the dispatcher
[dispatcher registerKey:"UnitData" object:[UnitModel class]];
```

Message Flow for Dispatch. Figure 2.15 shows the dispatcher delivering unitData objects through two routes. (Note that each data object consumer must respond to the -deliver: message, which has the data object as a parameter.) When UnitModel receives unitData objects, it either (1) updates an existing UnitModel instance or (2) creates a new instance. To determine if a specific UnitModel instance exists, UnitModel maintains a class variable,[7] instanceList. This class variable contains all UnitModel instances and their associated unit names. When a data object is delivered, UnitModel uses the object's unit name to find the associated UnitModel instance. If an instance exists, the UnitModel class sends it the -update: message, passing the unitData as the argument. The unitModel instance then propagates updates to its views.

If UnitModel does not find the unit name in its instanceList, it creates a new UnitModel instance and adds it to the "world" of tactical data by sending sitmapModel the message -addToOverlays: with the new unitModel as an argument. Because sitmapModel does not know to which overlay the unitModel belongs, it sends the unitModel to all its overlay models, using the message -addObject:. In Fig. 2.15, unitOverlay responds by sending the -addUnit:

---

[7] In this implementation, a *class variable* is an instance variable for factory objects. Cf., a class variable that is *shared* by all instances of a class.

Figure 2.15
Object Dispatching.

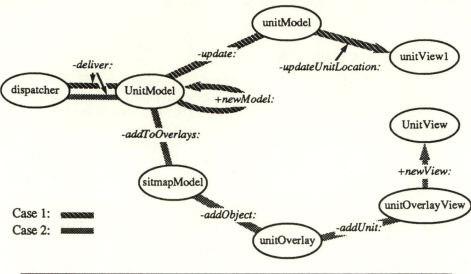

Case 1:
Case 2:

message to all its views. This causes unit OverlayView to create and display a new UnitView instance. In addition, because sitmapModel broadcasts new objects to all its overlays, several overlayModels can share the same submodels (that is, a friendlyUnitOverlay can share unitModels used by a commandUnitOverlay).

Unlike this example, because the data objects may be logically incomplete, dispatching data objects to real-time overlays is not always simple. For example, if a unitData's status information arrives before its location information, its corresponding unitViews cannot be displayed on map backgrounds since the unitData has no map coordinates. Under these circumstances, UnitModel distributes instances to sitmapModel only when they contain enough information to be displayed.

Discussion. Dispatching objects in this manner works well for low-volume information and infrequent updates. SITMAP's MVC design allows for multiple views of the same data and facilitates the difficult process of dispatching data objects while maintaining a highly interactive user interface. However, the user interface response time degrades with large volumes of information (e.g., a thousand navy radar tracks) because user and interprocess communication events have equal priority. Also, because it is difficult to manage large volumes of updates that arrive in a short period of time (for example, 10 updates that arrive in a matter of seconds can result in more than 20 updates to the display), we developed more efficient ways of updating the displays, including "batching" update messages to SITMAP views. To avoid this problem in the future, the application implementors will be able to explicitly filter incoming information and establish update intervals for selected events.

2.3.5 Interprocess Object Distribution

Because SITMAP's principal function is to present tactical information, it must obtain that information from various data sources, including a tactical database. SITMAP's acquisition of tactical data is both active (that is, when querying) and passive (that is, via notification).

Typically, data that are sent and received between processes are put into packets and transmitted using a family of network protocols common across machine architectures. Our goal was to provide an object-distribution mechanism that (1) offered a simple and intuitive interface and (2) hid the details of connection setup and teardown. For an object-oriented application, *objects* are the ideal form for data that are distributed between two or more processes, as opposed to a flat bit-stream, which is inert and meaningless without interpretation.

There are at least three approaches to *object distribution* that support passing data between two processes:

— Using distributed objects, that is, instances that are shared across machine address-spaces and whose locations are transparent to class consumers
— Distributing a copy of an instance (that is, the instance variables) and its class (namely, factory and instance methods)
— Distributing only a copy of an instance

None of these approaches to object distribution is currently available through Objective-C and its associated ICpaks.

Successfully implementing the first approach (distributed objects) would involve supporting co-routines and mediation between process-local and object-resident spaces [3]. The second and third approaches require interprocess communication to support instance distribution and a mechanism to represent and store the instance in a machine-independent form. In addition, the second approach requires dynamic method binding.

Although the first two approaches are interesting as research problems and would support distributing objects, their implementation was outside the scope of our project. Hence, we chose the last approach, distributing a copy of an instance. We will now discuss our design and implementation of this approach.

Design and Implementation. Objective-C's foundation library (ICpak 101) provides a class named AsciiFiler, which stores and retrieves objects to and from UNIX text files [12]. The methods -storeOn: and +readFrom: implement instance input and output (I/O) by creating and interpreting, respectively, a graph of the instance. Because these methods are also supported by the class Object (the root class in the class hierarchy), all objects have the capability for *automatic I/O* to and from ASCII files.

Ideally, objects should have the capability for automatic I/O through network connections to other processes (that is, across computer address-space barriers), as well as to files. However, it was not feasible to implement automatic network I/O for all ICpak 101 class consumers since such implementation would require a change to the class Object.

Although we use a NetFiler instance to support object I/O, our implementation is general, supporting I/O of *all instances* within the sender's and receiver's class hierarchy.

Socket. In UNIX systems that support the Berkeley 4.2 BSD Interprocess Communication (IPC) facilities, a socket is an addressable entity that represents a process endpoint of communication [8]. Thus we chose to encapsulate the information and actions needed for interprocess communication in the class Socket. Socket's purpose is to aid other classes (for example, NetFiler) that define and implement an I/O protocol by providing an interface between class consumers and transparently allocated and maintained network communication endpoints.

Although Socket defines methods for the setup and teardown of network connections, it does not provide methods for reading from, and writing to, the network connections; other classes must provide these functions. In this way, Socket remains general because it can be used by classes not only to exchange objects but also to exchange binary and ASCII data.

Following are code examples that create Socket instances that allow support for sending and receiving data between processes. Note that the class consumer must send additional messages (not shown) to ICpak 201's event-handling class to enable Socket instances to receive events [5, 13, 14, 15].

A sending Socket instance is established as follows:

```
newSocket = [Socket new];
if ([newSocket initForSending:"mars" at:2550 type:VIRTUAL_CIRCUIT] == nil)
    fprintf (stderr, "failed to establish send socket");
```

A receiving Socket instance is established as follows:

```
newSocket = [Socket new];
if ([newSocket initForReceiving:2550 type:VIRTUAL_CIRCUIT] == nil)
    fprintf (stderr, "failed to establish receive socket");
```

Here is an example of a Socket instance accepting a connection:

```
newSocket = [Socket new];
    if ([newSocket socketAccept:socketWithPendingConnectionRequest] == nil) fprintf
    (stderr, "accept of new connection failed\n");
```

Currently, Socket only supports Transmission Control Protocol/Internet Protocol (TCP/IP) and User Datagram Protocol/Internet Protocol (UDP/IP) communication styles. However, in its use of UNIX sockets, Socket does not limit access to, or use of, other network protocols: Whatever is supported by the operating system, and available through UNIX sockets, can also be supported by Socket.

NetFiler. NetFiler supports the sending and receiving of instances between processes. Only the *data portions* of an object are captured; the private and shared parts, including the object code for the methods, are not. Thus both sender and receiver must have the same class hierarchy for those sections that relate to the transmitted objects. In this way, correct object reconstruction is guaranteed.

The NetFiler class consumer is insulated from the details of connection management. NetFiler uses Socket instances to establish and maintain network connections between the sending and receiving processes. To prevent anomalous connections, NetFiler must create every Socket instance it uses; that is, user-created Socket instances are not considered valid by NetFiler instances. Presently, NetFiler only supports asynchronous object I/O due to restrictions on the current event-handling mechanism. Thus receivers cannot block and wait for objects.

The class consumer is also insulated from the details of translating the instance to and from its transmitted form (namely, an object graph) since NetFiler uses methods in Objective-C's AsciiFiler class to create and restore these object graphs.

The following example shows how NetFiler sends objects:

```
netFiler = [NetFiler create];
aSocket = [netFiler establishSendTo:"mars" at:2050
          type:VIRTUAL_CIRCUIT
          protocol:DEFAULT_PROTOCOL];
if (aSocket == nil)
    fprintf(stderr, "Failed to establish a connection\n");
else /*Try to send the object */
    [netFiler send:myObject over:aSocket];
```

Programs that use NetFiler to receive objects must specify a *client object* as the intended receiver. All objects received on the designated port are then sent to the client using the -dispatch: method. This is the sole protocol between NetFiler and a client. For example, in SITMAP the dispatcher (see Fig. 2.15) requests NetFiler to receive objects from other processes and dispatch them as follows:

```
netFiler = [NetFiler create];
if ([netFiler registerRecvOnPort:2050 type:VIRTUAL_CIRCUIT
        protocol:DEFAULT_PROTOCOL client:dispatcher] == NO)
    fprintf(stderr, "Registration to receive objects failed.\n");
```

2.3.6 Two-Dimensional Graphics Extensions

SITMAP needed a two-dimensional graphics package that (1) supported a Programmer's Hierarchical Interactive Graphics System (PHIGS)-like graphics hierarchy, (2) supported storing and retrieving composite graphics objects, (3) supported interactively creating primitive graphic objects using rubberbanding for visual feedback, and (4) could be integrated into existing user interface (UI) packages.

Although Stepstone's ICpak 201 provides classes for constructing window system independent UIs, and has partial support for two-dimensional *structured graphics*[8] (namely, through its Layer hierarchy), it has limited graphics capabilities and no primitive graphic object classes (namely, circles, lines, rectangles, and so on). To extend and exploit ICpak

---

[8] *Structured graphics* allows composite graphic objects to be treated as single entities. Because Layers are tree structures that propagate selected messages to their frontLayers (see Section 2.3.2 for description of layers), GraphicLayers must also propagate messages to their frontLayers. Thus the graphics attributes of the entire structure can be altered by sending messages to the root.

Figure 2.16

Graphic Extensions Class Hierarchies. (a) GraphicLayer Class Hierarchy. (b) GraphicObject Class Hierarchy. (c) GraphicCtlr Class Hierarchy.

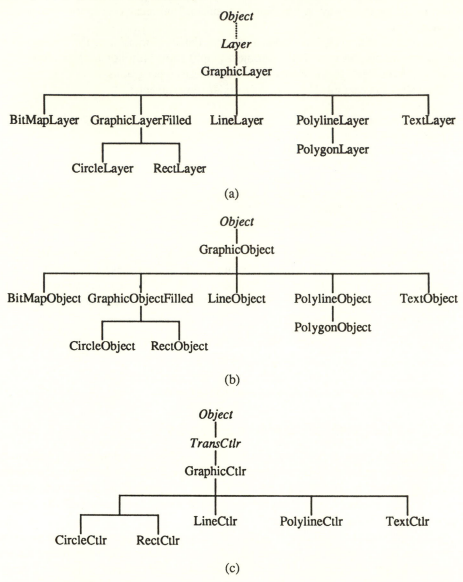

(a)

(b)

(c)

201's **Layer** functionality, we created new classes whose subclasses correspond to bitmaps, circles, lines, polygons, polylines, rectangles, and text objects (see Fig. 2.16). These classes also allow objects to be hierarchically grouped; procedurally and interactively (via mouse manipulation) created and defined; collectively displayed and selected; and stored to, and retrieved from, ASCII text files, via ICpak 101's automatic I/O facility.

GraphicLayer Classes. GraphicLayer, a subclass of *Layer*, inherits Layer's methods for hierarchical creation and manipulation and thus supports structured graphics. (See Fig. 2.16a). GraphicLayer is also an abstract superclass for primitive graphic objects, but unlike traditional abstract superclasses, whose instances are generally non-functional, GraphicLayer can also create transparent instances that function as root nodes for structured graphics. In addition, all GraphicLayer subclasses contain *graphic attributes* (namely, foreground and background color, line thickness, and line and fill patterns) that specify the appearance of instances. These attributes, which include support for transparency, can also be procedurally redefined.

For applications using the MVC paradigm, a GraphicLayer corresponds to a *view*. In support of this use, GraphicLayer has an instance variable corresponding to its *model*; however, GraphicLayer's implementation is actually constrained by ICpak 201's layer hierarchy from being a "pure" view. One reason is that, based on its bounding box and whether it is invisible, GraphicLayer functions as a preliminary event filter and as an interface for an instance of private GraphicObject classes (see the following section). (Because each GraphicLayer instance contains a pointer to a corresponding GraphicObject instance, the GraphicLayer and GraphicObject class hierarchies are identical, as shown in Fig. 2.16b).[9]

GraphicLayer instances inherit ICpak 201's Layer methods and thus use their bounding boxes to determine whether they can consume events via Layer's -processEvent method.[10] However, because this method assumes that all layers are opaque and rectangular, GraphicLayer overrides -processEvent to require the selection of some *visible portion* of its hierarchy. This allows a partially transparent layer (for example, a nonfilled circle) to pass an event to underlying layers, even if the event is within the transparent layer's bounding box (see Fig. 2.17 for an illustration of this example).

GraphicObject Classes. GraphicObject classes[11] are responsible for graphical rendering. Thus their instances contain class-specific representational data (for example, LineObject has starting and ending points instance variables) and graphic attributes. (With the exception of GraphicLayer's layer manipulation and processing methods, most GraphicLayer methods pass their arguments to associated GraphicObject methods.)

Although ICpak 201 classes support drawing lines and rendering text, they provide little

---

[9] The organizations of the GraphicLayer and GraphicObject class hierarchies contain class implementations that could be simplified if multiple inheritance were available. Specifically, PolygonLayer's and PolylineLayer's attributes and methods are *identical*, with the exception that PolygonLayer is *fillable*. In this case, multiple inheritance would allow PolygonLayer to inherit from *both* PolylineLayer and GraphicLayerFilled. (This observation also holds true for PolygonObject, PolylineObject, and GraphicObjectFilled.)

[10] Events are distributed using the layer hierarchy, which is a directed tree structure. Using a depth-first traversal, events are passed to successive layers (leaf nodes) only if the events occur within the layer's bounding box; layers can then elect to consume or ignore events.

[11] The raison d'etre for these classes is that ICpak 201 contains a class, DispObject, whose sole purpose is to render graphics into on- and off-screen display memory. Thus GraphicObject classes were designed analogously, and graphics rendering methods that would normally be implemented in view classes (namely, GraphicLayers) were implemented in these classes.

Figure 2.17
LineLayer Behind a Transparent CircleLayer.

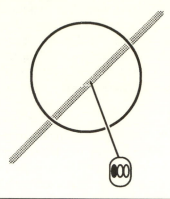

or no support for drawing filled or unfilled circles, polygons, polylines, and rectangles, or for applying paint attributes to graphic primitives (namely, transparency, thick lines, stencilling, and so on). Thus GraphicObject, BitmapObject, CircleObject, LineObject, Polygon-Object, PolylineObject, RectObject, and TextObject classes include flood-filling and appropriate bitmap rendering algorithms. An instance of these classes also has its graphics clipped to the bounding box of its parent GraphicLayer.

GraphicCtlr Classes. In the MVC paradigm, controllers define how views respond to user interactions. Because controllers are context-specific (namely, controllers service the needs of *models*), the graphic extension's default GraphicCtlr *classes* handle the interactive creation of new GraphicLayer instances. For this reason, there is limited similarity between the GraphicCtlr and GraphicLayer class hierarchies. (This is because the BitmapLayer class does not permit interactive definition, while the PolygonLayer class does not have a corresponding PolygonCtlr class since it uses the PolylineCtlr class.) In addition, these classes use rubberbanding to provide visual feedback when GraphicLayer instances are interactively defined via GraphicLayer's -userCreate and +fromUser methods.

Discussion. Figure 2.18 shows an example of structured graphics in which a transparent GraphicLayer has a RectLayer, a LineLayer, and a CircleLayer as its frontLayers; this composite graphic structure represents a unitView. Even though all the displayable GraphicLayer instances (that is, frontLayers) are contained within the backLayer's bounding box, the user can select the unit view only by clicking one of the frontLayers. Thus clicking point A will select the unit view, while clicking point B will not.

Because the interpretation of user-generated events is context-sensitive, the GraphicLayer must decide whether to dispatch an event to its controller. As an example, Fig. 2.19 shows a GraphicLayer that represents a Confirmer dialog. When the user clicks the mouse within aGraphicLayer's bounding box, aGraphicLayer first allows its frontLayers (namely, polygonLayers) to consume the left-button-down event.

Figure 2.18 _____
Composite Graphics Example.

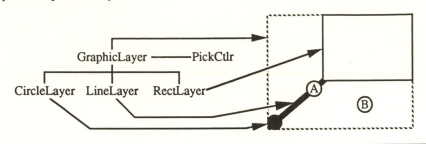

If point A is selected, aPickCtlr1's -leftButtonDown method performs [aPolygonLayer1 picked: aPolygonLayer1] *but does not consume the event.* (Note that both aPolygonLayer0 and aPolygonLayer2 ignore the event because its location is outside their bounding boxes.) After aGraphicLayer checks that none of its frontLayers consumed the event, it checks if any were *picked.* Because aPolygonLayer1 was picked, aGraphicLayer sends its controller, aConfirmCtlr, a -leftButtonDown message. After determining which polygonLayer was picked, aConfirmCtlr then sends the appropriate message to its model, aModel; this action effectively maps the mouse down event from the *view's domain* into a message in the *model's domain.*

If point B is selected, the left-button-down event is simply ignored, because none of aGraphicLayer's frontLayers will have declared themselves picked.

Because of their flexibility, the GraphicLayer classes, along with the associated support

Figure 2.19 _____
Event Processing Example.

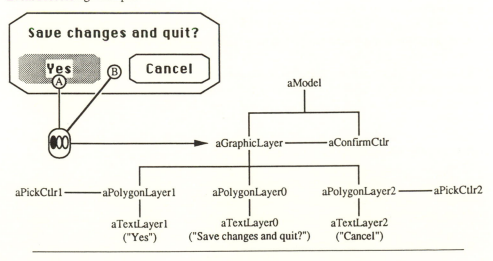

classes, have been heavily used to create SITMAP's unitViews (see "Unit MVC Example" for description of unitViews), as well as the Graphics Editor Module's (GEM's) visible palettes, discussed in the next section.

Unlike traditional graphics packages, which are normally *constrained* by UI toolkits, our two-dimensional graphics extensions are tightly integrated with ICpak 201 UI toolkit. (Thus, for example, the GraphicLayer class, CircleLayer, could be used to create *circular windows!*) This is a tribute to the power of class inheritance and the basic utility of ICpak 101's and ICpak 201's classes.

2.3.7 Designing for Reusability—Graphics Editor Module

To support the application-independent, interactive creation of graphic primitives, we designed the Graphics Editor Module (GEM). Its design requirements were (1) to be reusable for applications other than SITMAP, (2) to be extensible, (3) to allow applications windows to share a graphic editor, and (4) to provide nonmodal interactive graphics. To satisfy these requirements, three primary classes were designed: GraphicEditor, GraphicPalette, and GraphicPaletteView, the last of which is an abstract superclass. Figure 2.20 shows GEM's class hierarchies.

GraphicEditor Class. GraphicEditor provides methods to interactively define and create graphic primitives in an application-independent manner. The class consumer specifies the layer upon which the interactive graphics definition takes place, and the root layer (namely, ICpak 201's *baseLayer*) where the graphicPaletteViews are presented.

GraphicEditor instances create and manage graphic palette models and their associated views. Class consumers indirectly manipulate graphicPaletteViews through GraphicPalette instances (which correspond to graphic palette models), while users indirectly manipulate GraphicPalette instances by interacting with the graphicPaletteViews and their controllers.

Typically, the class consumer creates a GraphicEditor instance and specifies the baseLayer upon which the graphic palettes are rendered:

```
aGraphicEditor = [GraphicEditor newEditor: baseLayer];
```

This instance is then sent the -newPalette: message, specifying the layer (namely, an *edit layer*) upon which users may interactively define new graphic primitives. As a side effect, this method returns a new GraphicPalette instance that stores the current graphic palette settings:

```
aGraphicPalette = [aGraphicEditor newPalette: aLayer];
```

The GraphicPalette class consumer then indicates which object to notify after the user has interactively defined a graphic primitive. Thus the following represents GraphicPalette's callback protocol:

```
[aGraphicPalette        whenComplete: myObject
                        do: @selector (someMethod:)];
```

Figure 2.20 _____
GEM Class Hierarchy.

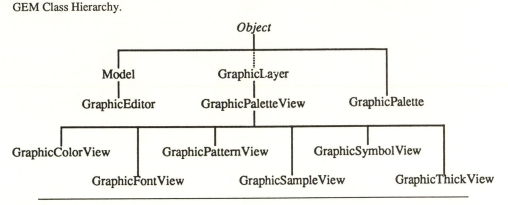

Finally, the GraphicPalette instance is sent a message to become the currently active graphicPalette for the graphicEditor's baseLayer; this makes graphicPaletteViews reflect the GraphicPalette instance's settings when sharing a graphicEditor:

| [aGraphicPalette activate];

Figure 2.21 shows the results of these actions, once -controlStart[12] has been sent to the baseLayer.

Once these actions are performed, and after the user has interactively created or updated a graphics primitive, the application is passed the new graphics primitive via -some-Method:. The application then becomes responsible for incorporating the new primitive into its views, replacing the primitive's controller with application-specific controllers, and freeing the primitive when it is no longer needed.

Because the GraphicEditor instance is effectively a GraphicPalette *factory*, multiple GraphicPalette instances may be created for a GraphicEditor instance; however, only one GraphicPalette instance may be active at a time. Thus, as shown in Fig. 2.22, unlike the Model-View-Controller paradigm, where a *model* has potentially *many views*, GEM's GraphicEditor instances manage *many models* with the *same view*.

GraphicPalette Class. GraphicPalette maintains paint and text attributes for interactively defined graphic primitives and allows consumers to define an interactively created graphic primitive's type, thickness, foreground and background colors, fill and line patterns, and font. Although GraphicPalette instances (which are exclusively created by GraphicEditor instances) are *views* within an application's domain, they are *models* within GEM's domain.[13]

---

[12] BaseLayer's -controlStart method causes the baseLayer and its children to be displayed. It also begins the application event loop, which accepts user inputs.

[13] Thus models and views are actually *context-dependent concepts*. That is, application "views" actually could be implemented as *models* with dependent views!

Figure 2.21

GEM Desktop Elements.

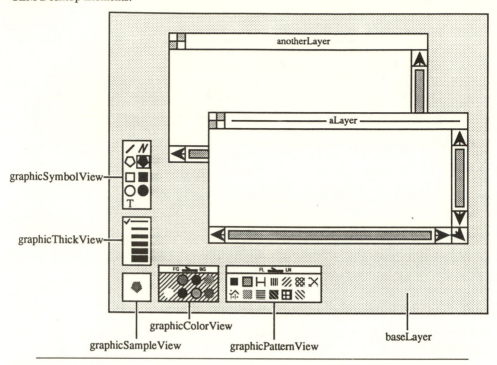

GraphicPaletteView Classes. GraphicEditors also manage graphicPaletteViews, which display the currently active GraphicPalette's symbol type, line thickness, color, patterns, and a sample symbol derived from these settings. (Note that GraphicPaletteView is a subclass of GraphicLayer, described in Section 2.3.6). The subclasses for this abstract superclass are GraphicSymbolView, GraphicThickView, GraphicViewView, GraphicColorView, GraphicPatternView, and GraphicFontView. Although these palette views are owned by GraphicEditor instances, applications may update these views by sending messages to GraphicPalettes. Color Plate 2.1 shows the graphicPaletteViews on SITMAP's desktop.

Discussion. To provide nonmodal interactive graphics, GEM's third design requirement, GraphicEditor, creates a *temporary layer* the same size as passed edit layer (see the preceding description of GraphicEditor's -newPalette: method). This temporary layer is attached to the edit layer's parent, but *in front* of the edit layer. This ordering allows the temporary layer to intercept all events normally consumed by the edit layer. The result is that the edit layer appears to be in a dedicated, interactive graphics creation mode. (In this mode, the input keyboard and mouse semantics are dependent upon the selected GraphicPalette's symbol.) If the user either completely defines the graphic object or cancels the interaction, the temporary layer is deleted. Because of this implementation, users can reenter an edit layer and continue interactive graphics definition after having temporarily exited to work with

Figure 2.22 _____

GEM MVC Paradigm.

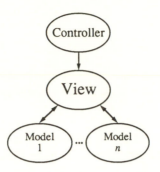

other layers (for example, in SITMAP, the user can scroll the map window and then continue drawing a circle).

In summary, GEM was designed and implemented to be an easily integrated, reusable module. It has allowed arbitrary UI applications to painlessly acquire a sophisticated, interactive graphics editing capability, with no impact on their design. Figure 2.23 shows the

Figure 2.23 _____

Graphics Editor Using GEM.

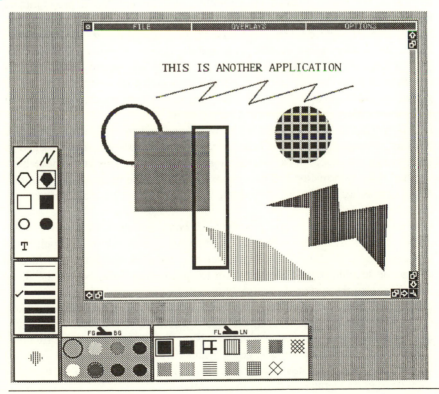

screen image of another application using GEM. Thus we were extremely successful in meeting GEM's design goal of reusability.

2.4 LESSONS LEARNED

Throughout SITMAP's development, we learned many lessons specific to training, programming tools, design, implementation, and project management.

- *Developers should be well versed in object-oriented programming.* Members of our group who were familiar with the concepts of object-oriented programming made the most contributions and were generally more productive during the development cycle.
- *Developers require more training than simply learning a specific object-oriented programming language.* Simply understanding how to use an object-oriented language does not necessarily make a programmer a good class producer. Extensibility and reusability are not realized if designers and programmers (1) are not skilled in object-oriented programming, (2) are not familiar with class hierarchies and class methods, and (3) do not communicate with each other. Also, programmers must adopt a philosophy of bundling components, instead of simply hacking code to implement a function. To paraphrase a speaker on an OOPSLA 1988 panel session, in an object-oriented programming environment "good programmers become better, and bad programmers become obvious."
- *When using a C-hybrid language, developers must exercise more discipline than those using a pure object-oriented programming language, such as Smalltalk-80.* With a C-hybrid language, it is too easy to deviate from sound object-oriented design principles. For example, a C-hybrid allows global variables, and the use of global variables violates the fundamental principle of encapsulation, making it difficult to understand, maintain, and extend code.
- *It is important to have a good class browser and debugger.* Since we lacked a browser, developers sometimes failed to read relevant class specifications and so accidentally overwrote or duplicated important methods. This could have been avoided if the information had been more easily available to the class consumer. Also, without a flexible class debugger, we found debugging tedious and time-consuming.
- *Given a rich set of classes, rapid prototyping is both possible and useful.* With such classes, a user interface can be developed ahead of the bulk of the application semantics and algorithms. This allows developers and users to experiment with user interaction techniques and enables them to spot design flaws before the flaws become part of the system.
- *During the design process, less emphasis should be placed on defining class hierarchies.* The design process should focus on defining objects and their components and the interaction between objects. New class hierarchies are difficult to define without complete knowledge of instance variables and methods. Not all instance variables and methods can be defined early in the development; therefore we refined class hierarchies during implementation.

- *Classes are only as good as their superclasses*. It is inefficient to subclass a defective or incomplete superclass to correct its flaws, because the correction might be needed in *all* the subclasses. Class designers should not hesitate to improve superclasses if deficiencies are found.
- *Multiple inheritance is useful*. In our development of 94 classes, we discovered that only three classes actually *required* multiple inheritance. Therefore, we agree with the general consensus that multiple inheritance is seldom required. However, in cases where multiple inheritance *is* required, its absence is noticeable—without it, resultant code is less maintainable.
- *Defensive programming helps prevent errors*. We discovered some defensive programming techniques that are specific to object-oriented programming. For example, a designer can restrict access to classes by overriding "standard" creation methods (for example, +new) with code to execute [self shouldNotImplement]. This prevents class consumers from inadvertently creating incomplete or inconsistent objects or referencing private methods.
- *When managing the project, allow more time for the design process*. Unlike the design of conventional programs, the design of object-oriented programs closely matches the implementation. Thus the greater part of the program structure is defined during the design process, and programmers need less interpretation to begin implementation. For example, we scheduled many design meetings and shared information by distributing class design sheets that later served as software specifications for programmers. Ideally, programmers need only implement methods and make class inheritance decisions.
- *The use of object-oriented programming made it possible to effectively manage and integrate the efforts of many developers*. Typically, adding more than a certain number of people to most large, complex projects tends to reduce productivity. In object-oriented programming, this appears not to be true because object-oriented programming allows the management structure to be similar to the program structure. We reduced the management costs by dividing the group into teams of two to three individuals; each team was tasked to implement a specific class set (for example, two-dimensional, graphics, object distribution). The teams required less management because the scopes of their tasks were well defined.
- *The cost of integration and testing is small*. Because object interfaces were resolved early in the development cycle, we gained a large productivity payback during software integration and testing. The process of integrating system components was relatively painless, compared with similar software programs coded in a traditional procedural language.
- *Team development also provides a form of project damage control*. Team development served to isolate the effects a poor class design or implementation may have on the entire system. Fortunately, poorly designed system components are easily replaced in an object-oriented system. To reduce the risk of missing project deadlines, novice object-oriented programmers should be assigned to less critical tasks.

The most important lesson we learned is that object-oriented programming works well in the development of real-world applications. Object-oriented programming was a success for us because it not only gave us very good tools with which to complete the task but it also helped to simplify the management of a large software project.

2.5 CONCLUSION

In this chapter, we described the implementation of a highly interactive graphics application called SITMAP. We elected to use object-oriented design and programming because, in a short period of time, they enabled us to produce a final program that is portable and configurable and can easily incorporate new features. We chose to spend more time in the design process; this led to a highly modular object-based system largely due to the nature of object-oriented techniques (encapsulation and messaging). Further, object-oriented programming allowed us to simplify project management and easily integrate the efforts of many developers.

Object-oriented programming environments can support both applied research and systems development. Objects are natural building blocks for experimental prototyping systems. At the same time they are robust components in operational systems. Most important, object-oriented techniques can be used to develop many different systems and allow the leveraging of multiple development efforts. By using the same set of tools, applications are implicitly integrated and share the same style of user interface. Object-oriented programming is ideal for large projects that wish to integrate multiple applications into a uniform and user-friendly environment.

References

[1] Adams, Sam S. "MetaMethods — The MVC Paradigm," *HOOPLA!,* July 1988, pp. 5–21.

[2] Cox, Brad J. *Object Oriented Programming—An Evolutionary Approach*, Addison-Wesley, Reading, MA, 1986.

[3] Cox, Brad J., "New Objective-C Tools and Concepts," Stepstone Inc. Confidential Technical Note, Sandy Hook, CT, January 1988.

[4] Davis, Michael; Schreier, Louis; and Wrabetz, Joan. "A Processing Architecture for Survivable Command, Control, and Communications," *IEEE MILCOM 87 Conference Record*, Washington, D.C., October 1987, pp. 639–647.

[5] Hamer Hodges, Kenneth J., and Watt, Alan. "Internal Design Note 201-20-1," Stepstone, Inc. Sandy Hook, CT, May 1988.

[6] Kaehler, Ted, and Patterson, Dave. *A Taste of Smalltalk*, Norton, New York, 1986.

[7] Krasner, Glenn E., and Pope, Stephen T. "A Cookbook for Using the Model-View-Controller User Interface Paradigm in Smalltalk-80," *Journal of Object-Oriented Programming*, August/September 1988, pp. 26–49.

[8] Leffler, S.J.; Fabry, R.S.; and Joy, W.N. "A 4.2BSD Interprocess Communication Primer," Computer Systems Research Group, Department of Electrical Engineering and Computer Science, University of California, Berkeley, 1983.

[9] Schmucker, Kurt J., *Object-Oriented Programming for the Macintosh*, Hayden Book, Hasbrouck Heights, NJ, 1986.

[10] Schmucker, Kurt J. "Object-Oriented Programming Course Notes," University of California Extension, Santa Cruz, 1988.

[11] Stepstone Inc. *Technical Specifications: ICpak 201 User Interface Software-ICs*, Sandy Hook, CT, October 17, 1987.

[12] Stepstone Inc., *Objective-C Compiler User Reference Manual*, Sandy Hook, CT, January 1988.

[13] Stepstone Inc., *ICpak 201 Graphical User Interface User Reference Manual*, Sandy Hook, CT, January 1988.

[14] Stepstone Inc., "Description of Event I/O Functionality," informal communications, Sandy Hook, CT, May 1988.

[15] Stepstone Inc. "Specification Sheets for Class Changes," informal communications, Sandy Hook, CT, May 1988.

Acknowledgments: The work described in this chapter was funded by the U.S. Army Communications-Electronics Command (CECOM), contract number DAAB07-86-D-A035, delivery order 0078, with additional funding provided by U.S. Army Europe (USAREUR) and SRI International. SRI International funded the writing of this chapter. Alan Algustyniak, Dean Mason, Ken Nitz, Keith Williams, Bill Wohler, and Dave Worthington contributed to the design and implementation of SITMAP. Joan Wrabetz provided managerial support and created an environment that allowed and encouraged technical innovation.

CHAPTER 3

Building Interactive Graphical Applications Using C++

Raghunath Raghavan
Mentor Graphics Corporation, Beaverton, Oregon

3.1 BACKGROUND

3.1.1 Corporate Background

Mentor Graphics Corporation is the market leader in providing software tools for electronic design automation. Founded in 1981, it has grown to be a $300 million company, with 2000 employees in offices worldwide. Its initial software tool offerings were interactive graphical applications for schematic capture and simulation, along with a proprietary system for technical documentation. Since then, the application base has grown to include software systems for printed circuit board (PCB) layout, integrated circuit (IC) layout, mechanical design and thermal analysis of electronic packaging systems, computer-aided software engineering, and electronic technical publishing.

3.1.2 The Development Environment

The development platform is a network of over 400 Apollo workstations. There is no single "host" machine involved; all the nodes on the network are peers. It is a true distributed computing environment.

The language selected for development in 1981 was Apollo Pascal, which is quite similar to Modula-2. This was a natural choice, since the Apollo operating system was itself written in Apollo Pascal. Also, in 1981 a Modula-like language was considered to be fairly "modern." Most of the developers prefer the native Apollo development tools—the Aegis operating system, the Display Manager pad editor (rather than Vi or Emacs), the various compilers, the source level debugger, the software profiling tools, and more recently, the DSEE software engineering environment.

3.1.3 The Old Application Development Framework

Until a year ago, all application development was based on the Idealib, a sophisticated library of complex reusable software components written entirely in Apollo Pascal. Initially architected by a small team in 1981, it has grown to over a million lines of code.

It is useful to understand the functionality provided by the Idealib, since it defines a lower bound for the functionality required from any new "replacement" system. The Idealib contains standard foundation components such as a heap memory manager and a dynamic string package. It also contains a number of more complex components, such as a human interface subsystem, graphics and text subsystems, a version management system, and a proprietary relational database system. These significant components are described in greater detail next.

The *HI system* is a pre-Macintosh user interface management system. It is not as icon- and mouse-oriented as the Mac interface, but it is considerably more powerful in many ways. It contains a user programming language that allows end users to write powerful scripts, define menus, define keys, and so on. Expert users can tailor the system infinitely by writing the appropriate "userware."

The *GSS system* is a display list data structure (with persistence) for doing two-dimensional graphics. The data structure represents a set of up to 256 layers, with graphical objects on each layer. Typical graphical objects are points, rectangles, polylines, polygons, stroke text, and so forth. GSS manages zooming, scrolling, and multiple windows onto the same display list.

GSS simplfies the implementations of applications wherein the user manipulates graphical representations of familiar objects. Such applications set up a GSS data structure that maintains all the graphic aspects of the application's data structure. The GSS data structure is manipulated via a procedural interface. Objects can be added, deleted, or edited. GSS takes care of all the actual graphical output to the screen.

The *TSS system* is the text analog of GSS. It is the basis for all displayed bitmapped text on the screen (except for stroke text embedded within pictures). It is roughly analogous to the text subsystem in the Mac toolbox.

A rather pragmatic approach to the design database problem has been taken by the Idealib. The *VMGR system* allows the creation of various typed "files" on top of the native file system. It also manages "interfile" references between these typed "files" (that is, design data links). The VMGR does not understand or in any way interpret the contents of the "files" managed by it.

Each VMGR "file" is a design database. File types include picture files, schematic files, IC layout files, PCB place files, and route data files. Each application (or each group of interrelated applications) can decide on the most appropriate data model and set up a corresponding VMGR file type. Idealib utilities like the DB relational database system and the B-tree indexing system may or may not be used to implement persistence for particular data models.

The components described thus far are general in nature and are not in any way specific to CAE/CAD applications. The Idealib also contains various special subsystems associated with the electrical network data model. This is a rather pervasive data model in the CAE domain and underlies all the Mentor Graphics schematic capture and simulation applications. Over time, the Idealib has grown to over a million lines of Apollo Pascal code, and it is considered to be largely unmaintainable. It is certainly hard to extend, given its somewhat outdated architecture and the nature of Apollo Pascal.

3.1.4 The New Object-Oriented Framework

In early 1986 C++ was chosen as the language for the second generation of applications and tools. The intention was to create a software base that would make obsolete the Idealib system and last well into the 1990s.

Selecting the Language. It was felt that an object-oriented language with inheritance was essential for building the second generation system. The Idealib system had been designed to support just schematic capture and simulation. Over time, it became increasingly difficult to have a single implementation that was optimized for all the numerous client applications. An object-oriented language with inheritance and polymorphism would certainly solve this problem by providing hooks for client applications to override and optimize certain fundamental behaviors.

There were a number of reasons why C++ was chosen. It is a very clean object-oriented extension to C. It is relatively mature, having been in use inside AT&T for quite a while. It has no special run-time support requirements, aside from the presence of the standard C libraries. Best of all, it is a very likely candidate for industrywide acceptance, just like Unix and C before it.

Some Requirements. The functional requirements on the new framework were rather stringent, since it had to replace the Idealib, which is a large and mature system. Fortunately, there was no requirement that the Idealib programming interfaces be supported directly and completely by the new system. Rather, for every capability in the Idealib, there had to be a functional equivalent in the new system. This requirement allowed the object-oriented design to be considerably cleaner.

One major complicating factor was the large number of fairly complex applications that used the Idealib. Given the product release cycle, an abrupt C++ rewrite of all the existing applications was not a real option. The approach taken was to repartition each of these applications so that its software structure was conceptually closer to the ultimately desired object-oriented structure. In the process, the application was modified appropriately to use the new framework rather than the Idealib. In many cases, significant amounts of code would remain in Apollo Pascal (for example, the place and route algorithms). This remaining code would be converted to C++ over the course of a release or two.

Some Architectural Issues. In the beginning, some thought was given whether to derive (that is, to subclass) all the classes in the framework either directly or indirectly from an abstract base class Object. Doing so usually results in an easy-to-use programming environment, where a consistent set of design and usage conventions prevails.

There are many class library systems where this is done (for example, Smalltalk, OOPS[1],

---

[1]OOPS stands for Object Oriented Programming Support. It is a C++ class library developed at NIH in Bethesda, MD, by Keith Gorlen.

MacApp). Using this approach with C++ has certain drawbacks, since C++ is a "hybrid" object-oriented language. The built-in types (int and float, for example) are not classes and therefore fall outside any class hierarchy. Also, the classes in the standard C++ libraries (for example, the I/O stream library) are themselves not derived from any common base class Object. Therefore, the framework's class library contains a number of classes, many that are quite independent of each other. The class inheritance structure, instead of being a tree rooted at base class Object, is a forest of highly optimized classes. Inheritance is used only where really needed for getting the required class behavior. Interestingly, it has turned out that this architecture is better suited to building a framework that includes contributions from a relatively large and diverse group of developers. There is no particularly clever taxonomy of objects in the framework library. Basically, the library is broken up into three big functional pieces: the core system (Core), the user interface management system (UIMS), and the design data management system (DDMS). The rest of this chapter describes how these pieces are constructed and how they are used to build interactive graphical applications.

3.2 THE CORE SYSTEM

The Core system is a foundation class set for object-oriented programming. It provides a number of very basic capabilities, some of which are discussed in greater detail in this section. What distinguishes the Core class library is its bottom-up design. Its classes and utilities have been created in the hope that they would be useful in the design and implementation of more complex components. Generally, however, there is no special knowledge about how or why these classes are used by particular clients. The major effort is in the correct design, implementation, and testing of the classes themselves, without being tied to any particular application domain or usage.

By contrast, the UIMS class library is designed for interactive graphics applications that share a common Mentor Graphics "look and feel." As a consequence, there is much more class inheritance, overall design coherence, and purpose among the UIMS classes.

3.2.1 Heap Memory Management

A general design philosophy in the Idealib that has been carried forward to the new framework is to have the programmer manage the free store (that is, heap memory). Languages like Pascal and C are not well suited to garbage-collection-based free store management. The discussion of the free store management philosophy is presented in two parts. First, the C++ hooks used to implement the scheme are discussed. Then, the overall impact on the programmer using this system is presented.

Building a Better Heap Management System. C++ simplifies storage management by the programmer considerably by allowing the operators new and delete to be overloaded. Exactly how this is done is explained by the expression

| new *type-name*

creates an object of type type-name from the free store and returns a pointer to it. Normally, the space for this object is obtained from the operating system by calling malloc(). The delete operator destroys an object created by the new operator. Usually, the space is returned to the operating system by calling free(). By overloading new and delete, it is possible to have a better free-store management than that afforded by calling malloc() and free(). Central to this scheme is class Heap.

Each instance of class Heap manages one or more large chunks of program free store, obtained via the malloc() system call. Heap services free-store allocation requests (new calls) and deallocation requests (delete calls) by further subdividing and managing these chunks very efficiently. The heap maintains a list of free elements in order to accomplish this.

As far as possible, allocation requests are satisfied by reusing elements (or parts thereof) in the heap's free list. If this is not possible, more free store is obtained from the system via malloc(). When a deallocation occurs, the newly returned chunk is added to the heap's free list. If it adjoins an element already on the free list, a coagulation is done.

The following is a partial listing of class Heap.

```
class Heap {
public:

    virtual ~Heap();                            // virtual destructor
    virtual void* allocate (long reqd_bytes);   // get free store
    virtual void clear ();                       // clear for re-use

protected:

    Heap ();
        // protected constructor because this is an abstract class.

    virtual void deallocate (void* element_p);
        // return element to the heap for possible future re-use.
};
```

The system new and delete operators are overloaded within the heap library so that they operate out of heaps instead. This is done very simply as follows.

```
extern void* operator new (long size_in_bytes);
    //   Overload the system new operator to get memory from the default heap.
    //   (This heap gets constructed automatically as a static global variable.)

extern void operator delete (void* ptr);
    //   Overload the system delete operator to return memory to the heap
    //   from which it was allocated, rather than perform the system call free().
    //   Each heap element "knows" which heap it was allocated from.)
```

Particular application classes can also overload the new operator so that the allocation is from a particular application-specific heap:

```
class Foo {
...

    ...
    void* operator new()
        { return appl_heap_p->allocate (sizeof (Foo)); }
    ...
    ...
};
```

Class **Heap** is an abstract class. When creating a heap, the programmer must choose from among one of its derived classes: **Genheap, Uniheap, or Fastheap**. Thus

```
Heap* appl_heap_p = new Genheap;
```

Class **Genheap** is the general implementation. It manages arbitrarily sized blocks and uses a boundary tag scheme for doing free element coagulation in constant time. Class **Uniheap** is an implementation that is optimized for heaps where all the elements are expected to be the same size. This situation often arises in practice. Class **Fastheap** is a special implementation for scratch heaps, that is, heaps that get used for a period of time and then get thrown away altogether. In this situation, deallocate can be a no-op.

Using the Better Heap Management System. The programmer using the heap system should first create one or more application-specific heaps. For example,

```
Heap* gen_heap_p    = new Genheap;
Heap* pin_heap_p    = new Uniheap (sizeof (Pin));
Heap* net_heap_p    = new Uniheap (sizeof (Net));
```

In order to do the allocation from the appropriate heaps, the programmer defines operator new() for all the appropriate classes to operate out of the appropriate heap(s).

```
class Pin : public ... {
    ...
    void* operator new()    { return pin_heap_p->allocate (sizeof (Pin)); }
    ...
};
```

Nothing special need be done in the constructor. The constructor code can be written, assuming that the space allocation has already been taken care of through operator new() before the constructor body is entered.

For proper deallocation, all the class destructors must behave responsibly. There are just two rules of thumb:

1. All abstract class destructors are made virtual. This ensures that the appropriate destructor of the appropriately derived class is called.
2. Each class destructor should remember to call delete for all subordinate heap-based objects that are "hanging off" the object via pointers. (Shared objects must be managed

carefully.) Member variables that are objects (and not pointers to objects) are managed automatically by the system.

It is clear from this discussion that reimplementing the free-store management scheme has a very minimal impact on the client programmer. On the other hand, it has a significant impact on system performance by allowing the programmer to better manage the usage of the virtual address space, by minimizing calls to malloc() and free(), and so forth.

3.2.2 Dynamic Strings

An important part of the object-oriented framework is class String, which provides all the usual string manipulation functions, for example, assignment, comparison/lexicographic

---

Listing 3.1 _____

Definition of Class String.

```
class String {
    ...
public:

    String ();                          // default
    String (const String&);             // for parameter passing
    String (const char*);               // to make a String from a char*
    String (const char*, int len);      // Pascal compatibility
        //Constructors

//   Assignment operators
String& operator= (const String& src);
String& operator= (const char* src_p);

//   Concatenation operators
friend String operator+ (const String& op1, const String& op2);
String& operator+= (const String& op);

//   Comparison and ordering functions
friend Boolean operator==      (const String& op1, const String& op2);
friend Boolean operator!=      (const String& op1, const String& op2);
friend Boolean operator<       (const String& op1, const String& op2);
friend Boolean operator>       (const String& op1, const String& op2);
friend Boolean operator<=      (const String& op1, const String& op2);
friend Boolean operator>=      (const String& op1, const String& op2);

//   Indexing, substring and searching functions
    char operator[] (int index);
    Substring sub (int start_pos, int length);
    Substring search (const char* reg_exp);
};
```

ordering, indexing, concatenation, substrings, regular expression searching, and so forth. Listing 3.1 is a partial listing of the definition of class String.

With class String in the framework, there should be very little reason for clients to deal with entities of type char*. One of the main design goals with class String was to hide completely all the usual string storage allocation/deallocation functions. The client could then treat an instance of class String just like a scalar, assigning to it, passing it about by value, and so forth.

From a storage management point of view, having clients deal with instances of String (rather than String*) has some major advantages. The job of making sure that the constructors and destructors do get called, and in the right order and at the right places, is left up to the C++ compiler. This is accomplished by making class String simply a small header record, with a pointer to the actual string store. The client of class String is not aware of the existence of this secondary store, which grows and shrinks dynamically as required.

The store can be shared between a number of String instances. A reference counting scheme is used to properly manage and control the sharing (see Fig. 3.1). The store is replicated only if (1) it is shared among many strings and (2) some string wants to change it. This scheme makes assigning strings (passing them by value, and so on) cheap since the secondary store does not have to be replicated or copied.

An interesting and useful aspect of the dynamic string system is class Substring, which is derived from class String. An instance of Substring provides read/write access to a portion of the secondary store of its parent, String. Assigning to a Substring actually changes the parent string by modifying its secondary store. (The reference counting scheme guarantees that other strings sharing that secondary store are not affected.) All types of assignments are supported: String to String, String to Substring, Substring to String, and Substring to Substring.

Being a derived class of String, Substring provides all the usual String functions. Furthermore, a Substring can be passed as an argument to any function that is expecting a String argument.

Figure 3.1 _____
Dynamic Strings and Reference Counting.

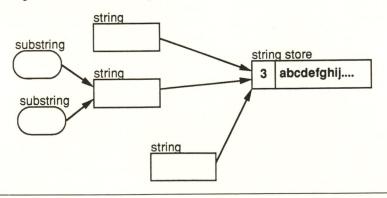

3.2.3 Container Classes

The term *container classes* refers to data structures such as linked lists, hash tables, and dynamic arrays. Though they are not particularly difficult to implement, such data structures represent the "glue" that holds most large software systems together. Implementing such classes properly once, and establishing a common usage protocol, promotes the overall software quality and maintainability.

Unfortunately, C++ does not as yet have a parameterized type capability. Such a structure would have allowed container classes to be built, wherein the element type could be specified as a constructor parameter. (This capability is planned for a future release of C++.)

Lacking this capability, a decision had to be made regarding the element type for container classes. Basically, there were two choices:

1. Make the elements be of type Object (an abstract base class). This technique is widely used to build object-oriented framework libraries such as Smalltalk. However, it is entirely too awkward for C++. The major reason is that the common built-in types (for example, int and float) are not classes. It would therefore be awkward to have, say, a list of ints. In any case, there is not much conceptual leverage in having everything derived from a common base class Object.
2. Make the elements be of type void* (that is, universal untyped pointers). This scheme is not without its drawbacks. The type-checking provided by the system is entirely turned off for the items, and it is left to the user to do all the proper type casts. Also, all the items have to have been allocated on the heap.

This alternative was chosen. The other alternative was essentially ruled out since the framework class library is not based on an abstract superclass Object. Figure 3.2 shows the basic container class hierarchy.

Class Container is an abstract base class representing unordered collections of items of type void*. Class Bag is a concrete implementation of it. Class List is an abstract class representing all types of sequenced collections. There are three actual implementations—singly

Figure 3.2 _____
Container Class Hierarchy.

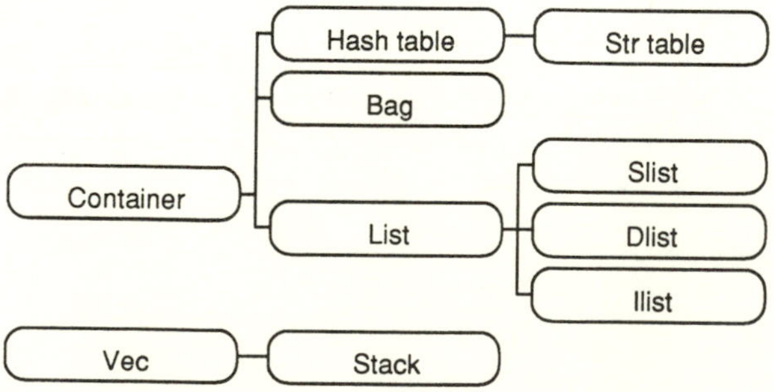

linked lists, doubly linked lists, and inverted lists (linked blocks of pointers to the actual items).

The details of the various class definitions are easily inferred and therefore will not be reproduced here. As expected, the various container classes provide facilities to insert and delete member items, operators for assignment, concatenation, and so on. They do not, however, provide facilities to traverse over all the member items. This is left to a separate associated scanner class. Separating the scanning function from the container class itself is of crucial importance. It makes the various container classes stateless with respect to scanning, thus allowing multiple concurrent scans of a particular collection. Also, this architecture supports thinking of a scanner as being, in addition to an iterator, either a pointer or an item marker.

All scanner classes are ultimately derived from base class Scanner. This promotes the use of a common protocol for scanning all types of collections. The existence of such a common protocol has proved to be a major boon to developers. Listing 3.2 is a partial listing of the definition of class Scanner.

Because class Scanner is an abstract base class, the actual implementations of the listed functions are delegated to derived classes. For each concretely derived class of base class Container, there is an associated scanner class that is derived from class Scanner, for example, Bag_scanner, Slist_scanner, Dlist_scanner, Hash_table_scanner, and so forth.

Listing 3.2 _____
Definition of Class Scanner

```
class Scanner {
...
public:

Scanner (Container&);              // constructor
virtual ~Scanner ();               // destructor

//   Ways to move the scanner
virtual void reset();
virtual void position (int index);
virtual Boolean operator++();
virtual Boolean operator--();

//   Checking the scan point
virtual Boolean at_valid_item();
virtual int position ();

//   Access to item
virtual void* item();              // get function
virtual void item (void* new_item);   // set function

};
```

In addition, the framework contains a dynamic array class Vec, and derived from it is class Stack. Class Vec is designed to allocate the storage for a particular index location only if that index location was actually assigned. If a particular index location is accessed within an expression before the location has been assigned, a value of 0 is returned even though the actual storage for it has not have been allocated. This scheme provides a user view of an infinite array initialized to 0 and requires distinguishing between array indexing on the left side of an assignment operator and array indexing in expressions. The following partial listing illustrates how this is done:

```
class Vec {
...
public:
...
    Vec_item operator[] (int index);        // note that an actual value is not returned
...
};
    class Vec_item {
...
    public:
...
    operator void*();                       //rvalue usage. return 0 if not allocated.
    void* operator= (void* item);           //lvalue usage. allocate if necessary.
...
};
```

3.2.4 Geometric Classes

Two very widely used classes, especially in the implementations of the user interface management system and the graphics system, are Point and Rectangle. Being very simple classes, their member functions are mostly implemented in-line. The result is a very rich vocabulary for programming with Points and Rectangles. At the same time, there is no procedure call overhead associated with calling the various Point and Rectangle member functions.

A point is a simple tuple (x, y) of ints. This coordinate system is adequate for the typical two-dimensional graphics required for most CAE/CAD systems. (The Mentor Graphics three-dimensional mechanical drafting application has its own point type, which is a triple (x,y,z) of doubles.) Listing 3.3 is a partial listing of the definition of class Point.

A rectangle is represented by a pair of points, representing two diametrically opposite corners. Pt0 is the (min x, min y) corner and pt1 is the (max x, max y) corner. Since rectangles are maintained in this canonical form, there is no built-in bias regarding the origin of the coordinate system. Consequently, the same class is used to implement both the window system (origin at the top left corner of the screen) and the graphics display list system (origin at the bottom left corner of the screen). Listing 3.4 is a partial self-explanatory listing of class Rectangle.

Classes Point and Rectangle both contain numerous other member functions that are not included in Listing 3.4.

Listing 3.3 _____

Definition of Class Point

```
struct Point {
    ...

    Point ();
    Point (int x, int y);

    //  Comparison operators. Useful for containment checks in class Rectangle.
    friend Boolean operator==      (const Point& op1, const Point& op2);
    friend Boolean operator!=      (const Point& op1, const Point& op2);
    friend Boolean operator<       (const Point& op1, const Point& op2);
    friend Boolean operator>       (const Point& op1, const Point& op2);
    ...

    friend Point min       (const Point& op1, const Point& op2);
    friend Point max       (const Point& op1, const Point& op2);
    friend Point abs       (const Point& op1, const Point& op2);

    //  Translation operators
    friend Point operator+     (const Point& op1, const Point& op2);
    friend Point operator-     (const Point& op1, const Point& op2);
    Point operator+=           (const Point& a);
    Point operator-=           (const Point& a);

    //  I/O operators
    friend ostream& operator<< (ostream& out, const Point& pt);
    friend istream& operator>> (istream& inp, Point& pt);
};
```

3.2.5 The Virtual Display Driver

Virtual Display Driver (VDD) is a subsystem that provides a pleasant object-oriented interface to the host operating system graphics and window manager system calls. It is responsible for "immediate mode" graphics output, keyboard and mouse input, and all interactions with the window manager of the host workstation. When VDD is initialized, it takes over a window of the underlying host window manager. It then controls all input and output for this window. Figure 3.3 shows the VDD architectural model.

The VDD subsystem is implemented as a small collection of classes. The more significant classes follow.

- Class **VDD** represents the host manager window. It provides event input and graphics output functions and has methods for interacting with the host window manager (for example, for window pop, grow, move, and iconify).
- Class Vcontrol is used to specify graphics output clipping and transformation information. Each drawing call takes a Vcontrol* argument.

Listing 3.4
Definition of Class Rectangle

```
class Rectangle {
    ...
    Rectangle ();
    Rectangle (int x0, int y0, int x1, int y1);
    Rectangle (const Point& pt0, const Point& pt1);

    int height();
    int width();

    Point corner (int x_extreme /* 0 or 1 */ , int y_extreme /* 0 or 1 */);
    Point center();

    Boolean contains (const Point& pt);
    Boolean contains (const Rectangle& r);
    Boolean overlaps (const Rectangle& r);
    Rectangle intersect_rectangle (const Rectangle& other);

    Rectangle expanded_by (int expansion_amt);
    Rectangle contracted_by (int contraction_amt);

    //   I/O operators
    friend ostream& operator<< (ostream& out, const Rectangle& pt);
    friend istream& operator>> (istream& inp, Rectangle& pt);
};
```

- Class **Vpen** is used to specify attributes for drawing lines, curves, and the edges of filled objects (for example, line width and line style). Each line drawing call takes a **Vpen*** argument.
- Class **Vbrush** is used to specify fill attributes for closed graphical objects (the fill patterns, the background and foreground colors, and raster ops, for example).

Figure 3.3
VDD Architectural Model.

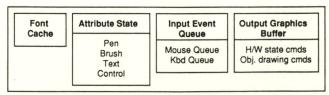

- Class **Vtext** is used to specify attributes for text, such as the font, justification, rotation, and slant.

Listing 3.5 is a representative sampling of class VDD. This listing leaves out much more than it reveals. Class VDD actually contains numerous member functions to control all aspects of the graphic interface. There are myriad little details, most of which are largely irrelevant for the purpose of this discussion.

Relationship to X Windows. X Windows is one of the many possible "host" graphics/ window management environments for VDD. However, it is not the only possible environment. The decision not to base all graphics directly on X was necessitated by the belief that current implementations of X do not adequately meet the company's needs. The issue is primarily performance. For example, on the Apollo workstation, the X-11 implementation is significantly slower than the native GPR and GSR graphics packages.

By basing all graphics on VDD, it becomes possible to select the best graphics system available on each workstation. Another advantage of using VDD is that it presents an object-oriented interface that fits in more naturally with the rest of the system.

Listing 3.5 _____
Representative Sample of Class VDD.

```
class VDD : public Rectangle {
    ...
    VDD();
    ~VDD();
    ...
    //  Graphic output methods
    virtual void polyline (Vcontrol* c_p, Vpen* p_p, Point pts[], int count);
    virtual void polygon (Vcontrol* c_p, Vpen* p_p, Vbrush* b_p, Point pts[], int count);
    virtual void rectangle (Vcontrol* c_p, Vpen* p_p, Vbrush* b_p, Rectangle& r);
    ...
    //  Event input methods
    virtual Boolean get_event (Vevent* ev_p, Boolean wait);
    ...
    //  Host window manager interface methods
    virtual void host_wmgr_grow_this ();
    virtual void host_wmgr_move_this();
    virtual void host_wmgr_pop_this();
    virtual void host_wmgr_iconify_this();
    ...
    //  Cursor control methods
    virtual void set_cursor_visibility (Boolean on);
    virtual void set_cursor_blink_rate (int times_per_sec);
    virtual void set_cursor_shape (String& font, char ch);
    ...
};
```

Multiple Implementations. Class VDD is an abstract base class. The actual implementation is left to derived classes. On the Apollo, GSR is the fastest native graphics system. Therefore, GSRDD is the concrete derived class of VDD for the Apollo. XDD is another concrete derived class that is based on X-11.

An interesting aspect of the design of VDD is that it can efficiently manage output to hardcopy devices, like printers and plotters. Therefore, there are yet other derived classes of VDD that represent the various hardcopy devices. This architecture allows a tremendous conceptual simplification.

3.2.6 MULE

MULE stands for Mentor Userware Language Environment. An interpreted language with a C-like syntax, it supports the common data types (integers, reals, strings, arrays, and so on). It has all the common C operators and control structures and even supports recursion. MULE is very much a stand-alone environment. (In fact, it can be invoked and used from the operating system shell.) Input is parsed and evaluated. If the input contains function definitions, they are parsed and stored in the MULE symbol table ("environment"). These user-defined functions can be subsequently invoked from expressions and the like.

What makes MULE much more than a simple shell-level programming language is that it provides full programmatic access to all its run-time data structures and operations. This feature allows clients of MULE to leverage its capabilities to the utmost, as described in the following section. MULE represents a very significant and complex chunk of reusable code. Exactly how it is used in various contexts is described in the coming sections.

Leveraging MULE. At the heart of the MULE run-time system is the MULE environment, a symbol tablelike data structure where variables and compiled definitions of functions (that is, instances of class Callable) are stored. The MULE environment is preloaded to hold the definitions of built-in operators and functions.

The MULE expression evaluator operates in the context of an environment. When evaluating an operator, it uses the operand name to search the environment for the current binding for that name. If the name represents a variable, the associated value is fetched from the environment. If it represents a function call, the name is bound to an instance of class Callable. The evaluator invokes the call() virtual function of class Callable to get the required value.

MULE clients exploit this process by defining appropriately derived classes of Callable to register their own functions with MULE. The call() virtual function can be overloaded appropriately to invoke the desired client functions. (At present, the UIMS is the most significant client of MULE; other MULE clients include VHDL-based applications.)

Application developers can create extensible applications by registering the primitive application functions with MULE. ("The MULE Interface," in Section 3.3.3, describes in detail how this is done.) The end user can extend this environment by writing higher-level MULE functions. The result is a RISC-based approach to application development. It places a lot of power directly in the hands of the end user.

The MULE Class Hierarchy. The diagram shown in Fig. 3.4 is a partial picture of the MULE class inheritance hierarchy.

Figure 3.4 _____

MULE Class Hierarchy.

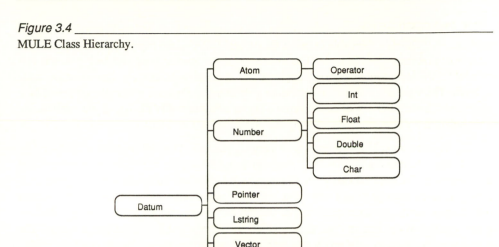

3.3 THE USER INTERFACE MANAGEMENT SYSTEM

The user interface part of any interactive graphical application is the agent that controls and manages all communication between the end user and the application. It features a variety of techniques for gathering input from the user, such as command lines, programmable function keys, strokes, menus, palettes, forms containing buttons, type-in fields, sliders, and gauges. The user interface also manages a set of windows that are used by the application for presenting graphical output to the user.

The user interface management system is a reusable software component that supports the design and implementation of user interfaces for particular applications. This section describes in some detail the object-oriented architecture of the Mentor Graphics UIMS.

3.3.1 Major Design Goals

A primary design goal in the UIMS was to achieve portability. This was largely facilitated by the use of VDD. The UIMS makes very few, if any, assumptions about the underlying workstation. It simply assumes that it owns one of the process windows managed by the native window manager of the host workstation. Another goal was to achieve a clean software architecture that allows extensive user customization of the interface. The UIMS is designed to allow a clear separation between the user interface part of an application and the underlying functionality of that application. There are a number of significant advantages in doing this.

1. This scheme allows the development of a common "look and feel" across a range of applications. This is achievable because the typical UIMS-based application contains very little user interface-specific code. The existence of a common look and feel makes it less painful for the user to move between applications. It also makes new applications a lot easier to learn. The separation of the user interface part of an application also makes it possible to experiment with a variety of user interface styles without really changing the application. This helps in the process of developing the common look and feel.

2. The common UIMS represents a very significant chunk of reusable code (see Fig. 3.5). There is tremendous software leverage in doing this, in terms of both development and maintenance. The common UIMS is usually extended/enhanced by the various application groups in small but significant ways. Typically, the enhancements add domain-specific user interface elements. For example, the user interface environment for simulation applications might contain waveform trace windows, which are not really relevant in other domains. The relevant application groups retain ownership and control of these domain-specific toolkit extensions. It is worth noting that these extensions are relatively small in comparison to the overall user interface environment.

3. Delegating the user interface functionality to the UIMS greatly simplifies the architecture of the application. The application does not have to ever bother with physical events (mouse moves, keystrokes, for example). Instead, it expects to receive "logical events" from the UIMS. A logical event is an encoded user-level command. It is simply a packet consisting of a name and an optional set of arguments.

When an application receives a logical event, it looks up the name of the logical event in a table to determine the appropriate logical event handler to execute in response. This is the basic mechanism for handling commands. The various UIMS gadgets (for example,

Figure 3.5 _____

Common User Interface Management System (UIMS).

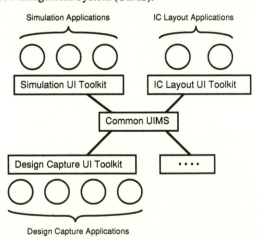

Figure 3.6
User Interface Management System Gadgets.

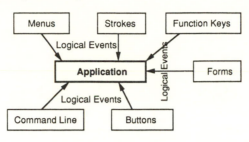

menus, command line, strokes, and function keys) are designed to send logical events to the application (see Fig. 3.6). Generally speaking, the application-specific code is unaware of how a particular logical event was generated. With this type of a scheme, adding new UIMS gadgets or refining existing ones has no direct impact on the architecture of the application.

4. This architecture also supports the goal of allowing the end user to customize the user interface extensively. This capability allows end users to impose their own "look and feel" extensions easily, without having to recompile the application. The UIMS provides an interpreted end-user programming language (MULE) that supports this customization. This language has a C-like syntax. It supports all the C control structures, up to and including recursion. Code written in this language is referred to as "userware."

Users can use this language to define their own commands. To do this, they specify the command name and bind it to the "userware" function that represents the logical event handler. These user-defined commands behave just like the built-in commands for all intents and purposes. This language also contains constructs that allow users to define their own menus, palettes, forms, function keys, strokes, window layouts, and so forth.

3.3.2 General System Architecture

This section presents a very high-level overview of the UIMS structure. Subsequent sections provide more detailed explanations.

The Process Model. The UIMS is designed to allow three different process models.

1. *The single process model.* Here, the user interface portion of an application is in the same process as the application-specific portion. This is the most common situation.

2. *The multi-display model.* Here, a number of displays are put into lock step. Any display can be used to interact with the application. All the displays have the exact same appearance at all time. This is a very useful facility for training and for communication. (See Fig. 3.7.) The implementation of this model can be hidden entirely beneath the VDD level. It involves having a set of VDD processes that are in lock step, with each VDD process

Figure 3.7 _____
High-Level Overview of UIMS Structure.

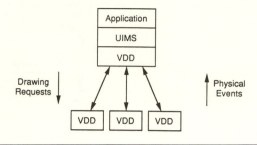

managing a display. Only one of the VDD processes has the actual application bound to it. IPC channels are used to keep the various VDD processes in sync.

3. *The multiprocess UIMS model* (Fig. 3.8). The user interface part is in a separate process from the rest of the application. Logical events are sent from the user interface to the application via IPC channels. Drawing calls are sent from the application to the user interface via IPC channels as well.

This latter model has a number of attractive features, the main one being its better utilization of network computing resources. This is very critical in certain application domains, for example, simulation. Typically, the back-end is the simulation kernel running on a big number cruncher, while the front-end is primarily a user-interface application that communicates in bursts with the back-end.

There are certain drawbacks; for example, dynamic dragging and rubberbanding that requires information from the back-end is not as visually responsive. Such situations are rare, and when they do occur, the end user appears not to mind.

Note that this scheme is different from the X-Windows client-server model. In the latter, the window manager is in a separate process (the server). The application, including its

Figure 3.8 _____
A Multiprocess UIMS Model.

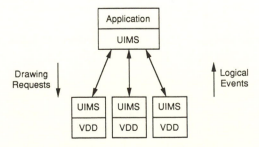

UIMS, is the client process and communicates with the window server as needed. The server is typically multiplexed between a number of clients.

The choice as to which process model to use is made by each application. The default choice for most Mentor Graphics applications is expected to be the single process model.

Operating System Dependencies. The UIMS is intended to run on UNIX workstations with relatively large bitmapped displays (for example, 1024 x 800 pixels). It is not particularly designed for operation from terminals, for example, VT 100. It is built on top of VDD, which is the portable virtual display driver interface. VDD takes over a window from the host workstation window manager and controls both input and output in this window. The UIMS itself does not contain any direct OS system calls. All such calls are embedded within the implementation of VDD.

Conceptual View of the Architecture. The UIMS has a layered architecture, as depicted in Fig. 3.9. At the base is VDD. Apart from being retargetable, it provides a pleasant object-oriented interface to the host system window manager and graphics system calls. VDD is built without any knowledge of the UIMS.

The next layer is the user interface core system. This layer implements the basic machinery that makes the whole system work. It contains such things as an area manager, an event manager, and facilities for managing off-screen bitmaps used for BLTs. It also includes the mechanisms for interfacing the UIMS with MULE, by introducing MULE primitives that are UIMS specific.

The toolkit layer contains various gadgets that can be used to construct user interfaces. Examples include buttons, menus, palettes, scroll bars, gauges, and text edit areas. This is a rather loosely organized collection of gadgets that adhere to a common "look and feel" policy as far as possible.

Applications are the next natural layer. To make the task of writing applications easy,

Figure 3.9 _____

Layered Architecture of the UIMS.

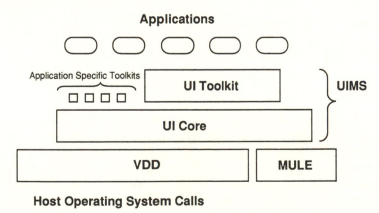

sample applications are included as part of the UIMS. These applications provide templates and road maps for "real" application architects.

These various layers are discussed in greater detail in the next section.

3.3.3 UI Core System

The UI Core System is a policy-free layer that implements the basic mechanisms for the UIMS. All the usual user interface gadgets (scroll bars, buttons, editable text fields, and so on) are built on top of the UI Core system. (These gadgets are all assumed to belong to the UI Toolkit layer built on top of the UI Core layer.) Functionally, this layer is similar to the Intrinsics layer of the X Toolkit (Xtk).

Area. The **Area** is the basic building block of the UIMS. It is a rectangular region that is capable of handling inputs ("events"). It has a bitmap into which it can paint things. (Actually, it shares a controlled portion of the screen bitmap.) The **Area** concept is very similar to the **Widget** concept associated with the X Toolkit.

Almost everything that a user sees and interacts with is based on class **Area**. UIMS artifacts such as menus, buttons, sliders, and gauges, are all derived classes of class **Area**. UIMS windows are also areas. Areas may contain any number of subordinate, or children, areas. The children must be wholly contained within the parent area, resulting in an area containment hierarchy that is rooted at the host display manager window.

The following is a high-level overview of the categories of member functions in class **Area**. Notice that **Area** is derived from **Rectangle**, which is very natural and very useful.

```
class Area : public Rectangle {
    ...
    // Constructors
    ...
    // Area hierarchy functions
    ...
    // Drawing functions
    ...
    // Physical event handling functions
    ...
    // Logical event handling functions
    ...
};
```

Event. The **Event** is the basic language of communication among areas. All areas are capable of handling events. An event handler is an appropriate member function of class **Area**. There are two types of events, physical events and logical events.

A Physical Event is generated by VDD and passed onto the UIMS event manager. Based on the mouse cursor location, the event manager figures out the destination area It sends the event to the appropriate area by invoking the appropriate event handler member function of that area. For each possible type of physical event, there is a corresponding handler function in class **Area**.

```
class Area : public Rectangle {
    ...
    // Physical event handlers
    virtual void mouse_move_act (Physical_event *);
    virtual void mouse_stop_act (Physical_event *);
    virtual void ascii_key_act (Physical_event *);
    virtual void function_key_act (Physical_event *);
    virtual void mouse_key_act (Physical_event *);
    virtual void other_key_act (Physical_event *);
    ...
};
```

A Logical Event is an artificial event. It consists of a name and an optional list of arguments. It is constructed by an area and sent to another area via the UIMS event manager. When an area receives a logical event, it looks up the name in its MULE environment (more on this later). If the name is known, the area responds by executing one of its member functions.

Unlike physical events, the number of logical events is open-ended. Each application area establishes (using MULE) the set of logical events to which it will respond. In addition, end users may create MULE userware functions that behave just like logical event handlers. Thus logical event handlers can be either built in (area member functions) or user written (MULE functions).

In the interests of promoting user interface consistency, there is a set of "standard" UIMS logical events to which areas will respond.

```
class Area : public Rectangle {
    ...
    //  Logical event handler
    virtual void act (Logical_event *);

    //  Standard logical event handlers
    virtual void move_act (Logical_event *);
    virtual void grow_act (Logical_event *);
    virtual void scroll_up_act (Logical_event *);
    virtual void scroll_down_act (Logical_event *);
    ...
    ...
};
```

Logical events augment the messaging capability provided by C++ virtual functions. When areas that are tightly related (that is, designed specifically to work together) wish to communicate, they will often do so by directly calling each others' member functions (that is, C++ messaging). When areas that are not related wish to communicate, they send logical events to each other (that is, UIMS/MULE messaging).

Since it is possible to query the logical event as to its name, arguments, and so forth, the UIMS messaging scheme has some significant advantages. For instance, if the logical event arguments are either incorrect or missing, the UIMS/MULE system throws up an auto-generated form to prompt the user for the right arguments. Also, context-sensitive on-line

Figure 3.10

Environment Chaining in the MULE Interface.

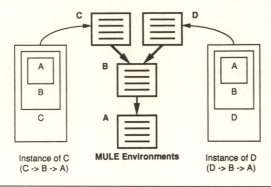

Instance of C   **MULE Environments**   Instance of D
(C -> B -> A)   (D -> B -> A)

helps can be tied to logical events, based on their names. Finally, logical event exchanges can be transcripted to get a replayable log. This is great as a form of crash protection, as well as being a testing/quality assurance tool.

The MULE Interface. Associated with each area class is a MULE environment. The first time an area of a particular class is constructured, the associated MULE environment is created and all the logical event handlers are registered as "callables" within this environment. Note that this need be done only once for each derived class of Area.

It is necessary to chain this MULE environment to that of the base area class so as to inherit all the userware capabilities inherent in the base class. This is easy to do, thanks to the order of constructor calls for base classes. Figure 3.10 illustrates this environment chaining. The notation in Fig. 3.10 is largely self-explanatory. Class C is derived from B, which is derived from A (that is, Area). Similarly, class D is derived from B and A. An instance of C is implicitly also an instance of B and of A.

The first time the C constructor is called, it immediately calls the B constructor, which in turn immediately calls the A constructor. (This is done automatically by C++.) The A constructor builds the MULE environment for class A before returning to the rest of the B constructor. The B constructor then builds the MULE environment for class B and chains it to the one for the base class A. Similarly, the C constructor can build and chain the MULE environment for class C.

Users can add their own Callables to a MULE environment by writing MULE functions and submitting them to the appropriate area. The area sends this function definition through to the MULE environment, where it gets parsed and saved.

When an area receives a logical event, its act() function (see earlier code fragment) looks up the name in the associated MULE environment for an appropriate binding. If a binding is found and it is a Callable, it gets call()-ed. Thanks to the polymorphic call() function, there is no need to worry about whether the Callable was a built-in one or a user-defined one.

Function keys and control keys are handled by reserving a set of function names corresponding to them. Thus, if a user defines a MULE function named f0(), the function key F0 is implicitly defined.

The Event Manager. The UIMS event manager is responsible for gathering, queueing, and dispatching events to areas. To ensure proper synchronization, logical events are dispatched before physical events. Within each event category, events are dispatched on a first-in, first-out (FIFO) basis.

Event addressing is fairly simple. Logical events are explicitly addressed by the senders at the time that they are queued. Physical event addressing is implicitly based on location, as follows. At any given instant, the event manager knows the root area for the area containment hierarchy. This root area defines the outer limits for event distribution. Physical events are always sent to the smallest containing area within which they occur. If a physical event occurs outside the root area, it is sent to the root area.

The notion of "grabbing" the event manager simplifies the design of certain inherently modal actions (like area move/grow). If the event manager has been grabbed by a particular area, it keeps sending physical events to that area until it is released (ungrabbed). A less invasive form of event grabbing is done by certain transient areas like pop-up menus. A transient area temporarily makes itself the root of the area-containment hierarchy. As long as a transient area is around, physical events are sent to it or to one of its children. It restores the original root when it goes away. This behavior can be nested, for example, to do pop-up menu cascades.

The following fragment of code describes a small portion of the event manager.

```
class Event_mgr {
    ...
    void queue (Area* dest_p, Logical_event* ev_p);
    ...
    void grab (Area* grabber_p);
    void ungrab ();
    void root (Area* new_root_p);
    ...
    void dispatch (Event* ev_p);
    ...
    void event_loop (Boolean wait);
    ...
};
```

Area Containment Hierarchy. Areas may contain any number of subordinate, or children, areas, which must be wholly contained within the parent area. The result is an area containment hierarchy that is rooted at the host display manager window.

```
class Area : public Rectangle {
    ...
    // Area hierarchy functions
    Area* parent ();
    Area* first_child();
    Area* next_child();
    virtual void add_sub_area (Area* child_p);
    virtual void remove_sub_area (Area* child_p);
    ...
};
```

A linear constraint mechanism is provided to help manage the area-containment hierarchy. Each area can be constrained to its parent via a simple linear constraint, as follows.

```
child left x = parent left x + delta1 + fraction1 * parent width
child top y= parent top y + delta2 + fraction2 * parent height
```

The complete constraint for an area can therefore be expressed as a set of four <delta, fraction> tuples.

When the parent area is resized, each constrained child area can be automatically resized by applying the constraint. Unconstrained children are resized by scaling them proportionally.

Areas and Output. Graphical output to an area is the joint responsibility of the UIMS and the "application" that controls that area. For each area, the UIMS maintains a list of rectangles that define the visible portions of that area. The following is a fragment of the definition of class **Area** as it pertains to output.

```
class Area : public Rectangle {
    ...
    //   Area output functions
    //   Functions often overridden by derived classes
    virtual void draw_contents_within (Rectangle& r);
    virtual void draw_border_within (Rectangle& r);
    //   Functions rarely overridden by derived classes
    virtual void draw ();
    virtual void undraw ();
    virtual void draw_contents ();
    virtual void draw_border ();
    //   Visible rectangles list
    Rectangle* first_vis_rect ();
    Rectangle* next_vis_rect ();
    ...
};
```

When an area is popped or resized or gets exposed, the UIMS causes it to redraw a specified portion of itself. All areas contain member functions that facilitate this (that is, draw_contents_within()).

An application client may wish to do graphical output to an area in order to reflect changes in the internal state of the application. In this case, it is the client's responsibility to clip the output to the visible rectangles of the area. The UIMS provides a simple utility that helps do this. Class **Area_output** is designed for controlled output to an area that may be partially obscured. It is a more convenient interface than using VDD directly. The following is a simplified version of the definition of this class.

```
class Area_output {
    ...
    Area_output (Area* area_p, Boolean clip_reqd);
```

```
   ...
void text (Point orig, String str);
void rectangle (Rectangle& r);
void polyline (Point coords[], int count);
   ...
};
```

This class also has a simplified attribute model. Each area maintains a Vcontrol*, a Vpen*, a Vbrush*, and a Vtext*. These member attributes are implicit arguments to the drawing calls in class Area_output. Class Area_output is used extensively to implement the various gadgets in the UI toolkit.

3.3.4 The UI Toolkit

The goal here is to provide all the common user interface components (scroll bars, buttons, menus, palettes, and so on) required to write interactive graphical applications. Though the gadgets in the toolkit are loosely organized, they embody a common "look and feel" policy. The goal is to achieve a consistent look and feel for the entire range of applications.

The set of building blocks is too large to describe in detail. This section provides a high-level overview of some of the more interesting capabilities in the toolkit.

The Text Subsystem. There is a widespread need within the UIMS for a simple single-font, multiline, text-editing capability. It is used as the basis for all sorts of things—pop-up helps, transcript windows, userware input pads, and so forth. Interestingly enough, it is also the basis for single-line text editing (rather than the other way about).

Class Text_area provides the desired functionality. It has all the usual primitive text editing functions.

```
class Text_area : public Area {
   ...
// Text editing functions
virtual void insert_char (char c);
virtual void insert_string (String s);
virtual void insert_newline ();
virtual void insert_tab ();
virtual void delete_char ();
virtual void backspace ();
   ...
};
```

Class Text_area also supports a rich set of ways of moving the insertion point. This feature is significant for supporting the selection model.

```
class Text_area : public Area {
   ...
// Insertion point cursor functions
virtual void cursor_left ();
```
(continues)

```
    virtual void cursor_right ();
    virtual void cursor_up ();
    virtual void cursor_down ();
    virtual void cursor_far_left ();
    virtual void cursor_far_right ();
    virtual void cursor_far_up ();
    virtual void cursor_far_down ();
    virtual void cursor_to_next (String pattern);
    virtual void cursor_to_prev (String pattern);
    virtual void cursor_to (int line_number, in char_pos);
    virtual void cursor_snap (Point loc);
    ...
};
```

The selection model is based on having any editing action (for example, insert_char(), insert_string(), backspace(), paste(), paste_file()) delete the selection range automatically. (This is somewhat similar to the Macintosh text model.) The selection range is defined by moving the insertion point cursor, mark()-ing one end of the selection range, moving it again, and select()-ing the other end of the selection range. In this context, it is easy to see why a rich set of primitives for moving the cursor around can be very useful.

The insertion point cursor and the selection range are very tightly coupled. In fact, the insertion point cursor is conceptually equivalent to a zero length selection range. Along with selection, class Text_area also supports cut and paste.

```
class Text_area : public Area {
    ...
    //   Selection functions
    virtual void mark ();
    virtual void select ();

    //   Cut and paste functions
    virtual void cut ();
    virtual void copy ();
    virtual void paste ();
    virtual void paste (String filename);
    ...
};
```

The following lists some of the other Text_area functions.

```
class Text_area : public Area {
    ...
    //   Scrolling functions
    virtual void scroll_up ();
    virtual void scroll_down ();
    virtual void scroll_left ();
    virtual void scroll_right ();
```

```
// Font and tab setting functions
virtual void set_font (String pathname);

// I/O
virtual void read (String pathname);
virtual void write (String pathname);
  ...
};
```

The diagram in Fig. 3.11 shows some of the area classes derived from base class Text_area. It is easy to appreciate the leverage afforded by this capability.

A very useful and powerful adjunct to class Text_area (and derived classes thereof) is that istream and ostream interfaces to class Text_area are supported. (Classes istream and ostream are the standard C++ I/O library stream I/O classes.) The ostream interface is provided via class Text_area_ostreambuf. This allows an ostream to be tied to a Text_area. Every time the buffer is flushed, its contents wind up being displayed in the Text_area as a side effect.

The ability to write to an ostream is widespread. In fact, most classes define an output to ostream operator (that is, operator<<()). The Text_area ostream interface means that all these classes can automatically write into Text_areas. This capability is also very useful in intercepting all output to the standard cout and cerr ostreams and displaying it in a Text_area. Thus system error messages can be diverted to Text_areas.

The analogous istream interface is provided via class Text_area_istreambuf. This class allows an istream to be attached to a Text_area for the purpose of reading its contents. The input operation has the side effect of moving the text insertion point cursor appropriately. This capability is most useful when MULE is parsing user-specified input from a Text_area based userware input pad. MULE thinks it is getting input from a normal istream. In fact, the input operation is moving the text insertion point cursor as a side effect. The result is that

Figure 3.11
Class Text and Its Hierarchy.

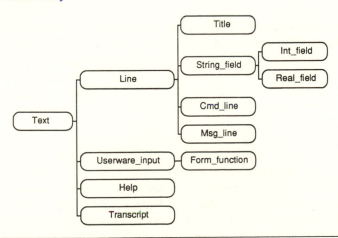

Figure 3.12 _____
The OGRE Class Hierarchy.

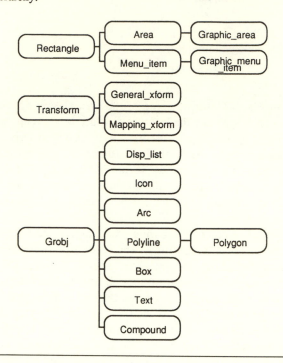

syntactic errors are automatically highlighted since MULE stops parsing at the point of an error and prints an error message.

The Graphics Subsystem. There are basically three options for graphics output:

1. VDD can be used directly. This is generally not advisable, since the user has to take care of clipping the output to the visible regions of areas, managing attributes, and so forth.
2. The UIMS includes a convenience class called **Area_output**. This is just like VDD, except that it takes care of clipping the output to the visible regions of the list. (This class has been alluded to earlier.) Class **Area_output** provides immediate mode graphics. This is entirely adequate for implementing all the UIMS gadgets (scroll bars, buttons, and so forth).
3. The OGRE system can be used. The rest of this section is a discussion of OGRE.

OGRE is a display-list-based structured graphics system. It simplifies the implementations of applications wherein the user manipulates the graphical representations of familiar objects. (Examples of such applications are schematic editors and layout editors.)

The OGRE model is a display list containing (pointers to) graphical objects. The objects are things like lines, rectangles, circles, text, and other display lists. They are all derived from base class Grobj. The display list is partitioned into a number of layers, representing the front-to-back stacking from the user's point of view. Attached to the display list is a set of one or more windows. OGRE displays the contents of the display list appropriately through each window.

Clients do graphics indirectly by adding, removing, or modifying objects in the display list. OGRE does the actual drawing as and when it sees fit. Figure 3.12 shows a partial picture of the OGRE class hierarchy.

OGRE has a very open architecture. Clients can add their own object types (derived from base class Grobj). They can also override the display list implementation if they so desire. Many application architects design optimized data structures that are derived from the OGRE display list and that support the application semantic view as well. Such a design avoids the registration problem wherein the same data are stored redundantly (such as in the application data structure as well as the graphics subsystem). The following is a partial listing of the definition of base class Grobj.

```
class Grobj {
    ...
    virtual Grobj* clone ();
    virtual Rectangle extent ();
    virtual void extent (Rectangle& r);
    virtual void draw (Graphic_area* area_p, Rectangle& clip_rect);
    ...
};
```

The Menu Subsystem. A menu is one of the ways of storing and sending logical events to other areas. Simply a regular array (typically a single column) of menu items, a menu supports both textual and graphical menu items. Each item has stored within it a logical event (and an optional list of arguments). When a menu item is selected, it queues its logical event for the area that is the current target of the menu.

There are three types of menus.

1. A *palette* is essentially a static menu. The target of a palette is determined by the common parent area of the palette and the target. (This is the Session Window, described in the next section.)
2. A *pop-up menu* is a transient menu that pops up right over its target area. Usually, the popping up and down of this menu is tied to some indivisible sequence of events, such as the left mouse button down/up. Certain items in the menu may have submenus associated with them. If the mouse happens to be within such an item, the submenu pops up ("cascades") to the right of that item.
3. A *pull-down* menu is a transient menu that is tied to an item in a static menu bar. When the left mouse button goes down within the menu bar item, the pull-down menu pops up right below the menu bar item. There may be cascading submenus underneath a pull-down menu.

The implementation of the entire menu system was simplified considerably by creating a single type of menu (that is, class Menu_area) but four different types of background areas for the various types of transient menus. When a particular type of transient area pops up, an appropriate type of background is first put up and the menu is placed within it. The background is responsible for saving and restoring the bitmap under the menu. It is also responsible for drawing the shadow, if any.

As long as it is around, the background is the root of the event distribution hierarchy. This guarantees that physical events are sent either to the background or to the menu, and nowhere else. By handling intelligently the events that it receives, the background helps define the apparent behavior of the transient menu. For example, the background for a cascaded submenu causes that menu to pop down if there are any mouse move events to the left of that menu. The implementation of each background type is about eight lines of C++ code. An indication of the leverage afforded by object-oriented programming lies in the fact that the entire menu system is less than 800 lines of C++ code.

The UIMS has defined a specific MULE extension that allows menus to be specified by the end user via MULE. Thus user menu definitions can be read in either at startup or at any other time.

The Forms Subsystem. A UIMS form is very much like its real-life paper counterpart. It provides a context for presenting a number of related pieces of information. It is used very often to solicit input from the user (in which case it is a dialog box). It is also used to present internal application state information.

When a form pops up, it is seen to contain a number of subareas. Some of these are part of the form background. They are present purely for informational purposes; their contents never change. The more interesting subareas are the dials, type-in fields, sliders, gauges, buttons, scrollable lists, and the like, that are used to display/set values. The user can interact with these subareas to change their values.

The forms facility is tied in very closely with the MULE userware function system. Conceptually, a form is the pictorial representation of the formal arguments of a MULE userware function. When a form first comes up, its active fields display the values determined by the default value expressions for the corresponding formal arguments. When a form is executed, the values in the active fields are used to call the userware function corresponding to the form.

This elegant and simple architecture makes it possible to have user-definable forms. A WYSIWYG form layout editor is an integral part of the UIMS, and makes the job even easier. The process of defining a form involves first laying it out and then defining its underlying function.

The various gadgets required to support forms are all seen as generators of values. Since each gadget corresponds to a function argument, it must be capable of producing a value for that argument when the form is executed. This fact causes a natural taxonomy for form gadgets, as shown in Fig. 3.13. Figure 3.13 is an incomplete enumeration of the form gadget classes; however, it is a representative sampling.

The Session Window. The Session Window concept is an embodiment of the Mentor Graphics common "look and feel" standard. It is the normal root of the area containment hierarchy and therefore it corresponds roughly to the host OS window obtained via VDD.

Figure 3.13 _____

Taxonomy for Form Gadgets.

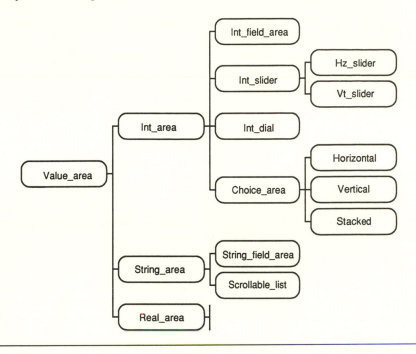

The Session Window contains particular areas that are considered to be a part of the common application framework:

— A window banner that shows the name of the design object being worked on, status information, various icons, and so on
— A menu bar across the top that provides access to appropriate application functionality
— A command line where a user can type in commands
— A message area for displaying text messages to the user
— A set of application areas

The Session Window may also contain palettes and other "torn-off" menus. It is responsible for defining appropriately the target area for these menus.

The application windows are typically framed windows, with titles, scroll bars, and the like. One application window is designated as being the current window within the session. This window is the target for the various resident menus, the command line, and so on. This concept provides a common "look and feel" upon entry into the application. Further interface consistency is evident in the lower-level gadgets as well.

3.4 WRITING INTERACTIVE GRAPHICAL APPLICATIONS

This section is a capsule summary of how an application architect uses the various capabilities described in the preceding section.

The following fragment of code is very representative of the main() program for UIMS-based applications:

```
main ()
  {
  Ui   ui;                    //  initialize the UIMS
  Ogre   ogre;                //  initialize OGRE (if used)
  new   Sample_session;       //  create the application session
  ui.run ();                  //  start running the whole system
  }
```

Clearly, this is a very simple setup. Most of the nasty details (such as initializing the graphics system) are taken care of automatically and transparently.

Typically, the application environment is embodied in an appropriately derived class of Session_window. As described earlier, the Session_window sets up a standard operating environment, including a command line, a message area, a title, and a menu bar with pull-down menus. The typical application session window extends the basic Session_window by adding commands to invoke the various component tools, windows, and so on. Thus,

```
class Sample_session : public Session_window {
    ...
    // Logical event handlers for application commands
    void quit_cmd (Logical_event *);
    void open_existing_object_cmd (Logical_event *);
    void create_new_object_cmd (Logical_event *);
    ...
};
```

The implementations of these commands will typically cause various application edit windows to be opened within the overall session window. For example,

```
void Sample_session::open_existing_object_cmd (Logical_event* ev_p)
    {
    String path_name = ev_p->arg (0);
    Area* edit_area_p = new Graphic_edit_area (path_name);
    Rectangle r = this->determine_new_area_position ();
    edit_area_p->change_exterior (r);
    this->add_sub_area (edit_area_p);
    }
```

This newly added area has its own command set, menus, and so on. In a sense, it is a miniapplication in its own right.

```
class Graphic_edit_area : public Ogre_area {
    ...
    // Logical event handlers
    ...
    void add_box_cmd (Logical_event* ev_p);
    void add_circle_cmd (Logical_event* ev_p);
    void add_line_cmd (Logical_event* ev_p);
    ...
};
```

From the user interface point of view, the primary duties of the application architect are (1) the design of the application's session window and (2) the design of the basic windows that will exist within the session window. In designing these windows, the focus is primarily on the determination of the command set. If OGRE is used, there is no need to worry about graphical output. Updating the OGRE display list is all that is needed.

Naturally, there is much more to designing even a simple application. There are such questions as what the data structure ought to be, what the editing paradigms ought to be, and which selection algorithm to employ. However, these issues are not relevant in considering the complexity of the application UIMS interface.

3.5 CONCLUSIONS

The process of introducing object-oriented technology into an existing product development environment is indeed quite challenging. The following are some of the more significant issues that were encountered:

- *What is the process for converting existing applications over to C++?* One important factor that made it at all possible was that existing Pascal and C code could coexist with the new C++ code. Thus it became possible to define a phased conversion process over to C++. Given the size of the application base, an abrupt conversion to any new language is just not feasible.
- *What is the process for converting Pascal and C developers over to C++?* This turned out to be the most challenging part of the project. An intensive in-house training program was instituted and is still continuing. The easy part is learning the C++ language. This is a language with a lot of power. Numerous subtle nuances must be mastered. The various C++ books out there are generally inadequate. The more difficult part is making good object-oriented designers out of experienced Pascal and C programmers. This requires a fundamental shift in mindset that takes a lot longer than expected. Languages like Pascal and C do not promote object-oriented problem solving.

  At this point in time, there are no widely accepted metrics for documenting and/or evaluating object-oriented designs. Thus good object-oriented design is still an art rather than a science. It has been observed that the object-oriented methodology is an amplifier for programming skills—the good programmers get better and the weak ones fall by the wayside.

- *What is a good, effective development environment for C++?* Putting together a solid development environment for C++ turned out to be another interesting task. Currently, C++ is just a language, not a programming environment. In order to have large teams of developers work effectively together, a C++ development environment is required. The first step was to figure out how to make the various native Apollo tools (such as source level debuggers and software profilers) work effectively with C++. The next step was to create an effective software engineering environment with source code control, configuration management, release management, and so on. The final step was to begin developing tools like class browsers to aid in the process of object-oriented design.

Tackling issues such as these was painful and time-consuming. However, the early indications are that the results are well worthwhile. The entire system as described was designed, implemented, and tested by a relatively small team in a relatively short period of time. In the process, a number of the developers have become very good object-oriented designers.

A tremendous amount of functionality was achieved with less source code than would have been needed with either Pascal or C. This fact is directly attributable to good object-oriented design and tremendous code reuse through inheritance.

Much of the credit for the success of this effort must go to the object-oriented approach in general and to C++ in particular. Mentor Graphics Corporation was a very early adopter of C++. In spite of the continuing evolution of C++, there have been very few "show stopper" type flaws in either the language or its implementation.

It is quite clear that object-oriented programming represents the wave of the future for commercial developers. The system described here has an extensible architecture that will allow it to survive more or less intact into the 1990s.

Development of a Visual Database Interface: An Object-Oriented Approach

C. Thomas Wu _____
Naval Postgraduate School, Department of Computer Science,
Code 52, Monterey, California

4.1 OVERVIEW

This chapter discusses our experience with object-oriented programming in implementing visual database definition and manipulation facilities. Actor is the particular object-oriented language we used for the project. It is an object-oriented language intended for writing Microsoft Windows applications. Actor itself runs under the Microsoft Windows environment.

Although some practical issues specific to Actor are discussed, the focus here is on the general object-oriented design techniques that we have learned from working on the project. Related to these design techniques, we present how the salient features of object-oriented programming, such as the notion of classes, inheritance, message passing, and polymorphism, have helped us improve the quality and quantity of our code. In other words, we show how the employment of object-oriented programming enabled us to develop an easily modifiable and very reusable code.

We initiate our discourse on object-oriented programming with background information of the project. Our research project on developing an easy-to-learn and easy-to-use visual interface to a database was conceptualized in late 1985. Although there were earlier proposals on visual interfaces to databases [4, 8, 9, 11, 13–15, 19, 20], we felt, and still do, that the research on user interface in general and visual user interface in particular was not fully explored (some of the more recent proposals are references [1, 3, 5, 7, 16–18]). We have just begun many new proposals, and the field is still in its infancy. There is no firm understanding of what constitute a good user interface, and at this early stage of research, we believe it is beneficial to experiment with as many different approaches as possible.

Our preliminary ideas were first reported in Wu [16]. Initially, we planned to implement our system on a workstation compatible with Sun Microsystem's. One master's student worked on a feasibility study by attempting to implement a data definition facility. It failed. Since the routines for the window management (such as sizing of window and displaying of scroll bars) are callable only from Pascal, FORTRAN, or C languages, we decided to use C, which we believe was a prudent decision. However, the available routines are too low-level and very difficult to use. For instance, a function to display a scroll bar requires more than several parameters. Needless to say, these parameters must be passed in a right sequence. Imagine writing code to handle the scroll bar movement and to adjust the content of the window's display area, which may require a dozen functions with more than several parameters. And that is just for handling the screen display, not to mention the C code to handle the logic of the application.

With a limited budget and limited manpower, we did not have an effective environment to conduct development research. We had to spend most of our time writing utilities necessary for window management using low-level routines. Because of its nature, the success of visual database interface research relies greatly on the success of experimentation. To experiment with different designs, without concern over low-level details, we needed a high-level software development tool that would allow us to produce a prototype rapidly. Utilizing a rapid prototyping tool was therefore critical to the success of our visual database interface research.

We began to doubt our decision to develop the whole software in C programming language. One colleague's project uses C programming language, many of whose components were written by master's thesis students. Because these students' codes were improperly documented and very difficult to comprehend, that project now employs professional programmers to "clean up" and document the students' code. We would like to keep our code, which would be developed by several people, comprehensible and manageable by the single main designer of the system.

So we started searching for a development tool that would be characteristic of so-called 4GL or CASE tools with good windowing routines. Desirable characteristics would include rapid prototyping, modifiability, and extensibility. The development language should be powerful enough to allow complex ideas and relationships to be expressed naturally without awkward structures and lengthy segments or excessive repetition of code. Concurrent to the search for an ideal development tool, we have been refining the design of our visual interface. The refined visual interface was reported in Wu [17]. In 1987 one of our new project sponsors, Naval Data Automation Command, added a new constraint, that the system run on IBM PC/AT-compatible MS-DOS machines. Since we did not wish to limit our system to a single hardware/OS platform, we decided to build the prototype in the requested environment with the intention of transferring it to other platforms (especially UNIX and Macintosh) later.

We first attempted the implementation with a Smalltalk system for PC, which seemed to have good windowing tools. And we were curious about the advertised effectiveness of object-oriented programming. After we familiarized ourselves with the language and environment, we started an initial implementation but hit upon a problem: We were not able to implement one particular function of the visual interface, and the company's technical support was not able to provide a solution. The reason was that the system lacked predefined classes for I/O objects such as dialog box, edit box, and buttons, and we could not afford to spend time in creating those objects by ourselves. In our search for another development tool, we saw a very promising advertisement for Actor in *Byte* magazine. Our experience with Actor and object-oriented programming is chronicled in the rest of the chapter.

In the next section, we describe the application for and explain the motivation behind a visual database interface and illustrate the latest version of our prototype. To facilitate a meaningful discussion, we list the characteristics of Actor that distinguish it from other object-oriented languages and programming environments. Then we explain our design decisions and discuss how we used the features of object-oriented programming and Actor in implementing the proposed visual database interface. Using our implementation experience, we then assess the features of object-oriented programming and present a set of design guidelines. We conclude the chapter with a plan for future implementation.

4.2 APPLICATION

Our research on a visual database interface is motivated by the lack of an easy-to-learn, easy-to-use query facility for accessing databases. Although relational query languages such as SQL and QUEL are much better than those for network and hierarchical systems, they are still not ideal languages for end users. For database systems to become truly useful as information managers, end-user participation is indispensable since otherwise data processing professionals must be used to develop application software. Such an arrangement is prohibitively expensive for the coming decades of information explosion. We believe a visual interface that supports a high-level semantic data model holds the best potential as an end-user interaction tool.

Our proposed visual interface GLAD (Graphics LAnguage for Database) provides a coherent interface method for both data definition and manipulation interactions. A coherent interface method would achieve a high degree of ease of learning and use. The key then is a simple database representation where users can visually interact with the system for data definition and manipulation.

We now illustrate GLAD by going through a sample session. The data manipulation and then the data definition components of GLAD will be described. At appropriate points during the illustration, we will present our visual interface principles and the core aspects of the GLAD data model. The illustration given in this section is limited to those features that have a direct relevance to our implementation efforts detailed in the chapter.

Figure 4.1 shows the top-level GLAD window.[1] All these menu choices apply to the manipulation of the database. The HELP option assists the user by explaining the other menu choices. The context-sensitive help system supports our first interface principle. *Interface Principle 1: Be able to provide more information when asked.* This principle covers a much wider area than does a simple help system. We will discuss this interface principle later in the section. The QUIT option exits the application. If the user removes any database during the session, the dialog box requesting the confirmation of removal appears before exiting GLAD. This confirmation supports our second interface principle, *Interface Principle 2: Be able to recover from the unintended or erroneous operation.*

Instead of selecting the QUIT menu option, the user may select the CLOSE option under the system menu box (see Fig. 4.1). The third way of quitting GLAD is double clicking (click

---

[1]All figures in this chapter are the actual screen dumps with minor adjustments. The text in italics and dotted lines were added for explanation. Because color images are reproduced here in black and white and all coloring appears as black shading, additional labels were added to tell the actual color.

Figure 4.1

Top-Level GLAD Window.

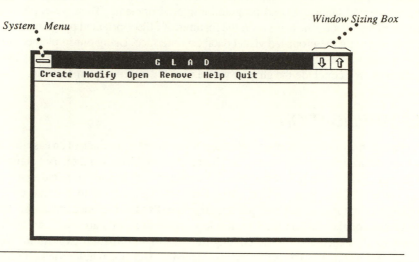

the mouse button twice in a quick succession) the system menu box. Letting the user perform the same operation in more than one way is our third interface principle, ***Interface Principle 3: Be able to perform the same operation in more than one way.*** Allowing more than one way of carrying out the same operation enables users to use the one they feel most comfortable with, thus supporting larger numbers of users. For example, novice users initially may prefer using the QUIT menu, but as they become more proficient in interacting with GLAD, they may prefer to close GLAD by double clicking the system menu box.

The system menu box and the QUIT menu choice will appear in every GLAD window. Their style and function are consistent over all GLAD windows. The user who knows how to use them in one window will know how to use them in any other GLAD window. This is our fourth interface principle: ***Interface Principle 4: Be able to perform the logically equivalent operation in a consistent manner.***

MODIFY, OPEN, and REMOVE options cause a dialog box with a list of databases to appear on the screen, allowing the user to either modify, open, or remove, respectively, any of the listed databases. The menu option OPEN is discussed now, and the option MODIFY is discussed at the end of the section. Figure 4.2 shows that the database "University Database" is currently highlighted and ready to be OPENed. When the database is properly opened, the user is presented the Data Manipulation window (see Fig. 4.3). It shows three rectangles captioned DEPT, EMPLOYEE, and EQUIPMENT. A rectangle represents both object type (database schema) and a set of objects (database instance) currently in the database. As such, there are two categories of operations: one that applies to a rectangle as an object type and another that applies to a rectangle as a set of instances. We call them *object type operation* and *object instance operation*, respectively. In the following discussion, we will use the terms *object* and *rectangle* synonymously. It should be clear from the context whether we are referring to an object type or a set of object instances.

Figure 4.2 _____

State After Selection of the Menu Option Open. A list of databases appears. The database "University Database" is currently selected and readied to be opened.

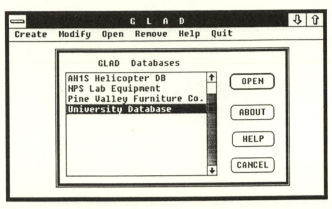

Describe, Expand, and ShowConnectn are the three object type operations. To initiate the menu options Describe and Expand, the user must first select one of the objects. When an object is selected by the user, the outer border line of the rectangle is thickened to reflect the most recently selected object. Operations will be applied to this rectangle. The color of the selected rectangle will also change. We see in Fig. 4.4 that the EMPLOYEE rectangle is selected. The selection is made by moving the cursor within the rectangle and clicking the left mouse button. Deselection is made by clicking the right mouse button. Whenever an inappropriate mouse button is pressed or an inapplicable menu option is selected, an error box with a corresponding message will appear. The user will not be able

Figure 4.3 _____

The Opened University Database. Three objects (DEPT, EMPLOYEE, and EQUIPMENT) are in this database.

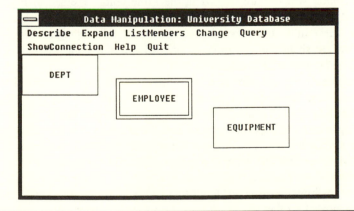

Figure 4.4

Selection of EMPLOYEE Object. The menu choices Describe, Expand, ListMembers, Change, and Query apply to the selected object.

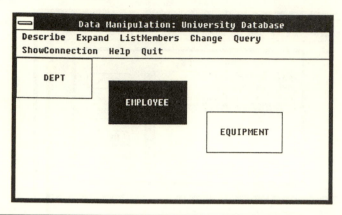

to continue without acknowledging the error (by pressing the OK button). This interaction is based on Interface Principle 2.

The Describe menu choice displays the relational information of the selected object. Figure 4.5 shows that the EMPLOYEE object has relationships Name, Age, Pay, Address, and WorksFor. The GLAD data model supports basically two semantic constructs: object type and relationship. The object types are categorized into *user-defined* and *system-defined*. The system-defined object types are those predefined by the system. Two system-defined types currently supported by GLAD are INT for integers and STRING for strings. The user-defined types are the application-specific types defined by the user. Only the user-defined object types are displayed on the Data Manipulation window. The object's characteristics (or attributes) are determined by its relationships to other objects. For example, age of employee is viewed as the relationship Age that relates the EMPLOYEE object to the INT object. If the related object is also user-defined, the object name and its corresponding rectangle in the Data Manipulation window are shaded in the same color. We see in Fig. 4.5 that the relationship WorksFor relates an employee object to another user-defined object, DEPT. The object name DEPT in the Describe window and the DEPT rectangle in the Data Manipulation window are shaded in the same color. Color referencing provides a clear visual representation of object relationships.

In other proposed visual interfaces [1, 3–5, 11, 15, 19], the whole database schema is presented to the user. If we applied the same idea to GLAD, we would be displaying every object type and relationship in the Data Manipulation window. We believe it would be too overwhelming to many users, especially for novices. We therefore decided to provide a sort of summary information first (Fig. 4.4) and display more information when the user requests it (Fig. 4.5) via Describe and other commands. The idea of displaying more information when requested is based on Interface Principle 1.

Users are not limited to just one Describe window. They can request the system to open Describe windows for other objects. Figure 4.6 shows the state where multiple Describe

Figure 4.5 _____

Describe Window After the Menu Option Describe Is Selected. Notice the use of coloring for showing the relationship.

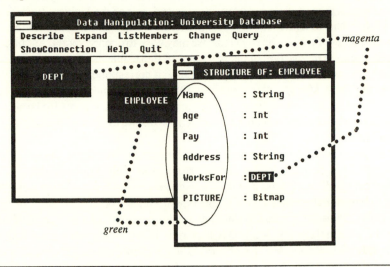

Figure 4.6 _____

The Describe Windows for all Objects. The objects and the Describe windows are repositioned to avoid any overlapping.

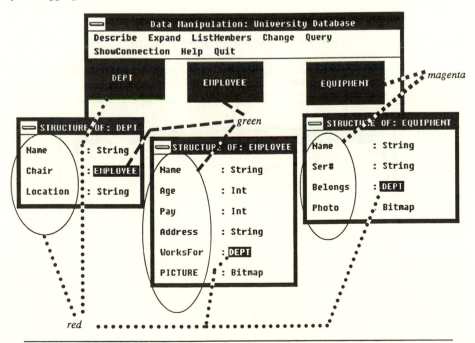

windows are displayed. The multiple-windows display, with each window conveying a certain amount of information, supports our fifth interface principle, ***Interface Principle 5: Be able to display multiple information at the same time***. This capability allows the user to see the varying degree of details. To the experienced user of the University Database, who is fully aware of other details, the three rectangles on the Data Manipulation window is enough. But first-time users of the University Database may wish to open several Describe windows to constantly remind themselves of the structures of those objects. The maximum number of Describe windows that can be shown on the screen corresponds to the number of objects present in the Data Manipulation window. Objects and windows can be moved in any position desired. Besides changing the position, the window size may also be adjusted; that is, it may be expanded to show more of its content or shrunk to show previously hidden parts of other windows.

We notice in Fig. 4.6 that there are three relationships among the objects. This feature is easily visible since the types of characteristics and their related objects in the Data Manipulation window are shown in the same colors. The user can also select ShowConnectn choice to globally display the relationships among the objects in a more concise form. In the ShowConnectn window, relationships are depicted by the directed lines drawn between the objects (see Fig. 4.7). This feature is based on our sixth, and last, interface principle: ***Interface Principle 6: Be able to display multiple views of the same information***. Through multiple display of the same information, the user gains confidence by verifying information via another view.

The Expand menu option may be applied to an object with an IS_A hierarchy. IS_A

Figure 4.7 _____

The ShowConnection Window. It globally depicts the relationship that exists among the objects. The arrow shows the direction of reference (not fully implemented yet).

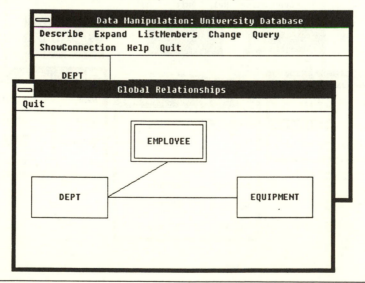

hierarchy is a special kind of relationship that exists between two objects. An object with an IS_A hierarchy is drawn as a nested rectangle. To view the IS_A hierarchy, the user clicks the Expand menu option after the object is properly selected. Figure 4.8 shows the state after the EMPLOYEE object is expanded. A nested Data Manipulation window appears on the screen, with the title caption "SubClass of: <selected object's name>." Except for ShowConnectn, this window has all the menu options that the Data Manipulation window has. Existence of nested Data Manipulation window supports Interface Principles 5 and 6.

We now illustrate the object instance operations. There are two additional windows, which we shall call AllAtOnce and OneByOne windows, to perform the object instance operations. These two windows allow the user to view and change data and formulate queries. The querying function is not yet fully implemented. Two menu options corresponding to these two windows appear in the pull-down menu under ListMembers. They are "All at Once" for the AllAtOnce window and "One by one" for the OneByOne window. The "All at Once" option is for viewing all the instances of the selected object. The number of data items viewed by the user at any given time depends on the size of the opened window. The "One by one" option is for viewing an instance of the selected object one at a time. We have provided users with two visual clues to maintain easy and quick association between the object in the Data Manipulation window and its AllAtOnce and OneByOne windows. The

Figure 4.8 _____

Two Levels of IS-A Hierarchy for the EMPLOYEE Objects. The nested objects' rectangles are drawn using the color of their parent's shading. So the rectangles for the objects FACULTY and STAFF are drawn in green, the shading of their parent EMPLOYEE. Similarly, the rectangles for TYPIST and TECH are drawn in magenta.

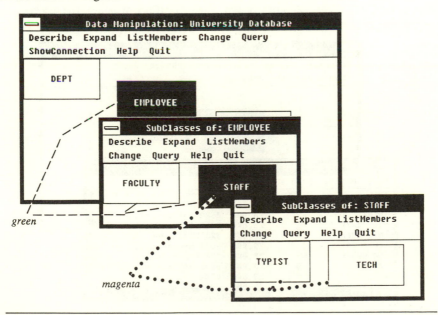

first clue is the object's name within the title caption. The second is the coloring of the attribute names with the same color as the object.

There are four menu options for the AllAtOnce window. Menu options HELP and QUIT are already explained. All GLAD windows have HELP and QUIT and the same functionalities, supporting Interface Principle 4. We will not elaborate on the option MODIFY other than to say it allows the user to modify the highlighted data. Menu option MORE provides the user with an additional window for viewing a particular instance in more detail, an especially useful feature when some values are too long to fit in the AllAtOnce window. The maximum length we allow for any value to appear on a line is 20 characters. Any value longer than 20 characters is cut off at the 16th character and concatenated with three dots and a space. Such a case is shown in Fig. 4.9, where the address values are longer than 20 characters. To see the complete address of a highlighted individual, the user chooses the MORE option. A OneByOne window appears with full address (along with the rest of information) in Fig. 4.10. This window is also used for modifying the data and specifying the search condition in a manner similar to QBE. This is the same window shown if a user chooses "One by one" from the Data Manipulation window's menu choice. If the OneByOne window is created from the Data Manipulation window and there is no AllAtOnce window, the first instance of the object will be displayed in the OneByOne window. Opening the same window from two different places supports Interface Principle 3. Opening both the AllAtOnce and OneByOne windows at the same time supports Interface Principle 5.

A simple yet useful browsing feature is supported by the OneByOne window. The user

---

Figure 4.9 _____

Instances of the EMPLOYEE Object Displayed in the AllAtOnce Window. The display is in the summary format. Notice that the full address does not fit in the allocated space.

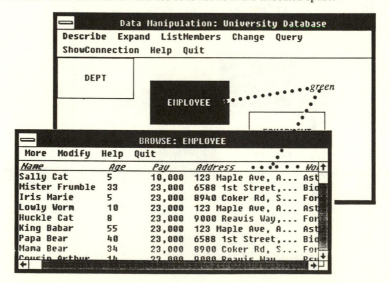

may browse through the instances of the selected object by selecting menu options Prev, Next, and GoTo. If the selected choice cannot be carried out correctly, an appropriate error dialog box will appear on the screen (Interface Principle 2). When the All menu choice is selected, an AllAtOnce window will appear. This window is, of course, the same one that appears if the user selects the "All at once" choice from the Data Manipulation window. If there was already an AllAtOnce window, the All option causes that window to be brought to the top of other windows.

When the two windows are present, as in Fig. 4.10, the user sees two views of same data. They can be opened in many different ways (Interface Principle 3). They are connected in a sense that an operation in one window will be reflected in the other window. The current data element in the OneByOne window corresponds to the highlighted one in the AllAtOnce window. When the Prev, Next, or GoTo option is selected in the OneByOne window, the new data are displayed in it and highlighted in the AllAtOnce window. When the user moves the cursor in the AllAtOnce window, the pointed row is highlighted and the corresponding data are displayed in the OneByOne window. We feel that this interface is beneficial to the user because it ensures the user that "what he is seeing is what he wants."

Figure 4.10 _____
OneByOne Window of Highlighted Instance of the EMPLOYEE Object.

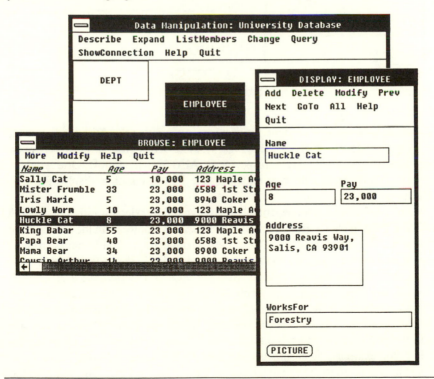

Figure 4.11 _____

Add Window for the EMPLOYEE Object. The user may add multiple EMPLOYEE objects.

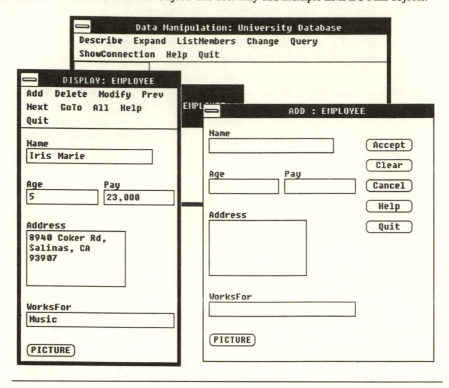

From the OneByOne window, the user may open either the Add window to add data or the Delete window to delete data (see Figs. 4.11 and 4.12). These windows are opened via the menu choices Add and Delete, respectively. Also from the OneByOne window, if the object has a bitmap image, the user may press the Photo button to display the associated bitmap image (see Fig. 4.13).

The data definition component of GLAD is invoked by selecting either the CREATE or the MODIFY menu choice from the top-level GLAD window. With the CREATE option, the dialog box asks the user for the name of the new database, and the system verifies that the chosen name does not conflict with names already existing in the system. After verification, the Data Definition window is opened. With the MODIFY option, the user selects the database to be modified from the dialog box listing of databases. Figure 4.14 shows the Data Definition window with the University Database selected for modification. Either way, the user may define a new object, delete the existing object, and change the existing object. The Data Definition window controls three different dialog boxes for these purposes. Integrity checking (for example, to ensure that no two objects have the same name or that the relationship is defined to the existing objects) is done by the Data Definition window.

Figure 4.12 _____

Delete Window for the EMPLOYEE Object. Various options for the deletion are available to the user.

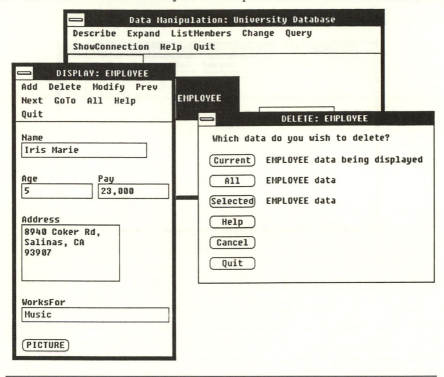

Figure 4.13 _____

Bitmap Window of the EQUIPMENT Object.

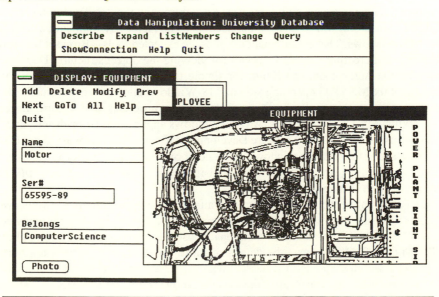

Figure 4.14 _____

Data Definition Window for University Database.

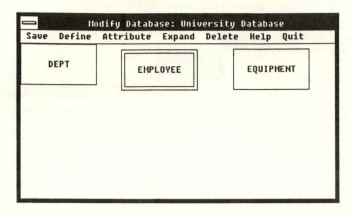

4.3 PROGRAMMING FEATURES OF ACTOR

In this section, we describe our development tool Actor. We assume the readers are already familiar with the basic concepts of object-oriented programming. Thus our objective in this section is to highlight the discriminating features of Actor. Actor is currently available for the MS-DOS machines. Its minimum hardware requirements are a hard disk, 640K main memory, and a mouse (or some pointing device). Though optional, an EGA or a VGA color monitor and extra memory are highly desirable. Our prototype was developed on an AT-compatible machine with an EGA color monitor and on a 386 machine with a VGA color monitor. Both do not have any extra memory beyond the required minimum.

Actor (its language and environment) is a programming tool for developing Microsoft Windows (henceforth MS-Windows) applications. The Actor environment itself operates under MS-Windows. That environment includes the expected tools—Browser for viewing, modifying, and creating classes; Inspector for viewing the object structure; Debugger for debugging the Actor code; and Editor for simple text editing. MS-Windows is a visual extension of the MS-DOS operating system. MS-Windows allows users to visually interact with the system to change the directory, copy files, run programs, and so forth, instead of typing textual MS-DOS commands. All MS-Windows applications (spreadsheet, database, and so on) use MS-Windows Software Development Kit routines (there are about 600) for operations such as displaying windows and dialog boxes, scrolling the scroll bars, creating buttons, and printing text. These software applications are called *MS-Windows applications*. Actor is one such Windows application.

Every Kit routine (about 600 of them) is available to Actor programmers. In other words, we may invoke any Kit routine from an Actor program. In this regard, Actor is equivalent to Microsoft C, which programmers traditionally used to program Windows application. Unlike Microsoft C, however, the details of these low-level Kit routines are normally encapsulated within the predefined classes (mostly in Window and descendant classes) from the Actor programmers. The result of this encapsulation is remarkable. Listing 4.1 shows the C program for displaying a window with the title "Hello World," as shown in Fig. 4.15.

Listing 4.1 _____

C Program to Print a "Hello World" Window.

```c
/* C program to open Hello,World window */

#include <windows.h>

long FAR PASCAL WndProc(HWND, usinged, WORD, LONG);

int PASCAL WinMain (hInstance, hPrevInstnce, lpCmdLine, nCmdShow)
HANDLE hInstance,hPrevInstance;
LPSTR  lpCmdLine;
int       nCmdShow;
{

        HWND hWnd;
        WNDCLASS WndClass;

        if (!hPrevInstance) {
                WndClass.lpszClassName = (LPSTR) "Hello";
                WndClass.hInstance = hInstance;
                WndClass.lpfnWndProc = WndProc;
                WndClass.style = NULL;
                WndClass.hbrBackground= GetStockObject(WHITE_BRUSH);
                WndClass.hCursor = LoadCursor(NULL,IDC_ARROW);
                WndClass.hIcon = LoadIcon(NULL,IDI_APPLICATION);
                WndClass.lpszMenuName = (LPSTR) NULL;
                WndClass.cbClsExtra = NULL;
                WndClass.clWndExtra = NULL;

                if (!RegisterClass (&WndClass))
                  return (NULL);
                }

        hWnd = CreateWindow ("Hello",
                "Hello World",
                WS_POPUPOVERLAPPEDWINDOW,
                CS_USEDEFAULT,
                CS_USEDEFAULT,
                CS_USEDEFAULT,
                CS_USEDEFAULT,
                NULL,
                NULL,
                hInstance,
                NULL);
```

(continues)

```
        ShowWindow(hWnd,ncmdShow);

        UpdateWindow(hWnd);

        return (NULL);
}

long FAR PASCAL WndProc(hWnd, msg, wP, IP);
HWND    hWnd;
unsigned msg;
WORD    wP;
LONG    IP;
{
        return DefWindowProc(hWnd, msg, sP, IP);
}
```

The same thing can be done in Actor as follows:

```
Win := defaultNew(Window,"Hello World");
show(Win,1);
```

where Win is a global variable assigned to a Window object created by the message defaultNew. The show message sent to Win causes it to be displayed on the screen. We should also remember that we must compile and link the C program before we can execute it. To execute the preceding display with Actor, we simply type the code in the Actor's WorkSpace window. As such, experimentation within Actor can be performed effortlessly. It is very easy to test and see how the different messages work in Actor. With C programming

Figure 4.15 _____
A Simple Window with a Title Caption "Hello World."

language, such experimentation is not practically feasible. To test one Kit routine, we must go through the whole sequence of compiling, linking, and executing the C program. We will discuss more on this point in Section 4.5.

As we can see from the preceding Actor statements, the most conspicuous difference between Actor and Smalltalk is syntax. By pushing the message passing paradigm to the extreme, Smalltalk ended up with a syntax that is quite different from any other prior languages. For example, every action and control flow in Smalltalk are results of sending messages to some object. As a consequence, Smalltalk has no control structure such as if and for-loop. Moreover, the message-passing expression is always in the infix format (that is, <receiving object> <message> <argument object>). Actor compromised this extreme uniformity and introduced control structures without sacrificing the basic tenet of the message-passing paradigm. Actor also mixes the infix and prefix format for the message-passing expression. This compromise resulted in a syntax that is much easier to learn, especially for those who already know other traditional languages such as C and Pascal.

The message syntax for Actor is

```
<message-name> ( <receiver>,[<argument-list>])
```

where the square brackets show the optional parts. In the previous example statement show(Win,1), the message show is sent to the Window object Win with the argument 1. (The argument 1 specifies that the window be displayed in the normal mode.) In Smalltalk, the statement will look like Win show: 1. Actor will allow a regular infix notation for certain kinds of messages, such as arithmetic messages. So, instead of +(4,5), we say 4 + 5 in Actor.

For every message name, there must be a corresponding method defined in the class where the receiver belongs. The syntax of method definition is

```
Def <method-name> (self [,<argument-list> [<temp-var-list>] ] )
{
    <statement-list>
}
```

where <method-name> is any sequence of alphanumeric characters, <argument-list> is a zero or more arguments passed to the method, <temp-var-list> is a zero or more local variables used only within the method, and <statement-list> is a sequence of Actor statements. The total number of arguments and local variables cannot exceed 16.

One frequent criticism of object-oriented language is its omission of static, or early, binding. Actor allows static binding as well as the normal dynamic binding of a variable. Dynamic binding is very useful for a rapid prototyping of application software, but it produces less efficient final software than static binding. Static binding, on the other hand, is not suitable for a rapid prototyping. By incorporating both kinds of binding, Actor allows developers to use dynamic binding to synthesize the application software quickly and to use the optional static binding to improve the performance of the final product. The static binding is done in Actor by attaching a class name to the receiver of the message. For example, we may statically bind the receiver of the message hideContent to MyWindow class at the compile time as

| hideContent(X : MyWindow)

We must be very careful in this case that the variable X is not assigned to any object but one from the MyWindow class prior to the execution of the preceding statement. The static binding in Actor becomes useful when used in conjunction with the inheritance mechanism. In our code, we have the method definition

```
Def start(self, dbName)
{
    newDbName := dbName;
    start(self : DMWindow, dbName)
}
```

in the class DDWindow (Data Definition Window), which is the descendant of DMWindow (Data Manipulation Window) class. The preceding definition states that starting a descendant DDWindow object is the same as starting its parent's, with one extra assignment statement. This is one form of reusing an existing code. It also clearly shows the logic of control and relationship of objects.

4.4 IMPLEMENTATION

In this section, we detail our implementation effort for the most recent version of GLAD with reference to an earlier version as appropriate. We have gone through two cycles of GLAD implementation. The purpose of the first cycle was to develop a rudimentary prototype to see whether the full implementation of GLAD by the object-oriented programming and Actor is feasible. The result of the first cycle was GLAD version 0.01, which was demonstrated to our sponsor in May 1988. Version 0.01 contains a subset of data manipulation facilities. Current version 0.02 has added a data definition component, a bitmap display capability, and some update facility to version 0.01. Our plan is to add more functionalities to successive versions. We discuss more on future versions in the concluding section. Besides these additional functionalities, some classes for version 0.02 are quite different from those of version 0.01. Both the design changes in application and the structural improvement of version 0.01 classes resulted in this change.

There is no question that an accepted strategy for implementing computer software is program modularity and reusability, which allow incremental development and easier modification and extension. The real question, of course, is how to realize program modularity and reusability. In other words, we have a well-defined strategy (modularity and reusability), but what are our tactics? Object-oriented programming provides a nice set of tactics: class, message passing, inheritance, and polymorphism. Just as any tactic, they must be used properly to have a desired effect. Badly designed classes, for example, are just as "spaghetti" as unstructured FORTRAN programs. How we have employed these tactics in our implementation is the subject of this section. We describe several classes to illustrate the point. In the next section, we evaluate the effectiveness of those tactics in achieving the strategy of modularity and reusability.

Figure 4.16 shows the class hierarchy for the GLAD version 0.02 classes. The shaded

Figure 4.16 _____

Class Hierarchy for the GLAD Classes.

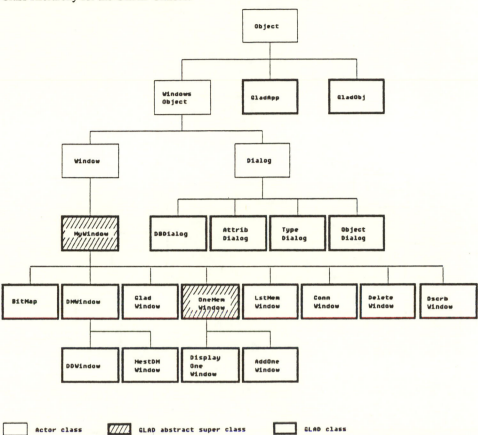

rectangle signifies that the class is an abstract superclass. In other words, there will be no instance of that class for running the GLAD application. The abstract superclass's purpose is to encapsulate a commonness among its descendants, so when a new descendant class is created, this new class can inherit all the common protocols. This eliminates the duplication of code, and thus a carefully designed abstract superclass increases the reusability of code. We have two abstract superclasses in version 0.02, while version 0.01 had none. One of the abstract superclasses is the MyWindow class. There are certain functionalities we need to have for almost all windows in the GLAD application. The MyWindow class encapsulates this commonness.

The class hierarchy of Fig. 4.16 shows only half the story of GLAD classes because it does not depict the dynamic relationship, that is, who sends what messages to whom and who creates whom. The connection graph of Fig. 4.17 does that; it shows the connection among the GLAD window and dialog objects. The solid line shows the creation relationship. DisplayOneWindow, for example, creates an AddOneWindow from its add method. Notice

Figure 4.17 _____

Connection Graph for the GLAD Window and Dialog Classes. The solid line shows the creation of one class by another. The dotted line shows the sending of message.

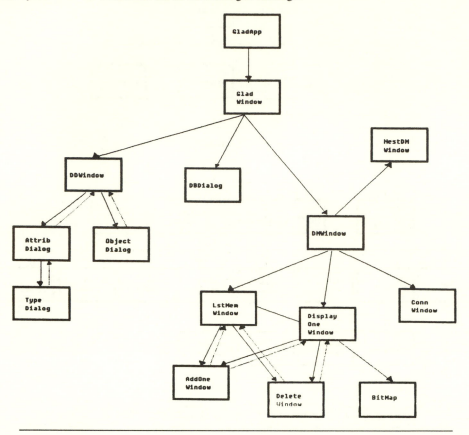

that it is not a control flow. The dashed line shows the message (with or without arguments) passed from one object to another. AddOneWindow sends the message addMembers to DisplayOneWindow to reflect the addition of new data values so the DisplayOneWindow object can update its internal state to remember the newly added data values. Not all the messages are shown. Messages such as those sent to system-defined classes are omitted.

Before we start our description of GLAD classes with the MyWindow class, we first discuss how the connection between Actor and MS-Windows is done. MS-Windows controls the actual devices such as keyboard, screen, I/O ports, and printers. It detects an event (for example, the user presses the function key, selects the window menu choice, clicks the mouse button, hits the accelerator keys, resizes the windows, and so on) and sends a corresponding message to the application software. MS-Windows essentially serves the purpose of Controller in the Model-View-Controller (MVC) triad [2, 12]. Whether to process or ignore messages sent back by the MS-Windows is up to the application software. In Actor, whenever we wish to handle an MS-Windows message, we simply add a method to an appropriate class.

If, for example, we wish to add a logic of handling right mouse button press to the application, we add the following method:

```
Def WM_RBUTTONDOWN(self, wp, lp)
{
/*some application specific code*/
/*wp - not used            */
/*lp - specifies the location    */
/* where the right button     */
/* is pressed           */
}
```

to a suitable class.
  The following methods

```
Def WM_COMMAND(self, wp, lp)
{
    command(self,wp,lp)
}
Def command(self, wp, lp)
{
}
```

are defined in the Window class. The message WM_COMMAND is returned when the user either selects the menu choice, presses the accelerator key, or hits the child controls (for example, buttons, listbox). Two parameters are passed with WM_COMMAND: wp and lp. The values of the two parameters determine which event has happened. For instance, if it is a menu choice selection, lp is 0 and wp is the identification number of the selected menu choice (each menu choice is assigned a unique integer value). The descendant windows redefine the command method for handling the menu choices, accelerator keys, and child control selections. (It is not obvious from this description that the purpose of the WM_COMMAND method sending the command message is to rename a sometimes obscure MS-Windows message to a more meaningful one in Actor. Perhaps the word processUserSelection instead of command is a better choice.) Listing 4.2 lists the command method for the DMWindow of version 0.01. Every descendant of the Window class must have a command method similar to the one in Listing 4.2 whenever it has a menu.
  One thing we did in the MyWindow class was to define an improved command method. The command method for the MyWindow class was defined as

```
Def command( self, wp, lp)
{
    if menuID[wp] then
        perform(self, menuID[wp])
    else
    ^0
    endif
}
```

Listing 4.2
Command Method for Version 0.01 DMWindow.

```
/*handles menu selection for DMWindow   */
/*Uppercase words (eg DESCRIBE_OBJ) are */
/*integer constants              */
Def command(self, wp, lp)
{
        select
          case lp <> 0
                is ^0
          endCase

          case wp == DESCRIBE_OBJ
                is describe(self)
          endCase

          case wp == EXPAND_OBJ
                is expand(self)
          endCase

          case wp == CONNECT_OBJ
                is showConnection(self)
          endCase

          case wp == LIST_MEM
                is listMembers(self)
          endCase

          case wp == ONE_MEM
                is query(self)
          endCase

          case wp == QUERY
                is query(self)
          endCase

          case wp == DMHELP
                is help(self)
          endCase

          case wp == QUIT_DML
                is close(self)
          endCase

        endSelect;
}
```

where the instance variable menuID is a Dictionary object. The perform message is similar to eval of Lisp. It applies the menuID[wp] message to self. This way, the descendant of MyWindow class needs only to set the menuID dictionary. There is no need for redefining the command method. It reuses the command method of its ancestor MyWindow. The setup of menuID for the DMWindow class of version 0.02 follows:

```
Def initMenuID(self)
{
    menuID := %Dictionary(1->#describe
                          2->#expand
                          3->#listMembers
                          4->#oneMember
                          5->#addMember
                          6->#deleteMember
                          7->#modifyMember
                          8->#query
                          9->#showConnection
                          10->#help
                          11->#close )
}
```

Thus we can avoid the undisciplined code of the version 0.01 LstMemWindow class's command method (see Listing 4.3). Instead of sending a message in the case clause, the actual processing is done inside the case clause. This requires a recompiling of the whole command method whenever there is a change in that part of processing. With the MyWindow class, the change is localized to the method for handling the menu choice. Also, use of initMenuID method serves as documentation and eases programming by eliminating need for the programmer to remember details. With the old way of redefining the command method for each descendant class, one must know about the variables wp and lp. With the MyWindow class, the programmers need not know about them. They only have to remember to define initMenuID method, which serves the purpose of documentation, and to define the

Listing 4.3 _____
Command Method for Version 0.01 LstMemWindow. Actual processing is done within the case clause, instead of sending messages.

```
/*handles menu selections for LstMemWindow*/
/*Uppercase words (eg LM_MORE) are integer*/
/*constants                    */
Def command(self, wP, IP)
{
  select
  case IP <> 0  /*exit if not menu*/
    is ^0
  endCase
```

(continues)

```
  case wP == LM_MORE
    is
      if selIdx
        if listMemObj.aOMWin
          displayNewMem(aOMWin,selIdx);
          Call BringWindowToTop(
                handle(listMemObj.aOMWin))
        else
        listMemObj.aOMWin := new(OneMemWindow,aDMWin,"GladOMMenu",
                                 listMemObj.name+" :READ MODE",nil);
        start(listMemObj.aOMWin,aDMWin, listMemObj,selIdx)
        endif
      else
        errorBox("WAIT","There is no highlighted line")
      endif
  endCase

  case wP == LM_MODIFY
    is
      if selIdx
        errorBox("Modify",asString(selIdx))
      else
        errorBox("WAIT","There is no highlited line")
      endif
  endCase

  case wP == LMHELP
    is errorBox("Help","will help")
  endCase

  case wP == QUIT_LM
    is close(self)
  endCase

 endSelect;

}
```

methods for handling the menu selections. Inheritance not only eliminates recoding but also aids in defining a conceptually higher-level routine for the descendant classes.

The second thing we did was to add scroll bars to the **MyWindow** class. The window style for the windows of **Window** class does not have scroll bars. Since the GLAD windows require scroll bars, the vertical and horizontal scroll bars were added to the **MyWindow** class. (Several window classes of version 0.02 are not yet using the scroll bars. We will be adding the scroll bars to them in the future versions. Currently, an explicit code is added to those window classes to remove the scroll bars.) More important than just adding the scroll bars is the handling of scroll bar messages. We did similar things to what we did for the command method. The horizontal and vertical scroll bar messages are handled by the following methods:

```
Def WM_HSCROLL(self, wp, lp)
{
    if hScrollID[wp] then
        perform(self, lp, hScrollID[wp])
    else
        ^0
    endif
}
Def WM_VSCROLL(self, wp, lp)
{
    if vScrollID[wp] then
        perform(self, lp, vScrollID[wp])
    else
        ^0
    endif
}
```

Here the instance variables vScrollID and hScrollID serve the same purpose as menuID.

The third addition was the handling of right mouse button click. The methods for handling it follow.

```
/*MS-Windows message for the right button down*/
Def WM_RBUTTONDOWN(self,wp,lp)
{
    if rbuttonDn
        ^0
    endif;
    rbuttonDn := true;
    Call SetCapture(hWnd);
    rbuttonDown(self,asPoint(lp))
}
/*MS-Windows message for right button up*/
Def WM_RBUTTONUP(self,wp,lp)
{
    if not(rbuttonDn)
        ^0
    endif;
    rbuttonDn := nil;
    Call ReleaseCapture();
    rButtonRelease(self,asPoint(lp))
}
```

We will not explain the details of the preceding two methods. The point is that they are taking care of low-level details. Once these methods are defined for the MyWindow class, the programmer of descendant windows simply redefines the rButtonDown and rButton-Release to handle the right button press and release, respectively. Notice that the variable wp is not passed to rButtonDown and rButtonRelease. The value of wp determines whether any virtual key, such as CTRL key, is pressed with the right button press and release. Since we do not use virtual keys in GLAD, there is no need to pass it to rButtonDown and rButtonRelease. Here again, as with the command and initMenuID methods, the preceding two methods hide the low-level details from the programmers of descendant classes.

We now describe two classes, DMWindow and GladObj, that illustrate the division of labor between the interactive and application objects. The terms *interactive* and *application* are equivalent to *view* and *model* in the MVC triad terminology. As expounded in Linton, Vlissides, and Calder [10], we separated the classes that implement user interface from the classes that implement logic of application. All the GLAD window classes are interactive objects that take care of the user interface. With version 0.02, GladObj is the only class, aside from system-defined classes such as TextFile, OrderedCollection, and Dictionary, that handles the application logic. This is expected since we are concentrating on the user interface at this point. More application objects will be added to future versions. Some will be mentioned in the concluding section.

The DMWindow class governs the data manipulation component of GLAD. Its basic functions are to display the database objects and to manage the data manipulation functions (by creating subordinate windows). In the sample University Database, there are three database objects: EMPLOYEE, DEPT, and EQUIPMENT. Information on each database object is stored in a GladObj object. In the following discussion, we use the terms *database object* and GladObj object synonymously. The DMWindow class encapsulates the knowledge of displaying the GladObj objects as rectangles (see Fig. 4.3), moving those rectangles, displaying and hiding the scroll bars, handling the scroll bars if present, and executing the selected menu choice. We notice from Fig. 4.17 that most of the menu choices result in the creation of new windows. For example, when the user requests the display of data for a database object one at a time, the DisplayOneWindow object is created to do that. The selected database object is passed to the DisplayOneWindow object, so this window will be able to communicate via messages with the passed GladObj object in order to get the necessary data to be displayed. This arrangement persists between the GladObj object and various window objects, as seen in Fig. 4.17. In other words, these window objects know how to display data (be it a database object itself as rectangle, single or multiple instances of database object, or the structure of the database object) and to interact with the users, but the data come from the GladObj object.

Only the GladObj object knows how and where to retrieve and store data. With version 0.02, data are stored in a simple textfile. We will modify the GladObj class in the future versions so that data may be stored in the relational back-end data servers or the ISAM files. Since this change will be localized to this class only, all the existing window classes are reusable without modification.

A selected database object may have multiple associated windows opened. In Fig. 4.10, the selected database object EMPLOYEE has two windows opened. A selected object may have windows for listing its data all at once (LstMemWindow), displaying its data one at a time (DisplayOneWindow), describing its structure (DscrbWindow), and showing its specialized object (NestDMWindow). Instead of closing the opened windows individually, the user may close all at once by deselecting the selected object. Who should take care of handling this event?

Certainly the DMWindow object should, since this is the "control" window for the data manipulation activities. The instance variable dbSchema (OrderedCollection) of DM-Window holds the GladObj objects, so we could add OrderedCollections to the members of dbSchema to remember their associated windows. This looks fine on the surface, but it turns out that it is not a good solution. The reason is that if DMWindow were to hold the information on associated windows for every database object, all communication among the associated windows would have to be done via DMWindow. For example, as shown in Fig. 4.10, LstMembersWindow and DisplayOneWindow are cross-referenced. A change in LstMemberWindow is reflected on DisplayOneWindow, and vice versa. For LstMemberWindow to find out whether there is a corresponding DisplayOneWindow, it must ask DMWindow. To do so, LstMemberWindow needs to send a message, say isThereDispOne(aDM,selObject), to DMWindow. The argument selObject is the instance variable of LstMemberWindow; it stores the database object associated with this LstMemberWindow. The corresponding method in DMWindow will search for this selObject in the instance variable dbSchema. Upon finding selObject, it checks to see if any DisplayOneWindow is opened for this selObject and returns the result to LstMemberWindow. A similar arrangement is necessary if DisplayOneWindow wants to know about the existence of its "sibling" LstMemberWindow. There needs to be a second method, say isThereLstMem(self,selObject), in DMWindow to handle that. This is not a good solution since whenever we wish to make a connection (that is, knowledge of each other's existence) between some window classes, we must write new methods similar to the above.

An alternative to sending messages to DMWindow is to add instance variables aDispOne to LstMemberWindow and aLstMem to DisplayOneWindow. These instance variables are used to remember whether there is any sibling window. When DisplayOneWindow opens a sibling LstMemberWindow, it will set its instance variable aLstMem to a newly created LstMemberWindow as

```
/*user asked to see the data all at once*/
/*so open the LstMemberWindow window */
Def more (self)
{
    if not(aLstMem) then
        aLstMem := new(LstMemberWindow, ... );
        start(aLstMem, self, selObject)
    else
        /*error: already opened*/
    endif
}
```

and send itself as argument for the start message to aLstMem. The start method of LstMemberWindow will set its instance variable aDispOne as

```
Def start(self, dispOne, gladObject)
{
    aDispOne := dispOne;
    /* rest of start up routine*/
}
```

The reverse arrangement is also required when LstMemberWindow opens a Display-OneWindow window.

By knowing each other, these two classes can communicate by sending messages. This is, however, a duplication of knowledge since DMWindow knows about the existence of all the associated windows and LstMemberWindow and DisplayOneWindow know about the existence of each other. It is not a good idea to replicate knowledge in such a way because this will make a degree of connectivity of one class to others higher than necessary. When one of the windows is closed, say LstMemberWindow, then it must send notification messages to both DMWindow and DisplayOneWindow so they have consistent information on its status. Sending two messages may not be bad, but if there are ten such connections, we must send ten messages. Tracking all the connections becomes harder and error-prone as the number of connections increases. Fewer connections implies easier class maintenance and modification. This is achieved by keeping one piece of information at one place.

We decided that the information on associated windows should be kept with the GladObj object itself because all the associated windows would know about their selected database object via their instance variable selObject. For example, when the selected database object X has the three associated windows LstMemberWindow, DisplayOne-Window, and DscrbWindow opened, then the instance variable selObject of these three windows is set to X. The GladObj class therefore has an instance variable assocWindows, an OrderedCollection, to keep track of all those opened windows associated with this database object. Thus we have exactly one place to store this single piece of information. Whenever any of those opened windows needs to know the existence of a sibling window, it simply asks its selObject.

With this setup, we only need one method to answer the inquiry from different associated windows regarding the existence of sibling windows. For example, if LstMemberWindow wants to know about the existence of DisplayOneWindow, it sends the message hasSibling(selObject,#DisplayOneWindow) to the selObject. The method to handle this inquiry is

```
Def hasSibling(self, windowType)
{
    do(assocWindows,
        {using(win)
            if class(win) = windowType then
            ^win
            endif } )
    ^nil
}
```

where the do message causes the receiver assocWindows to iterate over its members and apply the passed block to each member. The variable win is set to the visited member of assocWindows.

When the selected object (highlighted rectangle in DMWindow) is deselected, DMWindow sends a message to this GladObj object to close any opened associated windows. Via the instance variable assocWindows, we can easily close the opened associated windows as follows:

```
Def closeAssocWindows(self)
{
    do(assocWindows,
      {using(win) quit(win);
          remove(assocWindows,win)})
}
```

where quit is the polymorphic message. Notice that without a polymorphic message feature, the preceding method could not be specified in such a concise manner and, more important, a change would be necessary whenever a new associated window was added.

The hasSibling and closeAssocWindows methods can accommodate any new connection we wish to add later among the associated windows. No changes are required in these methods or in the instance variables of GladObj class. All we have to do is to add logic to send the message hasSibling from the newly connected windows. The changes are again localized to the affected classes only; that is, no changes are required to the existing classes. Properly designed classes (for example, right choice of instance variables and effective use of polymorphic messages) therefore facilitate easier modification and extension.

To illustrate how an improperly designed class would hamper modification and extension, we describe how we initially kept the information on associated windows. At first we had separate instance variables in the GladObj object for separate windows, so we had instance variables aDispOne and aLstMem in the GladObj object. We soon realized that this design was very poor because modification required a change in the already existing class GladObj. Every time we needed to add a new associated window, we had to create another instance variable, a very time-consuming task since all the existing methods had to be recompiled. Additionally, a method to handle a new message had to be composed. Moreover, the method to close the associated windows had to be modified and recompiled. The method may look something like this.

```
Def badCloseAssocWindows(self)
{
    if aLstMem then
        quit(aLstMem); aLstMem := nil
    endif;
    if aDispOne then
        quit(aDispOne); aDispOne := nil
    endif;
    /* and so forth for other windows */
}
```

This does not allow the effective use of a polymorphic message.

We now describe the data definition component of GLAD classes. DDWindow is the control window for handling the data definition component. We initially started to design the class as a completely separate one from DMWindow, but we soon realized that many common functions are required by both. DDWindow lets the user define a new object, and it must display the object just as we did for DMWindow. So we made DDWindow a child of DMWindow, as depicted in Fig. 4.16. It inherits all the knowledge of DMWindow and adds its specialized knowledge of handling a new set of menu choices. The arrangement looked proper. However, as we started writing this chapter and rethinking our design decisions, we realized that this is not actually a good hierarchy. DDWindow is inheriting something it should not. All those methods defined for handling the menu choices of DMWindow are also inherited by DDWindow. This is not logically correct.

We will modify this component according to the hierarchy shown in Fig. 4.18. The

Figure 4.18 _____

Modified Class Hierarchy for the GLAD Classes. The SchemaWindow class is added as a new abstract superclass.

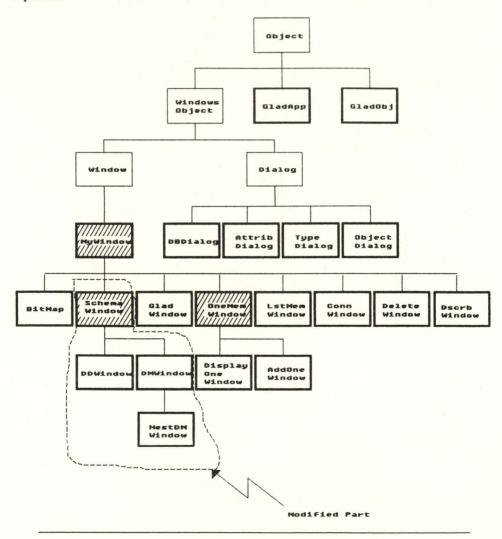

SchemaWindow class is the abstract superclass embodying the knowledge that DDWindow must inherit. In other words, it is a subset of old DMWindow and contains all the methods of old DMWindow except those pertaining to menu handling. DDWindow and DMWindow will inherit from SchemaWindow. Specialties of those windows are methods for handling their menu choices. This is a much more logical hierarchy because it shows the relationship more precisely.

Will it be easy to make such modification? Yes, thanks to the modular construction of classes. What we have to do is to define a new class, SchemaWindow, as a descendant of MyWindow. The SchemaWindow class has all the methods from the old DMWindow class except those pertaining to the processing of the menu choices. Then we will change one statement of DDWindow to specify that it is now a descendant of SchemaWindow. Finally, we will recompile the new DMWindow. No other classes will be affected; that is, no descendants of DDWindow and DMWindow need to be touched. Only the directly affected classes (SchemaWindow, DDWindow, and DMWindow) need to be modified. The new hierarchy shows a nice, logical relationship between the abstract superclass and its descendants.

Besides the one between MyWindow and its descendants, the relationship between the abstract superclass OneMemWindow and its descendants DisplayOneWindow and AddOneWindow also exhibits a logical hierarchy. OneMemWindow is an abstract superclass that knows how to "paint" the content of the window for displaying one instance of GladObj. It asks the GladObj object whether there is a defined template that specifies where each field will appear on the screen. If it has one, it uses the defined template and displays it. Otherwise, it creates a default template. DisplayOneWindow (for OneByOne window) inherits this knowledge. DisplayOneWindow also displays the data value (see Fig. 4.11). AddOneWindow, which allows the user to add data, also inherits the knowledge of displaying the template from OneMemberWindow. AddOneWindow adds the specialized knowledge on this to expand the window size to accommodate the control buttons and the logic to handle this button.

4.5 EVALUATION

The previous section described our design decisions and showed how we employed the features of object-oriented programming. In this section, by using our implementation experience as a yardstick, we assess the benefits of class, inheritance, message passing, and polymorphism.

4.5.1 Benefits of Class

The concept of program modularity is well supported by the object-oriented programming and Actor. Each window functionality, such as displaying database schema, listing data values, and showing database object structure, is implemented by a separate window class. A window class encapsulates the specific knowledge of a single functionality within its instance variables and methods. A clear division of labor by classes helps us develop finely structured, modular application software with excellent flexibility for modification and extension in a continued development.

The notion of class is a very powerful programming paradigm. However, just like any other powerful tool, it must be used properly to realize its true benefits. How do we know whether the given classes are well designed? We believe that notions of tight cohesion and loose coupling (from the traditional structured program criteria) also apply for object-oriented programming. A class must be tightly cohesive and it also must be loosely coupled with other classes. Tight cohesion means that the class implements a single, well-defined function and embodies a single piece of information. Loose coupling means that this single piece of information is not replicated among different classes. We next present some guidelines for designing a tightly cohesive and loosely coupled class.

4.5.2 Benefit of Inheritance

The availability of inheritance in an object-oriented language shortens the development time and increases the power of application without a major effort. Inheritance supports (or encourages) the natural way of organizing knowledge in a hierarchical manner, such as the taxonomic classification of organism. Hierarchical organization allows the human mind to grasp the knowledge faster and better.

Inheritance supports information hiding. As we have seen with the abstract superclasses of GLAD, the low-level details are hidden within those classes, providing conceptually higher-level routines to their descendants (or actually programmers of descendant classes). Once a class is defined, any new descendant class can be created easily via inheritance. All we have to do is define methods specific to the new class.

Although it seems that inheritance applies only to the downward direction, that is, creating a child from a parent, it is more flexible and powerful. Actually, there are two ways to create a hierarchy in object-oriented programming: generalization and specialization. With generalization, a commonness among classes is grouped and generalized into a class. We have shown the examples of generalization in the previous section. Three abstract superclasses (MyWindow, OneMemberWindow, and SchemaWindow) are generalized from the other window classes. Although not a requirement, normally the generalized class is an abstract superclass. The actual sequence of creating the classes may vary. A parent class may be created first and then the descendants, or vice versa. With the MyWindow class, we knew what kinds of windows we needed for GLAD at the design stage, so we created MyWindow first and then the descendants of MyWindow. For the newly designed SchemaWindow class, we will modify the already existing DDWindow and DMWindow classes, as explained in the previous section.

With specialization, a special subclass is created from an existing class. We may view NestDMWindow as a specialized DMWindow where data manipulation functions are exactly the same as for DMWindow. Yet it must have its objects' rectangles drawn in the color of the selected object in its parent DMWindow or NestDMWindow (see Fig. 4.8) window and has no ShowConnectn menu choice. To achieve the behavior of NestDMWindow, we first made it a subclass of DMWindow so it would inherit all the methods of DMWindow. We then modified some of the inherited methods, so the functionalities special to the NestDMWindow could be attained. To remove the ShowConnectn menu choice from the menu bar, we modified the start method to dynamically eliminate this menu choice from the available list.

We also modified the getPenColor method. The actual drawing is done by the display method defined in the DMWindow class. The display method determines the color to be used via the getPenColor method, which is defined as

```
Def getPenColor(self, hdc)
{
    ^Call GetTextColor(hdc)
}
```

in the DMWindow class. The variable hdc stands for a handle to display context. This data structure holds all necessary information about the window so the system can properly draw the window's content. The method returns the current pen color (normally a black) by making an MS-Windows call GetTextColor. The method is redefined as

```
Def getPenColor(self, hdc)
{
    ^color(genObj)
}
```

in the NestDMWindow class. The method now returns the color of genObj, an instance variable of the NestDMWindow that is set to the selected object in the parent window (either DMWindow or NestDMWindow). In Fig. 4.8, the genObj of the first NestDMWindow window (one with the caption "SubClasses of: EMPLOYEE") is set to the green-colored EMPLOYEE object, so the rectangles for the FACULTY and STAFF objects are drawn in green.

Instead of drawing a colored rectangle, the border of a NestDMWindow window is colored in version 0.01. To do the window border coloring, the paint method of NestDMWindow is modified to

```
Def paint (self, hdc)
{
    shadeOuterRegion(self,hdc);
    paint(self:DMWindow,hdc)
}
```

where the shadeOuterRegion message is sent to itself to color the border. Then the message paint is sent to itself for drawing the window's content. Notice that the receiver object is typed as self:DMWindow. It forces the paint method defined for the DMWindow class to be used, which is exactly what we want, because the drawing of NestDMWindow content is same as that of DMWindow except for border coloring.

The visual effects of version 0.01 and version 0.02 are thus quite different. Yet they only take very simple modifications of the inherited methods. Proper use of the inheritance mechanism therefore allows experimentation of different interface styles without a major coding effort. We conclude that the inheritance mechanism of object-oriented programming is a very powerful programming paradigm. It supports information hiding and allows a flexible way of creating a hierarchy, which makes an effective reuse of code possible. Since Actor does not allow multiple inheritance, we did not use the concept in our design of GLAD. Even if it did, we are not sure whether we would have used multiple inheritance. It would be interesting to do a comparative study of single and multiple inheritance.

4.5.3 Benefits of Message Passing

Message passing allows an incremental sharing of knowledge, thus easing the task of extending program functionality. Knowledge sharing does not mean knowledge duplication. A single piece of information must be kept in one class, but this information may (and should) be shared with other classes.

Consider the case of LstMemWindow and DisplayOneWindow, which we have described in the previous section. By adding a message-passing protocol between two classes that we developed separately, we were able to improve the quality of GLAD interface dramatically. LstMemWindow and DisplayOneWindow classes for displaying data were developed separately without any prior consideration of cross referencing at the later stage. During the development we realized that a change in one window should be reflected in another window. We were able to achieve this new functionality by again adding a few methods to these classes. What we did was quite simple. Inside every method that changes the content of a window, such as displaying new data and highlighting a new row, we added a message to be sent to another window. For example, inside the Prev method of Display-OneWindow class, we added the message hiLiteNewItem(aLMWin(selObject),idx) to be sent to the instance of the LstMemWindow class. The newly defined method hiLite-NewItem of the LstMemWindow class simply highlights the idx'th data of selobject. The same message was added to next, first, last, and ith methods of DisplayOneWindow class. Analogously, a new method, displayNewMem, was added to the DisplayOneWindow class. Corresponding messages were added to the methods in the LstMemWindow class so the changes in the LstMemWindow window would be reflected in the DisplayOneWindow window by sending the message displayNewMem to it.

While the message-passing mechanism of object-oriented programming facilitates an easier extension of programming functionality, it requires a major effort in a traditional process-oriented programming. Consider, for example, that we have two processes, PA and PB, that handle the update of equipment and employee information, respectively. Both equipment and employees have room assignments (where they are placed and where they work). The process PX controls the other two processes, PA and PB. What will happen when a new requirement specifies that when a certain type of equipment (nuclear, for example) is assigned to a room, all employees working in the room will get a bonus payment? We need to modify the subroutine calls made by PX to PA and PB by adding a status flag to signal the event (assigning of designated equipment types to a room). The control logic of PA and PB must also be modified to correctly set and use this status flag. We see that all PX, PA, and PB must be recompiled and tested again. With an object-oriented approach, we only have to add a method to the Employee class to handle the event and send a message from the Equipment class when the event occurs.

4.5.4 Benefits of Polymorphism

Polymorphism in an object-oriented language means an ability to send the same message to instances of different classes. The proper use of this concept could result in a cleaner code with less awkward control structures. It could also lead to an easier extension of code. A good example of this occurred when we were developing the cross-referencing capability between LstMemWindow and DisplayOneWindow classes.

When both the DisplayOneWindow and LstMemWindow windows are present, the messages hiLiteNewItem and displayNewMem are correctly sent to the intended receivers. However, when only one is present, we encounter an execution error. Let us take the case of hiLiteNewItem message. Suppose only DisplayOneWindow window is present. Since there is no LstMemWindow window, the message hiLiteNewItem (aLMWin(selObject), idx) inside one of the DisplayOneWindow classes will not be sent to an instance of LstMemWindow class. In other words, the object returned from aLMWin(selObject) is not an instance of LstMemWindow class because there is none. Instead, the returned object is Nil, which will be the message receiver. The object Nil is system-defined and belongs to the class called NilClass. To eliminate the execution error, we could replace every occurrence of

| hiLiteNewItem (aLMWin(selObject), idx)

to

```
<ListWin := aLMWin(selObject);
if ListWin <> Nil then
    hiLiteNewItem (ListWin, idx)
else
    /*some error handling here*/
endif
```

This will require the time-consuming task of finding all methods that contain the offending message and recompiling those methods. It also lengthens the code itself. The much better solution we adopted is to add a new method, hiLiteNewItem, to NilClass. This method will contain the logic for the else part of the preceding code. By this approach, no changes were necessary to the already defined methods, and thus no space-taking control structure is added. We only have to define and compile a single method in NilClass.

4.6 LESSONS LEARNED

In this section, we discuss the lessons we learned from our implementation effort. We present them here as a list of object-oriented design guidelines.

- *Create a class that implements a single functionality.* This makes the class cohesive and modular. We should be able to describe the function of the class in a single sentence. The class must be implementing either interactive or application objects, but never both. This single functionality rule also applies to a method. Instead of writing a long method, it is better to write many shorter methods, with each method implementing a clearly defined function. This makes later modification and extension easier.
- *Do not duplicate the knowledge among different classes.* Knowledge certainly must be shared among classes, but it must reside within a single class to easily maintain consistent information. This makes the classes loosely coupled. In this regard, the use of a global variable must be avoided because the value stored in a global variable is accessible and modifiable by all classes.

- *Do not violate the integrity of class (or, equivalently, do not violate the principle of encapsulation).* Instead of fully protecting the privacy of objects, a system may allow the programmers to access the instance variables without using the defined protocol. For example, as a tool for debugging and testing, Actor allows the programmers to use a dot notation to access the instance variables of objects. If Emp is an Employee object, then we can use the dot notation Emp.salary to access its salary instance variable. Since the dot notation is easier to use than sending messages to access the values of instance variables, we may be tempted to use it. However, the dot notation is, in essence, a duplication of knowledge and should never be used because it makes modification very difficult (when the Employee class is modified, for example). So instead of keeping the instance variable, the salary is now computed from the values of other instance variables, and all the dot notations Emp.salary must be corrected. Finding all the references is very time-consuming and error-prone.

- *Develop and test a class individually before using it in a program.* Besides checking for the correctness of the class, individual testing aids in determining the degree of class modularity. When the class cannot be easily tested separately, it means that the class is too intricately connected to the other classes. In other words, we have "spaghetti" classes.

- *Use an abstract superclass to effectively support the inheritance and information hiding.* Proper use of an abstract superclass allows the hiding of low-level details. Programmers for descendant classes can use conceptually higher-level routines in devising a solution. Although allowed, the methods of the descendant classes should not make references to the inherited instance variables directly, because, in essence, this uses a dot notation as discussed in the design guideline 3. When some instance variables of the abstract superclass are modified, all the methods of the descendant classes that were referring to the modified instance variables must be recompiled or completely rewritten. Instance variables of any other objects, whether inherited or not, should be referred via messages only. This allows easier modification and extension.

4.7 CONCLUSIONS

We close this chapter with a description of our immediate future plan for the GLAD project. First, we will add a full querying capability. We envision two querying facilities: form-based and language-based. The form-based query window is intended for novice users and operates in a fashion similar to Query-By-Example. The language-based query window is intended for more advanced users and allows them to type in query language statements. The query language is based on predicate calculus. From the user input, the form-based query window generates the statements of the same query language. We will be using two Actor classes, YaccMachine and Analyzer, to create a parser for the query language. This parser will generate an equivalent statement in Actor for execution.

Second, we will connect the GLAD interface to the underlying data server. We are envisioning an SQL-based relational data server and a prototype Multiple Backend Database System (MBDS) [6] as a possible high-performance back-end data server. The tasks of supporting database services such as backup, recovery, and concurrency are delegated to the back-end. We are also considering a B tree as an underlying data manager for a single-user system.

To facilitate the flexibility of interchanging the back-end data servers, we are planning to implement the connection by creating an Actor class DBset. The DBset class encapsulates within its methods knowledge of how the actual data are retrieved and updated. For instance, if the back-end is a simple B tree, then the method for the add operation will add the object into the B-tree structure. If the back-end, on the other hand, is the relational database server, then the method will send an appropriate message to the back-end to carry out the addition to the corresponding relational table. Notice that the parsing part (that is, all the classes that do the parsing) of the system is not affected by the interchanging of back-end data servers. In other words, a query specified in our query language is always translated into the same Actor statements irrespective of the back-end data server. The only methods we need to change are those that access the actual database such as do, exists, add, and delete in the DBset class. By redefining the do method, for instance, the system will retrieve and scan the data from B tree, relational database server, or whatever the back-end data server may be.

References

[1] Bryce, D., and Hull, R. "SNAP: A Graphics-Based Schema Manager," in *Proceedings of 2nd IEEE International Conference on Data Engineering* (Los Angeles, 1986), pp. 151–164.

[2] Cox, B.J. *Object-Oriented Programming: An Evolutionary Approach.* Addison-Wesley, Reading, MA, 1987.

[3] Elmasri, R.A., and Larson, J.A. "A Graphical Query Facility for ER Databases," in *Proceedings of 1985 Conference on Entity-Relationship Approach* (Chicago, 1985), pp. 236–245.

[4] Fogg, D. "Lessons from 'Living in a Database' Graphical Query Interface," in *Proceedings of 1984 SIGMOD Conference* (Boston, 1984), pp. 100–106.

[5] Goldman, K.J.; Goldman, S.A.; Kanellakis, P.C.; and Zdonik, S.B. "ISIS: Interface for a Semantic Information System," in *Proceedings of 1985 SIGMOD Conference* (Austin, 1985), pp. 328–342.

[6] He, X.G.; Higashida, M.; Kerr, D.S.; Orooji, A.; Shi, Z.Z.; Strawser, P.R.; and Hsiao, D.K. "The Implementation of a Multibackend Database System (MDBS): Part II—The Design of a Prototype MDBS," in D.K. Hsiao (Ed.), *Advanced Database Machine Architecture*, Prentice-Hall, Englewood Cliffs, NJ, 1983.

[7] Heiler, S., and Rosenthal, A. "G-WHIZ, a Visual Interface for the Functional Model with Recursion," in *Proceedings of 11th Conference on Very Large Data Bases* (Stockholm, 1985), pp. 209–218.

[8] Herot, C.F. "Spatial Management of Data," *ACM Transactions on Database Systems*, Vol. 5, No. 4 (Dec. 1980), pp. 493–514.

[9] Larson, J.A. "The Forms Pattern Language," in *Proceedings of IEEE International Conference on Data Engineering* (Los Angeles, 1984), pp. 183–191.

[10] Linton, M.A.; Vlissides, J.M.; and Calder, P.R. "Composing User Interfaces with InterViews," *IEEE Computer*, Vol. 16, No. 2 (February 1989), pp. 8–22.

[11] McDonald, N., and Stonebraker, M. "CUPID—The Friendly Query Language," Memo ERL-M487, ERL, University of California, Berkeley, October 1974.

[12] Pinson, L.J., and Wiener, R.S. *An Introduction to Object-Oriented Programming and Smalltalk.* Addison-Wesley, Reading, MA, 1988.

[13] Stonebraker, M., and Kalash, J. "TIMBER: A Sophisticated Relation Browser," in *Proceedings of 8th Conference on Very Large Data Bases* (Mexico City, 1982), pp. 1–10.

[14] Sugihara, K.; Miyao, J.; Kikuno, T.; and Yoshida, N. "A Semantic Approach to Usability in Relational Database Systems," in *Proceedings of IEEE International Conference on Data Engineering* (Los Angeles, 1984), pp. 203–210.

[15] Wong, H.K.T., and Kuo, I. "GUIDE: Graphical User Interface for Database Exploration," in *Proceedings of 8th Conference on Very Large Data Bases* (Mexico City, 1982), pp. 22–32.

[16] Wu, C.T. "A New Graphics User Interface for Accessing a Database," in *Proceedings of Computer Graphics Tokyo '86* (Tokyo, 1986), pp. 203–219.

[17] Wu, C.T. "GLAD: Graphics Language for Databases," in *Proceedings of 11th International Conference on Computer Software and Applications* (Tokyo, 1987), pp. 164–170.

[18] Wu, C.T., and Hsiao, D.K. "Implementing Visual Database Interface by Using Object-Oriented Language," in *Proceedings of IFIP TC-2 Visual Database System Workshop* (Tokyo, 1989), pp. 105–125.

[19] Zhang, Z.Q., and Mendlezon, A.O. "A Graphical Query Language for Entity-Relationship Databases," in *Entity-Relationship Approach to Software Engineering*, Elservier, New York, 1983, pp. 441–448.

[20] Zloof, M.M. "Query-by-Example: A Database Language," *IBM Systems Journal*, Vol. 4 (December 1977), pp. 324–343.

Acknowledgment: The author appreciates the efforts of Hank Fore, Rob Schuett, Mike Williamson, and Lon Yeary for implementing some portions of GLAD. Appreciation also goes to the technical staff of The Whitewater Group, especially Zack Urlocker and Mark Solinski.

CHAPTER 5

DoubleVision: A Foundation for Scientific Visualization

Mary Mock
Apple Computer, Columbia, Maryland

5.1 INTRODUCTION

Object-oriented programming is a well-established organizational and implementation approach, especially within the area of human–computer interaction. One reason is that many common examples of user interface concepts, such as windows, menus, and elementary interaction techniques, have been prepared with object-oriented languages. However, there are not many examples of object-oriented programming in specific application domains for which source code is available. A physicist who must write some of her own software, for example, would find little evidence that object-oriented programming is applicable to her field. Therefore, the physicist may be unlikely to consider undertaking the learning curve associated with object-oriented programming, even for the productivity gains reputed to accompany the use of object-oriented techniques. The DoubleVision application described here is one example available for evaluation by the scientific programmer.

The purpose of DoubleVision was twofold: first, to develop a sample program that all MacApp developers could use either as a guide for various techniques or as a starting point for their own applications, and second, to provide a general-purpose program that scientists can extend for their own specific applications with minimal programming required of them. Some techniques demonstrated in DoubleVision are multiple views of the same data, pseudo-color encoding of data values, palette manipulation techniques, selection techniques for continuous data, and use of off-screen pixel maps for the rapid display of voluminous data sets.

5.2 DOUBLEVISION FUNCTIONALITY

5.2.1 What the User Sees and Does

When DoubleVision is launched, the two "main windows" are displayed, as shown in Color Plate 5.1.* Each window displays one parameter of the data; for example, one window

---

*Color plates appear inside the back cover of this book.

displays temperature and the other pressure. These are standard Macintosh windows; hence they can be resized, moved, and closed [1]. They are initially positioned with one window occupying roughly the left half of the screen and the other occupying the right half. There are four distinct regions within each window. At the top is the color scale, which displays the mapping of data values to colors and can be used to manipulate the color palette. Below the color scale is a horizontal scale with labeled tickmarks to indicate one of the two dimensions of the data. A similar vertical scale is on the left side of the window. The remaining area contains the view of that window's parameter, with color used to indicate values of that parameter at each point. Each window has a vertical and a horizontal Macintosh scroll bar. Clicking in one of the scroll bar arrow buttons causes both the corresponding tickscale and the main view of the window to scroll in that direction. Scrolling will continue as long as the mouse button is held down. The scroll bar thumb may be dragged to any position between the buttons, and the tickscale and main view will be positioned proportionally to the position of the thumb within the scroll bar. So if the thumb in the vertical scroll bar is positioned one-third of the way from the top to the bottom, the vertical tickscale and main view will be scrolled to one-third of their depth.

The user can make several adjustments to these windows. As mentioned earlier, the user can use the color scale to adjust the color palette associated with that window. To do this, the user presses the mouse button inside one of the 16 squares in the color scale and drags the mouse to the left or right. The square gradually changes color to be closer to that of the adjacent square on the side dragged toward. This makes pixels in the data views in the color originally in that square animate to the square's new color. The most recent occurrence of this adjustment can be undone and redone via the Undo and Redo commands in the File menu. The complete set of menus for DoubleVision can be seen in Fig. 5.1.

In most Macintosh applications, the user can display several windows simultaneously. However, only one window is *active* at a time. The active window will not be even partially

Figure 5.1 _____

DoubleVision Menu Commands. While the program is executing, only those menu commands that make sense at a particular moment are enabled. A command that is disabled will still be visible in the menu, but its name will be dimmed.

File	Edit	Windows	Optional Windows	Settings	Palette	Enhance Data
Open...	Undo	Temperature	Scrolling Histogram	Entire Width	Color Scale	Add 10
Close	----------	Pressure	Static Histogram	Max X Resolution	Gray Scale	Add n...
----------	Cut			----------------	----------	----------
Save As...	Copy			Entire Height	Natural Contrast	Smooth n...
Save A Copy	Paste			Max Y Resolution	Higher Contrast	
In...	Clear					
Revert To	----------					
Original	Select All Rows					
----------	Select All Columns					
Page SetUp...	----------					
Print...	Show Clipboard					

Quit						

obscured by other windows; that is, it is always the front window. It is also the only one that can be manipulated directly. In typical Macintosh applications, if the user chooses Save from the File menu, only the data corresponding to the active window is written on the disk. Clicking the mouse button while the cursor is over an inactive window makes that window active. In DoubleVision, the active window may also be changed via the Windows menu. The Windows menu lists all windows currently displayed by DoubleVision, with a check beside the active window. Selecting any other window's name in the menu makes that the active window. The utility of this will be clear when the additional windows that can be displayed in DoubleVision are described.

The Palette menu allows the user to adjust the palettes used to display the data in two other ways. The menu items Color Scale and Gray Scale, as their names suggest, serve as a toggle between displaying the data with color or gray scales. The menu items Natural Contrast and Higher Contrast permit variation of contrast with the selection of colors for display. The difference between Natural Contrast and Higher Contrast is in the way that color values are assigned from the data values. With Natural Contrast, the assignment of color values from data values is by fixed intervals. For example, if the ith color is displayed for data values from 1 to 20, the $i+1$th color is displayed for data values 21 to 40, the $i+2$th color for data values 41 to 60, and so on. With Higher Contrast, the mapping of data values to colors contained within the data file is used. The scientist would typically set these values in the file to provide a high level of contrast at more interesting data values and a low level of contrast at less interesting values. The current mapping of data values to colors is displayed by the color scale. With both of these pairs of display choices, a check mark in the menu indicates which option is currently active.

Another pair of toggles available for the user are the Entire Width and Max X Resolution menu commands and the analogous Entire Height and Max Y Resolution commands, all in the Settings menu. When Max X Resolution is active, all data points in the horizontal dimension are available to be viewed, one data point per pixel. If the window's size is such that all the data cannot fit into the data view region of the window, the horizontal scroll bar is active and can be used to display regions of the data not currently visible. If there is surplus area within the data view region, that surplus area is left white. On the other hand, when Entire Width is active, the data are forced to fit the current size of data view area. So if the data view area is smaller than required to display all the data, the data are decimated to fit. However, if the data view area is larger than required, the data points are not replicated to "stretch" the data to fit the display region. Instead, the data are displayed at the resolution of one pixel per data point. Max Y Resolution and Entire Height behave correspondingly for the vertical direction. With any of these settings, the horizontal and vertical tickscales are adjusted appropriately. When the program is launched, Max X Resolution and Max Y Resolution are active.

Finally, to support the façade of the scientist's being able to "touch the data" and interact with it directly, the user can select a portion of the data with the mouse-controlled cursor. Three types of selection are supported: (1) contiguous rows of data, (2) contiguous columns of data, and (3) a rectangular area. To select a set of contiguous columns, called a *column selection*, the user presses the mouse button at either the leftmost or rightmost column desired in the selection, drags to the other side of the desired selection, and releases the mouse button. Color Plate 5.2 shows a column selection being created. If the motion of the mouse is primarily vertical, a selection of contiguous rows, a *row selection*, is made. If the motion of the mouse is primarily diagonal, a rectangular area is selected. In this case, the points at which the mouse button is pressed and released form opposite corners of the rectangle.

Any existing selection may be adjusted by holding down the shift key and pressing the mouse button. For a column selection, the side closer to the mouse-down point can be adjusted by dragging and releasing the mouse button. Color Plate 5.3 shows a column selection being extended. Similarly, for a row selection, either the top or bottom is adjusted. Notice that a row or column may easily be removed from the current selection by this technique. Adjusting a rectangular selection is a little different: The mouse-down and mouse-up points again form opposite corners of a rectangle, but the new selection is the union of this new rectangle and any existing selection. So, by extending a rectangular selection a few times, almost any area may be selected. Thus this type of selection is called an *area selection*. Color Plate 5.4 shows an area selection being extended. One drawback to this area selection user interface is that, unlike the row and column selections, once a point is selected it cannot be deselected by using selection adjustment. Finally, the user may select all the data via the Select All Rows and Select All Columns commands from the File menu. The distinction between all rows and all columns facilitates construction of the optional windows.

Once a selection is made, optional windows to view the selected data are available to the user with the Views menu. This menu has two commands, Scrolling Histogram and Static Histogram. Histograms are commonly used in many scientific disciplines; if a different type of plot is desired, a scientist is able to add it. The specific way a scientist would do this is discussed later in this chapter.

The histogram shows the relative frequency of one parameter's values for some subset of the domain. Two forms of histograms are available. The static plot uses all the points in the selected region to compute the relative frequencies. This form is available for any type of selection and is the only type of histogram available for an area selection. It is selected with the Static Histogram command. Color Plate 5.5 shows a nonscrolling histogram of a row selection. The scrolling histogram is available only when the current selection is a row selection or a column selection. This is a scrolling plot where a histogram of a single row's data (or column's data) is plotted at a time. A scroll bar is used to select and indicate which row or column of data is currently plotted. Color Plate 5.6 shows a scrolling histogram of the same selection. The scrolling histogram also indicates the starting and stopping points of the selection.

5.2.2 What the Programming End User Can Do

As mentioned earlier, the second goal for DoubleVision was to provide a type of data visualization system that scientists could extend for their own specific applications. Additionally, these extensions should be possible with a minimum of effort on the part of the scientist. We expect a scientist to extend DoubleVision by adding new data manipulation routines or by adding new data-rendering algorithms. In DoubleVision, templates for both of these extensions have been provided.

The Enhance Data menu is available for scientists to insert whatever filtering or other data manipulation techniques are appropriate for their area of expertise and nature of data. Only three menu items, Add 10, Add n..., and Smooth n..., are included. When the user selects Add n..., a dialog box appears in which the user can select a value for n, which is then added to all data values in the current selection. Add 10 provides similar behavior, except that, since no argument is required for the computation, no dialog box is needed to select the argument's value. Smooth n... performs a simple nearest-neighbor smoothing algorithm. This algorithm is applied to the selected data n times, where n is selected through a dialog box. Clearly, these are not especially useful on their own. More important, to add a new filtering technique, the scientist only has to determine whether a dialog box is required with the new technique. If not, the scientist can reuse the code that performs the Add 10 command, substituting the new filtering technique for the addition. If a dialog box will be required to set parameter values, then either the Add n... or Smooth n... command can be used as a model for the new technique. The new command can then be added to the Enhance Data menu by adding one line to the menu template. This line will be modeled after the existing entries for Add 10 and Add n... and will allow the command to be named as the scientist chooses. The Smooth n... command was not included in early plans for DoubleVision but was added to test the ease of adding a new filter. In fact, this filter was added to DoubleVision in only a few hours by a college student with limited MacApp experience.

Adding a new rendering algorithm for the data will be a little more difficult than adding a new filter. The scientist determines which existing optional window more closely resembles the desired new view. The code for the existing view can then be reused, and only the computational and rendering code needs to be modified. So the scientist has sample code that can display a window on the screen, install scroll bars, and draw tickscales beside the view. DoubleVision provides numerous methods for accessing the data conveniently, such as by row, by column, and by rectangle. Installing this view into the Optionals Windows menu is as straightforward as installing a new filter into the Enhance Data menu.

5.3 DESIGN OF DOUBLEVISION

5.3.1 MacApp Functionality

Before delving into the details of DoubleVision's class hierarchy, a short diversion into MacApp, Object Pascal, and Macintosh programming in general is necessary. A fundamental principle of Macintosh applications is that the user is in control of what happens. This makes developing a Macintosh application more complex—the program cannot predict what the user's next action will be and so must be prepared for the user to move the mouse, press the mouse button, type on the keyboard, insert a disk, select a menu command, and so forth, in any order. Most Macintosh programs are structured around an event loop, which continually tests for any sort of event [2]. When an event is detected, the event loop identifies the event and passes control over to the piece of the program that handles that sort of event. When that event has been handled, control is returned to the event loop. Since many of these events, such as printing or saving a file to disk, require significant amounts of code to handle, an application grows quickly in size and complexity.

MacApp was written with Object Pascal and can be used with both Object Pascal and C++. Object Pascal is ordinary Pascal with object-oriented extensions to the language. Developing a program in other hybrid languages often requires using a preprocessor to convert the program into another program in a non-object-oriented language. This second program is then compiled with an ordinary compiler. However, Object Pascal is compiled directly, without using a preprocessor. This feature may make life a little easier for the programmer, since errors may be more easily identified with only one compiler in use. Object Pascal depends heavily on inheritance but does not include multiple inheritance. Object Pascal's primary extensions over Pascal are its declarations of objects and method calls. An object is declared as follows:[1]

```
TMyObject = OBJECT(TSuperClass)
    fFirstInstanceVar:      INTEGER;
    fSecondInstanceVar:TAnotherObject;
    PROCEDURE TMyObject.AMethod;
    PROCEDURE TMyObject.AMethodWithParm(myParm: ParmType);
    FUNCTION TMyObject.AFunction : ReturnType;
    FUNCTION TMyObject.AnOverridingFunction : ReturnType; OVERRIDE;
```

This declaration appears in the TYPE declaration section of the program. The keyword OBJECT indicates that TMyObject is an object and a subclass of the TSuperClass class. Instance variables are declared next, along with their types. Instance variables can be either ordinary Pascal types, such as integers, user-defined types, or another object type. Following the instance variables are the methods, in any order. Methods may be either procedure or functions and are identified as such by the appropriate keyword. In the first method declaration, the method name is AMethod. If an object overrides a method in its superclass, the overriding method is identified with the keyword OVERRIDE, as shown with TMyObject.AnOverridingFunction above. The syntax of a method call is

```
 instance.method(parm1, parm2,...);
```

which is similar to its declaration. An overriding method may call its superclass's method via the INHERITED keyword. Finally, the keyword SELF refers to the object instance and can be used optionally to enhance readability.

Since a large amount of functionality and code would be replicated from one application to another, MacApp offers a division of labor with the programmer. That is, MacApp handles the basics of the Macintosh user interface, and the application programmer provides the portions that are specific to the application. For example, MacApp provides a standard Macintosh window class whose instances can be moved, resized, closed, and scrolled. The application programmer then provides the content of the window and any specialized behavior desired in addition to (or instead of) the standard behavior at the time that the standard behavior would be performed. In addition to providing a library of code that implements standard Macintosh behavior, MacApp also determines when an application's code is called. In these cases, the programmer overrides a MacApp null method to perform the specific behavior required.

---

[1]MacApp naming conventions include class names beginning with "T" (for "type") and instance variable names beginning with "f" (for "field"). The code segments included here conform to these conventions.

MacApp includes an object-level debugger, which is available when the application is built with the debug option. MacApp also provides an inspector, again available when the application is built with the debug option. Lastly, two browsers for the MacApp library are available. The most recent of these, Mouser, is reminiscent of a Smalltalk browser and can be used to browse application code as well as the MacApp class library.

5.3.2 Main Windows

As a data visualization program, DoubleVision relies extensively on MacApp's display class, TView, which is responsible for everything an application displays on the screen. In fact, many of the objects used in DoubleVision are subclasses of TView. TWindow is a subclass of TView and implements the standard Macintosh window. TDialog is also a subclass of TView and implements a dialog window. Another important subclass of TView is the TScroller class. A scroller object performs the coordinate translation required to scroll a portion of a window, but it is not readily identifiable with any specific object on the screen. A scroller usually works in concert with scroll bars, but not necessarily. The TScroller class figures prominently in the design of DoubleVision. TSScrollbar is an indirect descendant of TView and implements a Macintosh scroll bar that communicates user interactions to an associated instance of TScroller. These class inheritance relationships are shown in Fig. 5.2.

In addition to the class inheritance relationships of TView, MacApp organizes the instances of the view classes into a tree structure, called the *view instance hierarchy*. One hierarchy is established for each window. An instance of TWindow is always at the root of the tree, and thus is the *superview* of every other view involved in displaying that window. MacApp uses this hierarchy in two ways. First, the hierarchy is used to determine which object handles a mouse click or menu command. In general, if a mouse click is detected, the view instance that the mouse was over and that is a leaf node in this hierarchy has the first opportunity to handle the event. If that object does not handle the event, the event is passed up through the hierarchy. Each object in turn up the hierarchy has a chance to respond, until one of them does so. The document and application objects also have a chance to handle any menu commands not handled by an object within the view hierarchy. Also, each view instance has its own coordinate system, and MacApp's second use of this hierarchy is to assist in computing coordinate transformations between view instances.

The DoubleVision main windows have four regions, as described earlier: the color scale, the horizontal and vertical tickscales, and the main view. Each of these is a *subview* of the

Figure 5.2 _____

The Class Inheritance Tree for the MacApp View Classes Used in DoubleVision. The gray line indicates that other classes are between these in the MacApp class hierarchy.

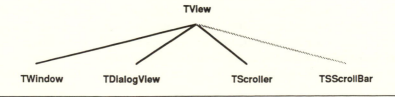

Figure 5.3

The View Instance Hierarchy for a DoubleVision Main Window.

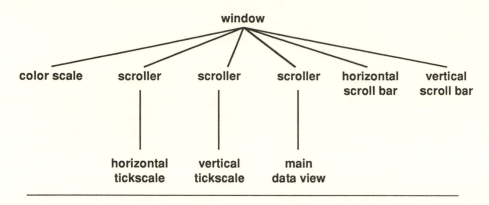

window object. Any view that can scroll must be the subview of an instance of TScroller. Since the color scale does not scroll, it is not a subview of a scroller but instead is a direct subview of the window. The other three regions are scrollable: The horizontal tickscale can scroll horizontally; the vertical tickscale can scroll vertically; and the main view can scroll in both directions. To accomplish this, there are three instances of TScroller in the main window's subview tree, each a direct subview of the window. One scroller instance only scrolls horizontally, and so only responds to the horizontal scroll bar; this scroller is the superview of the horizontal tickscale. Similarly, the second scroller instance scrolls only vertically, responds only to the vertical scroll bar, and is the superview of the vertical tickscale. The third scroller instance scrolls in both directions, responds to both scroll bars, and is the superview of the main view. The three scroller instances are necessary since the tickscales and main view have different scrolling behavior. If all three behaved the same way, one scroller object could serve as the superview for all three. Of course, if the tickscales scrolled in both directions, they could be scrolled out of the visible region of the window—which seems less than desirable. Finally, each scroll bar is a subview of the window. The view instance hierarchy is shown graphically in Fig. 5.3, and Fig. 5.4 shows the window regions these scrollers control.

A few other classes perform the translation of data values into their colored representations on the screen. The drawing of the main views actually takes place via an offscreen pixel map, which is then copied to the screen in one operation. Each main view has an fOffScreen instance variable, which is an instance of the TOffScreen class, which performs the drawing for that main view.

The Macintosh Palette Manager handles much of the color manipulation within DoubleVision. It allows the programmer to use and manipulate color without concern for the specific video hardware and the number of screens attached to the Macintosh. DoubleVision defines two palettes, one for color drawing and the other for gray scale drawing, each with 36 entries. In the color palette, the first two entries are black and white, followed by 16 colors, which are used to represent valid data points. The next entry is gray, which is used to represent

Figure 5.4 _____

The Regions That the TScroller Instances Occupy Within a DoubleVision Main Window. Horizontal stripes indicate the region of the scroller that scrolls the horizontal tickscale; vertical stripes indicate the region of the scroller that scrolls the vertical tickscale. Diagonal stripes indicate the region of the scroller that scrolls the main data region. Recall that the color scale does not scroll; hence no scroller is shown for the color scale.

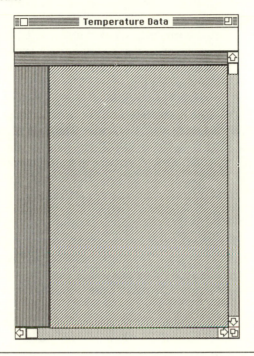

any invalid data values within the data set. The next 16 colors are "dimmed" versions of the 16 valid data colors, and the final entry is a dimmed gray. The 17 dimmed colors are used to highlight selected regions of data. The gray palette is similarly organized, with black and white, 16 values of gray for valid data, very dark gray for invalid data, and dimmed versions of the 17 gray shades for highlighting selections. The Palette Manager is used to assign a palette to a specific window and to modify the colors within the palette.

Each data value is stored as an eight-bit, unsigned integer. So these 256 values must be mapped onto 17 colors before they are displayed. This mapping is handled by an instance of the TCategorization class. This mapping takes any value outside the range of valid data values to 18, the index of dark gray within either palette. The mapping of valid data values depends on whether natural contrast or higher contrast is desired. For natural contrast, this mapping is linear; for example, the number of valid data values is divided by 16, and that number of consecutive data values is mapped to each color. For higher contrast, the mapping is that which is contained within the data file. Both categorizations are computed when a main view is initialized and are then stored in the main view's instance variables fCatLinear and fCatEqualized. The instance variable fCatCurrent identifies which categorization is currently in use.

Part of the pixel map data structure is a color table that maps pixel values to colors. The offscreen image object maintains two such tables. Its instance variable, fNormCTHdl, is a handle to a table mapping the data values to the 17 regular colors (or values of gray), and fDimCTHdl is a handle to the table mapping the data values to the 17 highlighted colors. These tables are computed using both the current palette and the current categorization. The offscreen image object's instance variable, fCTabHandle, indicates which is currently in use. Preparing these tables has the result that drawing is not explicitly performed by the program—just placing the data values into the correct area of video RAM will cause the corresponding colors to be "drawn" on the screen. The offscreen image object uses the Macintosh utility routine CopyBits to perform this, by copying the data from their location in memory to the portion of video RAM corresponding to the window's content region. This technique makes drawing much faster than looping through all data points, explicitly transforming each data point from its measured data value to the corresponding color, computing its location within the window, and drawing a single point of that color at that location.

5.3.3 Optional Views

The histogram views are implemented with four additional classes: THistogramView, TBarsView, THistogramControl, and THistogramScrollBar. The first three of these are immediate subclasses of the MacApp TView class, and THistogramScrollBar is, as its name suggests, a subclass of the MacApp TScrollBar class. The class inheritance relationships are shown in Fig. 5.5.

The first of these is the THistogramView class, which corresponds to the content of the window. An instance of this class maintains the minimum and maximum domain values, as well as the data that will be graphed within either a scrolling or static histogram. For a scrolling histogram, a count of data values is made for each row or column within the selection when the histogram is created. This way, there may be a short pause before the first histogram is plotted, but histograms plotted as the user scrolls will be plotted more quickly

---

Figure 5.5 _____

The Class Inheritance Tree for Histograms. The grey line indicates that other classes are between these in the MacApp class hierarchy.

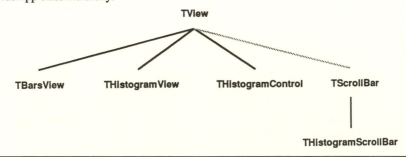

Figure 5.6 _____

The View Instance Hierarchy for a Static (Nonscrolling) Histogram.

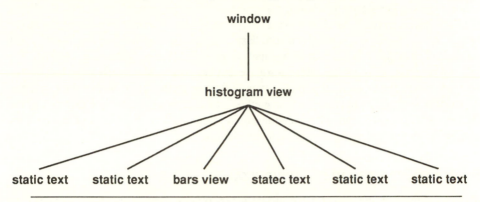

since the counts for those histograms have already been performed. This object also has methods to draw and erase itself and to normalize the histogram data to fit into the instance of TBarsView. The instance of THistogramView is a subview of the window and has six subviews. Five of these subviews are instances of the MacApp class TStaticText, which implements a static text item. These five instances correspond to the histogram's labels. The remaining subview is an instance of TBarsView.

The TBarsView instance corresponds to the portion of the window in which the histograms are actually drawn. It has instance variables to determine the background color and the color in which the bars will be drawn. By default, these are gray and red, respectively. This class also has methods for drawing and erasing itself. The view hierarchies for a static histogram window and for a scrolling histogram window are shown in Figs. 5.6 and 5.7, respectively.

Figure 5.7 _____

The View Instance Hierarchy for a Scrolling Histogram

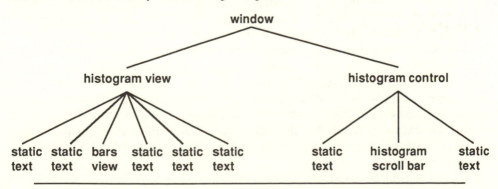

THistogramControl and THistogramScrollBar are only instantiated for a scrolling histogram. The instance of THistogramControl is a subview of the window. It uses information from the THistogramScrollBar instance to determine which row or column of data should be drawn by the TBarsView instance. It also sets the domain range for the data to be plotted. An instance of THistogramScrollBar is a subview of the THistogramControl instance. THistogramScrollBar is a subclass of the MacApp class TScrollBar. The TScrollBar class performs the interaction a user expects with a Macintosh scroll bar, that is, handling mouse clicks within the arrow boxes and dragging the thumb within the scroll bar. THistogramScrollBar overrides a few methods so that these actions are directed to the THistogramControl instance for transformation into selection of the appropriate data for plotting rather than effecting a coordinate translation.

5.3.4 *Implementation of Commands*

MacApp eliminates the need for the programmer to code explicitly the main event loop common to most Macintosh programs. What the programmer *does* have to do is code the actions desired when a *user event* occurs, such as clicking or dragging the mouse, and selecting a menu item or typing a menu item's keyboard equivalent. So the MacApp programmer only needs to prepare the code to write a document's data to a disk file, for example, but does not need to detect that the user selected Save from the File menu or used command-S, the keyboard equivalent of Save.

Instances of four classes can handle user events; all of these are descendants of the abstract superclass TEventHandler. These instances are an application's views, windows, document, and the application itself. Each of these instances is responsible for handling only those events directly associated with it. A view handles manipulation of the objects it displays. A window is responsible for handling mouse clicks in the close box, zoom box, and grow box. The document handles reading and writing data to disk files. The application handles user events that could occur when no window is open, such as Quit, About, and Open. In general, these instances each have an opportunity to handle a given event, in the above order. If the instance chooses not to handle the event, it does nothing and MacApp passes the event on to the next event handler. For views, the next event handler is its superview. If the window does not handle the event, the document and application, in turn, have an opportunity to do so. So when the user generates a Save command, a view would typically do nothing in response. Similarly, the window would do nothing. When MacApp passes the Save command on to the document, the document would write its data to the disk file. Since the command has now been handled, the application object does not receive the command.

The programmer overrides just a couple of methods to implement the actions required to handle a user event. To handle a menu command, regardless of whether it comes from highlighting a menu command or from the keyboard equivalent, DoMenuCommand is overridden. Similarly, DoMouseCommand is overridden for handling mouse activity outside the menus and DoKeyCommand is overridden for keystrokes that do not involve the command key. Other methods within MacApp call these methods at the appropriate time. These methods can either perform the command themselves or, frequently, create a *command object* to perform the command.

Command objects are MacApp's way of making undo- and redoable user operations easier for the programmer. There are two types of command object, simple commands and complex commands. A simple command cannot be undone and does not require the mouse to be tracked. For example, the Save As... menu command, once done, cannot be undone, because the file has already been written on the disk.[2] So Save As... is a simple command. Typically, complex commands are performed by a command object and simple commands are performed procedurally in DoMenuCommand, DoMouseCommand, or DoKey-Command. The selection capabilities in DoubleVision require tracking the mouse and thus require a complex command. In DoubleVision, the simple commands include Natural Contrast, Higher Contrast, Color Scale, and Gray Scale, and the complex commands are those for selection and adjusting the color palette.

The level of contrast can be set separately for each main window. So the Natural Contrast and Higher Contrast commands are handled by the DoMenuCommand of the active window's main view. All that is required to implement these commands is to check whether the command requires a change to the view's current categorization. If so, the view's offscreen image is instructed to change its categorization, which recomputes the pixel map's color tables. Then the color scale and the main view are told to redraw themselves. The color scale uses the new categorization to redraw itself, and the main view instructs its associated offscreen image object to redraw the visible portion of the view, using the revised color tables.

Although the selection of color or gray scale primarily affects the view instances, the Color Scale and Gray Scale commands are handled by the DoMenuCommand of the document. The change, however, is applied to all windows that the application has open. An alternative design would permit each window to have its own pair of color and gray palettes. In this case, the Color Scale and Gray Scale commands would only apply to the front window. In DoubleVision, a single pair of color and gray palettes are used by all documents open by the application. This design choice results in more efficient usage of the color table. In performing the command, a check to determine whether the palette needs to be changed is performed first. If it does need to be changed, the offscreen image of each window's main view is told to change to the new palette. The offscreen image object recalculates the pixel map's color tables using the new palette, and the new palette is assigned to each main window. Next, the visible portion of the color scale view and the main view of each window are redrawn with the new palette. The MacApp application method ForAllWindowsDo simplifies this operation. Code segments that perform these operations are given in Listing 5.1.[3]

Selection in DoubleVision is more complex than in many applications. Most Macintosh applications deal with discrete objects displayed on the screen, for example, icons on the desktop or objects in a CAD application. In such an application, data are discontinuous and the way selection occurs is similarly discontinuous. However, the data in DoubleVision are continuous over the domain, and so selection in DoubleVision is an exception to the usual approach. Object-oriented programming handles the complexity of three types of selections, each of which know how to adjust themselves. This is done by using a *selection object* that

---

[2]Save As... is usually performed by MacApp, not by the application programmer.

[3]In this listing, as well as Listing 5.2, the source code was simplified to enhance clarity. Features such as memory management, segmentation, error testing and handling, and compiler directives were removed from the shipping version of DoubleVision.

Listing 5.1 _____
Methods That Perform the Color Scale and Gray Scale Menu Commends.

```
{This method is called by MacApp when the document is given an opportunity to handle
a menu command. If the argument is the command number corresponding to either
Color Scale or Gray Scale, the action is performed here. Otherwise, the INHERITED
method is called to let MacApp pass the command along to the next event handler.}
FUNCTION    TDVDocument.DoMenuCommand(aCmdNumber: CmdNumber):
  ...TCommand; OVERRIDE;
BEGIN
  DoMenuCommand := gNoChanges;

  CASE aCmdNumber OF
    cColorPalette, cGrayPalette:
      SELF.ChangePalette(aCmdNumber = cColorPalette);
    OTHERWISE
      DoMenuCommand :=
        INHERITED DoMenuCommand(aCmdNumber);
    END; {Case}
END;{TDVDocument.DoMenuCommand}

PROCEDURE TDVDocument.ChangePalette(wantColor:BOOLEAN);

  PROCEDURE ChangeToNewPalette(aWindow: TWindow);

  VAR
    itsMainView:  TMainView;

  BEGIN
    {Tell Palette Manager to assign the new main palette to this window}
    SetPalette(aWindow.fWMgrWindow, gMainPalette, TRUE);
    ActivatePalette(aWindow.fWMgrWindow);

    {Find the main view & update palette in its offscreen object}
    itsMainView := TMainView(aWindow.FindSubView('MAIN'));
    IF itsMainView <> NIL THEN
      BEGIN
      itsMainView.fOffScreen.SetPalette(gMainPalette);
      aWindow.ForceRedraw;
      END;
  END;

BEGIN   {TDVDocument.ChangePalette}
  {First, check whether this command will change the current color state. If not, do
    ...nothing and return.}
  IF wantColor <> gUsingColor THEN
    BEGIN
    {Determine which palette to change to.}
    IF wantColor THEN
      gMainPalette := gColorPalette
    ELSE
      gMainPalette := gGrayPalette;
```

```
    {Change the palette for all application windows. If the window has an offscreen
    ...object, update its palette & color tables.}
    gApplication.ForAllWindowsDo(ChangeToNewPalette);

    {If the previous command object is a color tuner command, commit it. Otherwise,
    ...executing Undo or Redo will cause a 'real' color to appear in the gray palette or
    ...a shade of gray in the color palette.}
    IF Member(gLastCommand, TColorTuner) THEN
        gApplication.CommitLastCommand;

    gUsingColor := wantColor;
    END;
END;   {TDVDocument.ChangePalette}
```

corresponds to the selected portion of the data, and a *selection command object* that tracks the mouse and (usually) creates a selection object. Specifically, the selection object will be an instance of TByRowSelection, TByColumnSelection, or TByAreaSelection. These three classes are all subclasses of their abstract superclass TSelection, which handles everything common to all three types of selection objects.

When the user clicks in the main view in either main window, MacApp calls that view's DoMouseCommand method. In general, DoMouseCommand is responsible for handling any sort of mouse activity within the view; in DoubleVision different behavior is required depending on whether the shift key is pressed and whether there is any existing selection. If the shift key is pressed, the existing selection, if any, will be adjusted. If the shift key was not pressed, a new selection is desired and any existing selection is deleted. If there is no existing selection, pressing the shift key is ignored. A *discriminator command object* is created. This command object takes control of tracking the mouse until the user moves the mouse far enough vertically, horizontally, or diagonally, depending on whether the user wants a row selection, a column selection, or an area selection, respectively. At this point, the appropriate *row selection command object, column selection command object*, or *area selection command object* is created. This object provides feedback appropriate for the type of selection and takes care of everything else associated with making a selection. This selection command object checks the points at which the mouse button is pressed and released to ensure that at least one row, column, or pixel is included in the selection. If a selection is to be created, then the selection command creates the appropriate *selection object* and control returns to MacApp.

This selection object can be created by either a selection command object or by the menu commands SelectAllRows and SelectAllColumns. The selection object knows how to adjust itself if the user presses the shift key; it does this by creating a command object to track the mouse while the adjustment is taking place. Specifically, if the shift key is pressed and there is an existing selection, the selection's CreateSelectionCommand method is called by DoMouseCommand. The CreateSelectionCommand method creates a new selection command of the same type that created the selection originally. The selection then passes control to this command object. When the mouse button is released, the selection command object checks whether there is already a selection object. If there is, the selection object's Adjust method is called. Otherwise, the selection command creates a new selection object and initializes it with values that the selection command determined by tracking the mouse.

The color adjustment command is the only undoable command in DoubleVision. This command object is created if the user clicks the mouse button when the cursor is over the color scale at the top of either main window. This mouse action is "caught" by the color scale view's DoMouseCommand, which creates and initializes the *color tuner command object*. As with any command object, MacApp calls the color tuner command object's TrackFeedback and TrackConstrain methods repeatedly while the mouse button is held down. When the mouse button is released, the command object's DoIt method is called. The DoIt method is usually where the real action of a command takes place; in DoubleVision the palette entry is changed, or *animated*, within TrackFeedback each time the mouse moves. Animating a palette entry changes every pixel drawn with that color, without redrawing any other pixel on the screen. Thus the color change happens very smoothly, without any screen flashing that may distract the user. The command object's TrackConstrain method keeps the mouse location within the rectangle fDragLimits. While the cursor on the screen is not moved, this adjustment of the mouse coordinates makes computing the new color easier. When the mouse button is released, the DoIt method is called. This method checks for the presence of any non-animating graphics device and updates any portion of any window that is displayed on such a device. If the user selects the Undo menu command, then the object's UndoIt method is called. UndoIt saves the new color entry and restores the original one. If the user selects Redo, then the RedoIt method is called to swap the original and the new palette entry again.

MacApp will preserve this command object instance until the command object's Commit method is called. At that time, the command can no longer be undone or redone, and MacApp will free the command object. This happens when another undoable command object is created, when a modal dialog appears, or when the previous command is explicitly committed. In DoubleVision, creation of a new color tuner command will commit any previous one. Unfortunately, using either the Add n... or Smooth n... commands will also commit a color tuner command since these commands each use a modal dialog box to determine the value for *n*. Finally, any existing color tuner command is explicitly committed when the Gray Scale command is executed. This prevents replacing a shade of gray in the gray palette with the most recently animated color in the color palette. Thus a change to the color palette will remain undoable through many user actions, including changing to the resolution, saving data to a file, reverting to the original data, and changing contrast level. The source code for TColorScaleView.DoMouseCommand and the TColorTunerCommand methods is given in Listing 5.2.

Listing 5.2 _____
Methods That Perform Color Palette Animation.

{This method is called by MacApp when a mouse press is detected over an instance of TColorScaleView. First, check whether the mouse is within the color bar, and we're using the color scale and natural contrast. As a design choice, we don't animate the shades of gray or when the enhanced contrast mapping is in use. If all this is true, create, initialize & return a color tuner command object. Otherwise, do nothing — indicated by returning gNoChanges to the MacApp routine that called this routine.}

```
FUNCTION TColorScaleView.DoMouseCommand(
     VAR theMouse: Point;
     VAR info: EventInfo;
     VAR hysteresis: Point):TCommand; OVERRIDE;

VAR
  colorTuner: TColorTuner;

BEGIN
  IF PtInRect(theMouse, SELF.fColorBarBounds) & gUsingColor &
     (SELF.fMainView.fCatCurrent=SELF.fMainView.fCatLinear)
  THEN
     BEGIN
     New(colorTuner);
     FailNIL(colorTuner);
     colorTuner.IColorTuner(SELF, theMouse);
     DoMouseCommand := colorTuner;
     END
  ELSE
     DoMouseCommand := gNoChanges;
END;   {TColorScaleView.DoMouseCommand}

{Initialize the color tuner command object.}


PROCEDURE TColorTuner.IColorTuner(aColorScaleView: TColorScaleView;
  ...anchorPoint: Point);

VAR
     thisRGB, preRGB, postRGB:       RGBColor;
     thisHSV, preHSV, postHSV:       HSVColor;
     thisHue, minHue, maxHue:        Fixed;
     preHueDH, postHueDH:            INTEGER;
     limitRect:                      Rect;

BEGIN
  {Call the superclass's initialization method}
  SELF.ICommand(cTuneColor, aColorScaleView.fDVDocument, aColorScaleView,
     ...NIL);

  {Determine the window this color scale is in. We'll need this for Palette Manager
     ...routines.}
  SELF.fWmgrWindow := TWindow(aColorScaleView.GetWindow).fWmgrWindow;

  {Determine which block the mouse went down in and set SELF.fItem to be the palette
     ...index of that block's color.}
  SELF.fItem := ((anchorPoint.h - kColorBarHOffset) DIV aColorScaleView.fItemWidth)
     ...+ kTolerants;

  {Set the fields of the superclass that we want to be initialized differently than the way
     ...ICommand set them.}
  SELF.fConstrainsMouse := TRUE;
```

(continues)

```
SELF.fViewConstrain := FALSE;
SELF.fCausesChange := FALSE; {This command does NOT change the data!}

{Determine RGB color of the item mouse went down in, convert to HSV and set
   ...SELF.fOrigHSV & SELF.fNewHSV to be that color.}
GetEntryColor(gMainPalette, SELF.fItem, thisRGB);
RGB2HSV(thisRGB, thisHSV);
thisHue := SmallFract2Fix(thisHSV.hue);
SELF.fOrigHSV := thisHSV;
SELF.fNewHSV := thisHSV;

{Use colors in color blocks adjacent to this one to set bounds on how much the color
   ...in this block can change. This limit is actually performed by constraining the
   ...mouse.}
GetEntryColor(gMainPalette,
   (SELF.fItem-kTolerants-1+kColors) MOD kColors + kTolerants,
   preRGB);
   RGB2HSV(preRGB, preHSV);
maxHue := SmallFract2Fix(preHSV.hue);
preHueDH := BSR(LoWrd(maxHue-thisHue), 5);

GetEntryColor(gMainPalette,
   (SELF.fItem-kTolerants+1) MOD
      kColors + kTolerants, postRGB);
RGB2HSV(postRGB, postHSV);
minHue := SmallFract2Fix(postHSV.hue);
postHueDH := BSR(LoWrd(thisHue-minHue), 5);

{Set the drag limits}
WITH anchorPoint DO
   SetRect(limitRect, h - preHueDH, v, h + postHueDH, v);
SELF.fDragLimits := limitRect;
END;   {TColorTuner.IColorTuner}
```

{This method is called when the mouse button is released.}

```
PROCEDURE TColorTuner.DoIt; OVERRIDE;
BEGIN
   {Set both palette entries corresponding to this item being tuned}
   SELF.SetEntryPair;

   {Compute new color tables in offscreen object & update any direct devices}
   SELF.UpdateGraphics;
END;
```

{This method is called when Redo is selected from the Edit menu.}
```
PROCEDURE TColorTuner.RedoIt; OVERRIDE;
BEGIN
   {Restore new color & update graphics environment}
   SELF.SetHSV(SELF.fNewHSV);
```

```
{Set palette entries corresponding to this item being tuned}
SELF.SetEntryPair;

{Compute new color tables in offscreen object & update any direct devices}
SELF.UpdateGraphics;
END;  {TColorTuner.RedoIt}


PROCEDURE TColorTuner.SetEntryPair;

VAR
   thisRGB:RGBColor;
   tempRGB:RGBColor;

BEGIN
   {Get 'animated color' (high order byte) for this entry via GetEntryColor}
   GetEntryColor(gMainPalette, SELF.fItem, thisRGB);

   {Put this color into 'set color' (low order byte) via SetEntryColor}
   SetEntryColor(gMainPalette, SELF.fItem, thisRGB);

   {Do the same for the dimmed version of this item}
   GetEntryColor(gMainPalette, SELF.fItem + kDeltaDim, thisRGB);
   SetEntryColor(gMainPalette, SELF.fItem + kDeltaDim, thisRGB);
END; {TColorTuner.SetEntry}
```

```
{This method animates the changed color and its dimmed version in the palette.}
PROCEDURE TColorTuner.SetHSV(hsv: HSVColor);

VAR
   rgb: RGBColor;

BEGIN
   {Convert new color from HSV to RGB}
   HSV2RGB(hsv, rgb);

   {Animate 'normal' palette entry, using Palette Manager.}
   AnimateEntry(SELF.fWmgrWindow, SELF.fItem, rgb);

   {Compute 'dimmed' version of the new color}
   WITH rgb DO
     BEGIN
     red := BSR(red, 1);
     green := BSR(green, 1);
     blue := BSR(blue, 1);
     END;

   {Animate 'dimmed' palette entry, using Palette Manager.}
   AnimateEntry(SELF.fWmgrWindow, SELF.fItem + kDeltaDim, rgb);
END;  {TColorTuner.SetHSV}
```

```
{Adjust mouse coordinates to force it within the limits set in IColorTuner.}


PROCEDURE TColorTuner.TrackConstrain(anchorPoint, previousPoint: VPoint; VAR
   ...nextPoint: VPoint); OVERRIDE;
```
(continues)

```
      VAR
         vhs: VHSelect;
   BEGIN
      FOR vhs := v TO h DO
         nextPoint.vh[vhs] := Max(SELF.fDragLimits.topLeft.vh[vhs],
            Min(nextPoint.vh[vhs], SELF.fDragLimits.botRight.vh[vhs]));
   END;{TColorTuner.TrackConstrain}
```

{Provide feedback as the mouse drags}

```
   PROCEDURE TColorTuner.TrackFeedback(anchorPoint,
         nextPoint: VPoint; turnItOn, mouseDidMove: BOOLEAN); OVERRIDE;

   BEGIN
      IF mouseDidMove & turnItOn THEN
         BEGIN
         SELF.fNewHSV.hue := LOWrd(SELF.fOrigHSV.hue -
         BSL(nextPoint.h - anchorPoint.h, 5));
         SetHSV(SELF.fNewHSV);
         END;
   END;{TColorTuner.TrackFeedback}
```

{This method is called when Undo is selected from the Edit menu.}

```
   PROCEDURE TColorTuner.UndoIt; OVERRIDE;

   BEGIN
      {Restore original color.}
      SELF.SetHSV(SELF.fOrigHSV);

      {Set palette entries corresponding to this item being tuned}
      SELF.SetEntryPair;

      {Compute new color tables in offscreen object & update any direct devices}
      SELF.UpdateGraphics;
   END;{TColorTuner.UndoIt}
```

{This method computes new color tables & handles direct (non-animating) graphics
devices. A Mac II can have multiple screens, and they can be different types!}

```
   PROCEDURE TColorTuner.UpdateGraphics;

   VAR
      theOffScreen:        TOffScreen;
      thisDevice:          GDHandle;

      PROCEDURE CheckInterSection(aWindow: TWindow);

      VAR
         frame:          VRect;
         windowRect:     Rect;
         deviceRect:     Rect;
         interRect:      Rect;
         interVRect:     VRect;
```

```
BEGIN
    IF aWindow.Focus THEN
        BEGIN
        {Get bounds of this window in its screen coordinates}
        aWindow.GetQDExtent(windowRect);
        LocalToGlobal(windowRect.topLeft);
        LocalToGlobal(windowRect.botRight);

        {Get bounds of this screen in global screen coordinates}
        deviceRect := thisDevice^^.gdRect;

        {If intersection of windowRect & deviceRect is non-empty, convert intersection
            ...to window's coordinate system & invalidate. Invalidating the intersection
            ...marks it for re-drawing next time re-drawing occurs.}
        IF SectRect(windowRect, deviceRect, interRect) THEN
            BEGIN
            GlobalToLocal(interRect.topLeft);
            GlobalToLocal(interRect.botRight);
            aWindow.InvalidRect(interRect);
            END;
        END;
    END;
PROCEDURE UpdateOffScreen(aWindow: TWindow);
{Find window's main view & update colors in its offscreen object}

    VAR
        itsMainView:TMainView;

    BEGIN
        {If the window is a main window, tell its associated offscreen image object to begin
        using the changed palette.}
        itsMainView := TMainView(aWindow.FindSubView('MAIN'));
        IF itsMainView <> NIL THEN
        itsMainView.fOffScreen.SetPalette(gMainPalette);
        END; {UpdateOffScreen}

BEGIN
    {Re-compute color tables & assign to offscreen objects.}
    gApplication.ForAllWindowsDo(UpdateOffScreen);

    {Now find any direct (non-animating) devices & update them.}
    thisDevice := GetDeviceList;
    WHILE thisDevice <> NIL DO
        BEGIN
        {If this is a direct device, see if it intersects any DoubleVision window}
        IF thisDevice^^.gdType <> 0 THEN
        gApplication.ForAllWindowsDo(CheckIntersection);
        {move to next device}
        thisDevice := GetNextDevice(thisDevice);
        END;
END; {TColorTuner.UpdateGraphics}
```

5.4 ANALYSIS OF OBJECT-ORIENTED PROGRAMMING IN DOUBLEVISION

DoubleVision is a very young application, and so it is difficult to evaluate it fully. The evaluation criteria are based on its original goals: to provide scientists with a general purpose foundation program that they can extend to more specific visualization programs, and to provide developers with a sample program from which they may select pieces of code for reuse. At this time, research geophysicists are using DoubleVision as a foundation for other data analysis software, but it is still too early to fully evaluate its overall success in this area.

Two specific goals through which DoubleVision was designed to assist scientists are in the addition of filters and optional plots of data. So far, we have observed mixed success in meeting these goals. Adding a new filter to DoubleVision requires only a small amount of effort by the programmer, via the following steps:

1. Add the new menu item to the menu template. This requires editing the file containing resource templates and then adding two lines to this file.
2. Insert a new program constant for the new command.
3. Include this new command in the appropriate object's DoMenuCommand method.
4. Write the subroutine or method that will actually perform the filter operation. This is facilitated by the numerous methods already present that provide for convenient access to the data by row, by columns, by rectangles, as well as for presenting dialog boxes to the user.
5. Recompile the DoubleVision application.

In this process, the programmer is not concerned with drawing the new menu item when the user pulls down the menu, highlighting the menu items within the window, or directly accessing the data. Instead, the bulk of the programmer's work is preparing the filter routine. Other tasks, such as modifying the resource template file, are done easily since the existing definitions provide a sample of the desired result.

As mentioned earlier, the Smooth n... filter was not included in the original plans for DoubleVision but was written as a way of determining exactly how much effort would be required to add a new filter. Since adding this filter to DoubleVision required only a few hours, we believe we have succeeded in making DoubleVision flexible enough for this sort of extension.

However, extending DoubleVision to include new optional views or plots may not be as easy, although the scientist will still have the numerous data access methods available. This part of the application was developed last, and time constraints for completing the project resulted in a less general design than originally desired. Another design could have included an abstract superclass for the THistogramControl class. This class would have included much of the functionality of THistogramControl, but it could then have been subclassed for classes that handle scrolling of histograms and other plots. This would be a fairly simple modification of DoubleVision's class design since the existing THistogramControl class is already well isolated from the THistogramView class. However, an abstract superclass for the THistogramView class would not be necessary since THistogramView is a subclass of

MacApp's TView class. TView includes all the functionality associated with drawing within a window, and so developing another plot would require only subclass(es) of TView, as was done with THistogramView.

The use of an abstract superclass resulted in greater code reuse in several classes within DoubleVision. For example, the TSelectionCommand class is the abstract superclass of TRowSelectionCommand, TColSelectionCommand, and TAreaSelectionCommand, and it handles much of the functionality required to form a selection. Specifically, TSelectionCommand methods perform initialization and freeing behavior for instances of any of the three subclasses, as well as provide feedback while the mouse is being tracked. Another method performs the transformation between screen coordinates and the corresponding rows and columns of the data. TRowSelectionCommand only overrides three methods, all of which perform behavior specific to forming a row selection. One of these methods, TRowSelectionCommand.MakeRect, handles forming the rectangle to be highlighted while the mouse is dragged, using the vertical coordinates of the mouse-down point and the current mouse location to determine the top and bottom of the rectangle. The left and right sides are determined using the full width of the data. This is in contrast to TColSelectionCommand.MakeRect, which uses the full height of the data and sets the left and right sides of the rectangle from the horizontal coordinates of the mouse points. This is a powerful technique of object-oriented programming, resulting in increased code reuse and increased factorization of functionality, both of which should make subsequent code modification easier.

Developing DoubleVision did provide some insight into using MacApp for medium-sized applications. MacApp provides an efficient path to developing a highly structured Macintosh application, especially for a commercial developer desiring robust applications. MacApp *correctly* handles or simplifies many programming areas that are prone to errors and are especially trying to Macintosh programmers—such as scrolling window contents, memory management, and making commands undoable and redoable. Much of the functionality of DoubleVision is, in fact, included in MacApp.

Since MacApp is a relatively mature library, it is stable and fairly close to complete. DoubleVision would have been easier to develop if MacApp included a unit that handles offscreen graphics objects. The TOffScreen object in DoubleVision could form the basis for such a unit, but currently it does not include much of the functionality desired for such a unit. For example, TOffScreen includes the capability to change the color table mapping, but adding clipping, stretching, and shrinking pixels, reallocating the pixmap, and changing the depth of the pixels would be necessary to make it a general-purpose unit for MacApp.

5.5 SUMMARY AND LESSONS LEARNED FROM DOUBLEVISION

The first conclusion reached from developing this application is that an application's design is largely influenced by the class library being used. Duplicating the functionality of DoubleVision with a different class library would most probably result in a dramatically different design. In fact, this happened with DoubleVision. DoubleVision's predecessor,

FalseImage, was written using MacApp 1.1, while DoubleVision used MacApp 2.0. This project was originally conceived as merely the port of the major classes, where the port would be accompanied by a few changes in functionality. These changes were to change the program from one used only by geophysicists to a more general visualization program. However, MacApp underwent major architectural changes between the 1.1 and 2.0 releases, most in the TView class and descendant classes of TView such as TScroller. For example, scroll bars and scrolling were implemented very differently between the two releases. The result of these changes was that most of the program was redesigned and reimplemented, and only about 20 percent of the existing code was ported without significant modification.

Another lesson learned is that well-factored code is easier to produce with object-oriented programming. While this fact is widely recognized within the the object-oriented programming community, it was demonstrated by the development of DoubleVision. For example, the TOffScreen object was completely reimplemented to take advantage of 32-Bit Color QuickDraw, a new part of Macintosh system software that became available halfway through this project. Since this functionality was encapsulated into an object, the changes to accommodate 32-Bit Color QuickDraw could be made without any changes to the rest of the application.

The next conclusion showed up in several aspects of the program. The further something is from the "usual" way of doing things, the more difficult it is. MacApp sample programs and recipes demonstrate commonly used techniques. Scrolling different parts of a window differently and using a scroll bar to control different scrollers were included in an existing sample program. However, since few programs require multiple types of selection, developing this feature required more effort. Reinterpreting scrolling to mean determining which line of data should be sent to another object for display is even further from typical; this feature required subclassing TScrollBar, a MacApp class that is rarely subclassed by an application programmer.

Finally, the learning curve for a large class library is substantial. It does appear that this is time well spent and that this investment is recovered in the next application developed. There seem to be two types of learning associated with a large class library. The first type of learning deals with the question, What class, or what method in this class, does what I need to do? Novices have sometimes duplicated functionality because they simply had not noticed that it was already present within the class library. The time and effort required for this learning process is decreased by the availability of a source code for the class library, as well as an on-line browser for the source code. The second type of learning deals with the question, How did I get here? which arises during debugging and testing. Since MacApp controls much of the flow of execution, this concern is dramatically more significant than in traditional, procedural programming. MacApp's object-level debugger provides significant help in dealing with this part of learning a large class library.

References

[1] Apple Computer. *Human Interface Guidelines: The Apple Desktop Interface*, Addison-Wesley, Reading, MA, 1987.

[2] Apple Computer. *Programmer's Introduction to the Macintosh Family*, Addison-Wesley, Reading, MA, 1988.

Acknowledgments: Several of my colleagues at Apple provided large amounts of assistance in this project. Kurt Schmucker read the manuscript and suggested several changes. Geoff Pascoe and Joost Kemink implemented several features in DoubleVision in remarkably little time, and Tom Charuhas included the Smooth n... command to test the ease of adding a new filter. Andrew Donoho helped solve a few especially persistent bugs, and along with Chuck McMath, served as a beta-tester.

Special acknowledgment for the development of the predecessor of DoubleVision goes to Colleen Barton and Larry Tesler. Their program is in extensive use by research geophysicists and includes many features not in DoubleVision. Without this program, as well as their support and encouragement, this project would not have been possible.

DoubleVision is available from MacApp Developer's Association, P. O. Box 23, Everett, WA 98206, (206) 252-6946.

Object-Oriented Design of a Branch Path Analyzer for C-Language Software Systems

Lewis J. Pinson and Richard S. Wiener
University of Colorado at Colorado Springs

6.1 PROBLEM STATEMENT AND SPECIFICATIONS

This chapter describes the design and implementation, using the object-oriented paradigm, of a branch path analysis software system for the C language. A specific approach to completion of an object-oriented design is presented and used in developing the branch path analyzer. The system was designed and prototyped using Smalltalk-80 on the Sun 3/50 workstation. All file-naming conventions presented in this chapter are consistent with those on the Sun 3/50. This first section presents a statement of the problem, the requirements, and the specification for a C-language branch path analyzer (CBPA).

6.1.1 Statement of the Problem

Software written in modern languages contains branch paths. A branch path is a block of code whose execution may be conditional on the value of one or more parameters. The value of a parameter may change for different test runs of the software. It may depend on inputs to the program or may be the result of other program steps. A typical test run will exercise only part of the branches in a software system.

One goal of software testing is to verify through multiple test runs that all branches of the software system have been successfully exercised without producing run-time errors. In support of this goal of software testing, a branch path analyzer has the following twofold objective:

— Automatically identify the branch paths in a software system
— Maintain updated statistics during testing on which paths have and have not been exercised

The statistic of primary concern is a binary yes or no that a path has been exercised. Each time the software is run, the branch path statistics must be updated in a cumulative and non-destructive manner.

During initial development and subsequent maintenance of a software system, new branch paths may be added and old branch paths may be removed in a particular component of the software system. A branch path analyzer must compensate for these changes and retain previously acquired testing statistics for all current branch paths in the software component.

Selective enabling/disabling of branch path analysis for each component of a software system allows the user to optimize testing efficiency. A software component is identifiable as a separate source file. Its compiled object file must be linked with the software system prior to execution.

6.1.2 Functional Requirements

Operational Overview. CBPA is a testing tool that monitors the logical branches of one or more C files and determines the branches that have and have not been executed. Separate data files are maintained for each C file (software component) that is monitored. These data files contain branch coverage statistics, gathered cumulatively as testing progresses.

Results of the branch path analysis may be examined with the view option at any time. The view option generates a file (that may be examined using any text editor) consisting of the original C source file with the comment,

| @@@@@@@@@@ BRANCH NOT EXECUTED @@@@@@@@@@

inserted at the beginning of logical branches that have not been executed. This provides easy identification of all unexercised branches of the software component. The developer of a C software component may wish to test the unexercised branches with additional test code or test data.

The first step in the branch path analysis is to have the CBPA software *instrument* a C source file. The first objective of instrumentation is to identify and mark all branch paths. The second objective is to insert code for monitoring the exercise of any branch path and for updating a data file. The final objective of the instrument option is to create and initialize the data file. Marking and instrumenting of branch paths consists of adding a procedure call, keyed to the branch number, to the C source file at the beginning of each branch. As the instrumented software system is run, marked branches are recorded in the data file as they are executed.

For branch path analysis, an instrumented file must be recompiled and the system relinked to include the object code for the instrumented file. Outside of a small run-time penalty, the user should not be aware that the software system is running under branch path analysis.

CBPA allows any subset of files in a C software system to be instrumented and monitored independently of other files in the system. If a reusable software component is being tested, there is no need to include the main driver program or any other files of the software system in the branch path analysis. This option minimizes the penalty of slower execution time.

After a file is instrumented by CBPA, it may be modified (that is, branches added or deleted) without losing any of the test data for the branches that are not modified. This feature allows a software developer to start performing branch path analysis on C files early in the development and testing process.

Specifications. The following specifications define the functional operation of the C-language branch path analyzer.

- Branch path analysis is to be provided for software systems developed using the C language.
- Branch path analysis may be performed on any part(s) or all of a software system under direct user control for a given test run. The smallest part of a software system that may be subjected to branch path analysis is the source code contained in a single file.
- The branch path analyzer instrument option identifies all the branch paths in a specified software component (a single source file), adds code for use by the branch path analysis, and creates a corresponding data file. For each branch path in the source file, the data file contains a unique identification number and an associated boolean variable initialized to false to indicate that a branch path has not been executed.
- The user specifies which source files in a complete software system are to be instrumented for branch path analysis. Additional source files may be instrumented at any time for inclusion in the branch path analysis. Source files may be deactivated (removed) from the branch path analysis at any time by using the strip option of CBPA.
- As a branch path in an instrumented file is executed, its boolean parameter in the data file is set to true.
- Modifications to the source file of the software system may result in the addition of new branch paths or the deletion of existing branch paths. The modified source file must be reinstrumented, recompiled, and relinked to the software system. A new data file is generated that reflects the addition of new branch paths. *Most significantly, the results of prior testing on branch paths that were not changed by the modification are maintained.*
- The view option of the branch path analyzer produces a source file with unexercised branch paths identified with the comment

@@@@@@@@@@ BRANCH NOT EXECUTED @@@@@@@@@@

inserted at the beginning of the branch path. The generated view file may be examined using any text editor.

Files used by CBPA. In the following paragraphs, we describe the files used by the CBPA.

Input Source Files. Only syntactically correct C source files that end in the extension .c can be instrumented. *An attempt to use the branch path analyzer on C source files that have syntax errors will produce unpredictable results.*

CBPA Driver File. The user must create an ASCII text file that contains the names of the files to be instrumented as well as a directory for saving the data file. For purposes of discussion, this file is given the name driver. A user may choose any valid file name for this file. The format for the driver file is given as follows.

```
data_directory_string
file_name1 file_name2 file_name3 ...
```

Spaces, tabs, or newline characters may be used as separators between file names. These parameters have the following meaning:

— data_directory_string—the directory path wherein data files are to be kept. The directory must exist.
— file_name1 file_name2 file_name3—a list of C source files that are to be marked for branch path analysis. These filenames *must not include the .c extension*. The files must exist.

CBPA supports *error handling*. CBPA will report, on the display screen, errors in the user's driver file. If the subdirectory specified for the data files does not exist, this error will be reported. If any of the given source files do not exist, such an error will be reported.

An example of the driver file is

```
/usr/user1/my_data_dir/
file1 file2 file3
```

For this example, the data files will be written to the subdirectory /usr/user1/my_data_dir/. The files file1.c, file2.c, and file3.c will be instrumented.

Files Produced by the Instrument Option of CBPA. Three files are produced for each file that is instrumented. Instrumentation of file file_name.c produces the following three files:

— file_name.c—the instrumented source file to be compiled and used in CBPA testing (the original file_name.c is overwritten),
— file_name.bps—branch-path source that is the original file_name.c file with comments added to identify branch paths,
— file_name.bpd—branch-path data file, created and initialized in the directory specified in the driver file.

The instrumented file_name.c file contains inserted code for monitoring and updating branch path information during execution of the software system. This is the file to be compiled and linked with a software system.

The file_name.bps file is a copy of the original source file. However, it contains comments inserted at the top of every branch indicating logical branch numbers. These comments are needed internally by CBPA for use in reinstrumenting the file if any changes are made to the file during software maintenance. Once testing is completed, these comments can be removed by using the strip option of CBPA, thus producing a clean file with no traces of instrumentation.

The file_name.bpd file is written to the subdirectory specified in the user's driver file. Every time a new branch in the monitored source file gets executed for the first time, its data file gets updated.

Files Produced by the View Option of CBPA. When a user invokes the view option of CBPA, the file file_name.bpv is generated. This file consists of the original source file with the comments

| @@@@@@@@@@ BRANCH NOT EXECUTED @@@@@@@@@@

inserted at the beginning of all the logical branches that have not yet been executed. This file_name.bpv file is generated in the current subdirectory. Its contents may be examined by any text editor to identify unexercised branches of the software component.

Execution of CBPA. Four options or steps are identified for use of the CBPA software system. Descriptions and commands for each step are described next.

1. *Instrument* option. The purpose of this step is to instrument C source file(s) for inclusion in the branch path analysis. An example of the instrument command option is

| cbpa driver

For this example, assume the driver file generated in the previous section is used. Data files file1.bpd, file2.bpd, and file3.bpd will be written to the subdirectory /usr/user1/my_data_dir/. The files file1.c, file2.c, and file3.c will be instrumented. Files file1.bps, file2.bps, and file3.bps will be written to the current directory.

The next step is to recompile and relink file1.c, file2.c, and file3.c into the software system. Subsequent execution of the software system will produce branch path updates for the file1, file2, and file3 software components.

2. *Monitor* option. This option is in effect during testing of a software system that includes instrumented software components. The branch path analyzer is transparent to the user during this step except for a possible penalty of increased execution time. The monitor option is effected by executing the software system with recompiled and relinked instrumented components.

3. *View* option. This step generates a source file with all nonexercised branch paths identified. The view source file is created from information stored in files file_name.bps and file_name.bpd. An example of the view command option is

| view file1 driver

This above example generates view file file1.bpv on the current directory. The specified file must be included in the driver file; otherwise, an error message is returned. The driver file argument is necessary so the system knows where the data file is stored. This command checks to ensure that file1.bps and /usr/user1/my_data_dir/file1.bpd exist.

4. Sourcefile *strip* option. This step is used after all branch path testing has been completed for a particular software component. It removes all branch path identifier comments from the file_name.bps file and can be used to produce a clean file_name.c source file. An example of the *strip* command option is

| strip file1.bps

This command strips out all the branch path identifier comments from file file1.bps. *The clean file is returned as* file1.bps. The .bps extension is required in this command. The instrumented file1.c is not affected. It is the user's responsibility to perform any additional file maintenance on choice of file names and to recompile the stripped file, relink it, and continue testing.

6.1.3 Constraints on the Usage of CBPA

Maintenance of an Instrumented Software Component. If maintenance is to be performed on any instrumented component of a software system, *all modifications to the source code should be made to the file* file_name.bps. *All embedded comments that indicate branch path numbers should be left intact unless an entire branch containing those comments is being removed.*

After adding or removing code from the file_name.bps file, rename it to file_name.c. Define a new driver file that contains only the modified component file names and invoke CBPA with the modified driver file. As an example of maintenance with CBPA, assume software component file1 is to be modified.

1. Modify file1.bps using a text editor.
2. Rename file1.bps to file1.c (replaces current file1.c).
3. Recompile file1.c to verify no compile errors.
4. Create new_driver with the following contents:

| /usr/user1/my_data_dir/
| file1

5. Reinstrument file1 using the command

| cbpa new_driver

6. Recompile the newly instrumented file1.c and relink the software system. Subsequent execution of the software system will include the maintenance changes.

Deactivation of an Instrumented Software Component. An instrumented software component that has been compiled and linked into a software system will be monitored by the branch path analyzer each time the software system is run until that software component is deactivated by the user. Deactivation of an instrumented software component consists of (1) creation of a clean file file_name.bps using the strip option of the branch path analyzer, (2) renaming file_name.bps to file_name.c, and (3) recompiling and relinking the clean source file file_name.c into the software system. Deactivation may be desirable for any software component that has been fully tested.

Known Restrictions. CBPA has two known restrictions. They are

1. If macros containing logical branch paths are used in a program, these paths will not be instrumented.
2. If, because of a macro, a single line statement following a FOR, WHILE, or IF structure does not contain a terminating semicolon (that is, this semicolon is tucked into the macro), the program will insert a closing right brace in the wrong place and possibly render the instrumented file syntactically incorrect. The solution is to remove the semicolon from the macro and place it into the code.

6.1.4 Tutorial Example on the Usage of CBPA

To illustrate the use of CBPA, a small C software system consisting of the files file1.c and file2.c is given in the following example. The example shows

— The initial source file contents (file1.c and file2.c) for the software system
— The resulting instrumented new files (file1.c and file2.c) for the two components
— The file1.bps and file2.bps files created by instrumenting
— View files for the two instrumented files (file1.bpv and file2.bpv) before running the software system
— View files for the two instrumented files (file1.bpv and file2.bpv) after running the software system and exercising selected branches
— A new source file file1.bps after a maintenance modification (This file is changed to file1.c recompiled and reinstrumented.)
— The newly generated file1.bps after reinstrumenting the modified file1
— A new file1.bpv created after the modification to file1 and before running of the new software system
— A new file1.bpv after running the new software system

Original Software Component file1.c

```
#include <stdio.h>

extern test();

main()
{
```

```
    int i;
    char ch;

    printf( "\nEnter the value of i: " );
    scanf( "%d", &i );
    fflush( stdin );
    if ( i > 0 )
        printf( "\ni > 0" );
    else
        printf( "\ni <= 0" );
    while ( i > 0 )
    {
        printf( "\ni = %d", i );
        printf( "\nEnter the value of i: " );
        scanf( "%d", &i );
        fflush( stdin );
    }
    printf( "\nEnter the value of i: " );
    scanf( "%d", &i );
    switch ( i )
    {
    case 1: printf( "\ni is equal to 1\n" );
        break;
    case 2: printf( "\ni is equal to 2\n" );
        break;
    case 3: printf( "\n is equal to 3\n" );
        break;
    default: printf( "\ni has some value\n" );
    }
    fflush( stdin );
    printf( "\n\nDo you wish to invoke the function test? (y/n)? " );
    scanf( "%c", &ch );
    fflush( stdin );
    if ( ch == 'y' )
        test();
}
```

Original Software Component file2.c

```
void test()
{
    printf( "\nIn function test.\n" );
}
```

After instrumentation, the new files file1.c and file2.c are as follows. Code added to the original files by the instrumentation operation are shown in italics in these two listings.

Instrumented Source File file1.c

```
/* This file has been instrumented for branch path analysis.
The following code has been added by the instrumentation program:
*************************************************************************
*/

extern int bpa_calibrate();

static int bpd_set_size = 1;

static int bpd_file_loaded = 0;

static char bpd_file_name[] = "/usr/usr1/my_data_dir/file1.bpd";

static unsigned *bpd_set;

#define branch_executed( branch_number ) \
( !bpd_file_loaded || \
( !( bpd_set[ branch_number / 32 ] >> branch_number % 32 & 1 ) ) ) ? \
( bpa_calibrate( branch_number ) ) : ( branch_number )
/************************************************************************
*/

#include <stdio.h>

extern test();

main()
{
branch_executed( 0 );
{
    int i;
    char ch;

    printf( "\nEnter the value of i: " );
    scanf( "%d", &i );
    fflush( stdin );
    if ( i > 0 )
{
branch_executed( 1 );
    printf( "\ni > 0" );
}
    else
{
branch_executed( 2 );
    printf( "\ni <= 0" );
}
    while ( i > 0 )
    {
branch_executed( 3 );
{
    printf( "\ni = %d", i );
    printf( "\nEnter the value of i: " );
```

```
        scanf( "%d", &i );
        fflush( stdin );
        }
    }
        printf( "\nEnter the value of i: " );
        scanf( "%d", &i );
        switch ( i )
        {
    {
        case 1:
    branch_executed( 4 );
        printf( "\ni is equal to 1\n" );
            break;
        case 2:
    branch_executed( 5 );
        printf( "\ni is equal to 2\n" );
            break;
            case 3:
    branch_executed( 6 );
        printf( "\n is equal to 3\n" );
            break;
            default:
    branch_executed( 7 );
        printf( "\ni has some value\n" );
        }
    }
        fflush( stdin );
        printf( "\n\nDo you wish to invoke the function test? (y/n)? " );
        scanf( "%c", &ch );
        fflush( stdin );
        if ( ch == 'y' )
    {
    branch_executed( 8 );
            test();
    }
    }
    }
    static int bpa_calibrate( branch_number )
    int branch_number;
    {
    #include <stdio.h>
    #include <malloc.h>
    static FILE *bpd_f;

    if ( !bpd_file_loaded )
    {
    bpd_set = ( unsigned int * ) malloc( bpd_set_size * sizeof( int ) );
    if ( bpd_set == 0 )
    {                                                           (continues)
```

```
printf( "\n\nHeap error in allocating bpd_set in file %s", bpd_file_name );
exit( 1 );
}
bpd_f = fopen( bpd_file_name, "r" );
if ( bpd_f == 0 )
{
printf( "\n\n Error opening %s", bpd_file_name );
exit( 1 );
}
fseek( bpd_f, 4, 0 );
fread( bpd_set, sizeof( int ), bpd_set_size, bpd_f );
fclose( bpd_f );
bpd_file_loaded = 1;
}
if ( !( bpd_set[ branch_number / 32 ] >> branch_number % 32 & 1 ) )
{
bpd_set[ branch_number / 32 ] |= 1 << branch_number % 32;
bpd_f = fopen( bpd_file_name, "r+" );
fseek( bpd_f, 4, 0 );
fwrite( bpd_set, sizeof( int ), bpd_set_size, bpd_f );
fclose( bpd_f );
}
}
```

Instrumented Source File file2.c

```
/* This file has been instrumented for branch path analysis.
The following code has been added by the instrumentation program:
*************************************************************************
*/

extern int bpa_calibrate();

static int bpd_set_size = 1;

static int bpd_file_loaded = 0;

static char bpd_file_name[] = "/usr/usr1/my_data_dir/file1.bpd";

static unsigned *bpd_set;

#define branch_executed( branch_number ) \
( !bpd_file_loaded || \
( !( bpd_set[ branch_number / 32 ] >> branch_number % 32 & 1 ) ) ) ? \
( bpa_calibrate( branch_number ) ) : ( branch_number )
/*************************************************************************
*/
void test()
{
```

```
branch_executed( 0 );
{
    printf( "\n\n function test.\n" );
}
}

static int bpa_calibrate( branch_number )
int branch_number;
{
#include <stdio.h>
#include <malloc.h>
static FILE *bpd_f;

if ( !bpd_file_loaded )
{
bpd_set = ( unsigned int * ) malloc( bpd_set_size * sizeof( int ) );
if ( bpd_set == 0 )
{
printf( "\n\nHeap error in allocating bpd_set in file %s", bpd_file_name );
exit( 1 );
}
bpd_f = fopen( bpd_file_name, "r" );

if ( bpd_f == 0 )
{
printf( "\n\n   Error opening %s", bpd_file_name );
exit( 1 );
}
fseek( bpd_f, 4, 0 );
fread( bpd_set, sizeof( int ), bpd_set_size, bpd_f );
fclose( bpd_f );
bpd_file_loaded = 1;
}
if ( !( bpd_set[ branch_number / 32 ] >> branch_number % 32 & 1 ) )
{
bpd_set[ branch_number / 32 ] |= 1 << branch_number % 32;
bpd_f = fopen( bpd_file_name, "r+" );
fseek( bpd_f, 4, 0 );
fwrite( bpd_set, sizeof( int ), bpd_set_size, bpd_f );
fclose( bpd_f );
}
}
```

The branches in each file may be seen by examining the contents of the generated file1.bps and file2.bps as seen in the following listings. There are nine branches (labeled 0 to 8) in file1 and one branch (labeled 0) in file2. The inserted branch comments are shown in **boldface** in the two listings.

Instrumented Source File file1.bps

```
#include <stdio.h>

extern test();

main()
{ /*@0*/
    int i;
    char ch;

    printf( "\nEnter the value of i: " );
    scanf( "%d", &i );
    fflush( stdin );
    if ( i > 0 ) /*@1*/
        printf( "\ni > 0" );
    else /*@2*/
        printf( "\ni <= 0" );
    while ( i > 0 )

     { /*@3*/
        printf( "\ni = %d", i );
        printf( "\nEnter the value of i: " );
        scanf( "%d", &i );
        fflush( stdin );
    }
    printf( "\nEnter the value of i: " );
    scanf( "%d", &i );
    switch ( i )
    {
        case 1: /*@4*/ printf( "\ni is equal to 1\n" );
            break;
        case 2: /*@5*/ printf( "\ni is equal to 2\n" );
            break;
        case 3: /*@6*/ printf( "\n is equal to 3\n" );
            break;
        default: /*@7*/ printf( "\ni has some value\n" );
    }
    fflush( stdin );
    printf( "\n\nDo you wish to invoke the function test? (y/n)? " );
    scanf( "%c", &ch );
    fflush( stdin );
    if ( ch == 'y' ) /*@8*/
        test();
}
```

Instrumented Source File file2.bps

```
void test()
{ /*@0*/
    printf( "\nIn function test.\n" );
}
```

Prior to execution of the software system, the view option may be exercised to test that none of the identified branches have been executed. The resulting file1.bpv and file2.bpv are shown in the following listings.

View File file1.bpv *Before Running Software System*

```
#include <stdio.h>

extern test();

main()
{
@@@@@@@@@@ BRANCH NOT EXECUTED @@@@@@@@@@
    int i;
    char ch;
    printf( "\nEnter the value of i: " );
    scanf( "%d", &i );
    fflush( stdin );
    if ( i > 0 )
@@@@@@@@@@ BRANCH NOT EXECUTED @@@@@@@@@@
        printf( "\ni > 0" );
    else
@@@@@@@@@@ BRANCH NOT EXECUTED @@@@@@@@@@
        printf( "\ni <= 0" );
    while ( i > 0 )
    {
@@@@@@@@@@ BRANCH NOT EXECUTED @@@@@@@@@@
        printf( "\ni = %d", i );
        printf( "\nEnter the value of i: " );
        scanf( "%d", &i );
        fflush( stdin );
    }
    printf( "\nEnter the value of i: " );
    scanf( "%d", &i );
    switch ( i )
    {
        case 1:
@@@@@@@@@@ BRANCH NOT EXECUTED @@@@@@@@@@
            printf( "\ni is equal to 1\n" );
        break;
        case 2:
@@@@@@@@@@ BRANCH NOT EXECUTED @@@@@@@@@@
            printf( "\ni is equal to 2\n" );
        break;
        case 3:
@@@@@@@@@@ BRANCH NOT EXECUTED @@@@@@@@@@
            printf( "\n is equal to 3\n" );
        break;
        default:
@@@@@@@@@@ BRANCH NOT EXECUTED @@@@@@@@@@
            printf( "\ni has some value\n" );
    }
```

(continues)

```
    fflush( stdin );
    printf( "\n\nDo you wish to invoke the function test? (y/n)? " );
    scanf( "%c", &ch );
    fflush( stdin );
    if ( ch == 'y' )
@@@@@@@@@@ BRANCH NOT EXECUTED @@@@@@@@@@
        test();
}
```

View File file2.bpv *Before Running Software System*

```
void test()
{
@@@@@@@@@@ BRANCH NOT EXECUTED @@@@@@@@@@
    printf( "\nIn function test.\n" );
}
```

The files file1.c and file2.c are next compiled, linked, and run. The inputs are entered as follows. User responses are given in boldface.

```
Example Run-time Session

Enter the value of i: 2

i > 0
i = 2
Enter the value of i: -5

Enter the value of i: 3

is equal to 3

Do you wish to invoke the function test? (y/n)? y

In function test.
```

Next, the view option of CBPA is again invoked to create an updated view file on both file1 and file2. Results are shown in the following listings. Note that several of the branches have now been executed. A walk-through of the preceding run-time session will verify the accuracy of the results.

View File file1.bpv *After Running Software System*

```
#include <stdio.h>

extern test();

main()
{
    int i;
    char ch;
```

```
    printf( "\nEnter the value of i: " );
    scanf( "%d", &i );
    fflush( stdin );
    if ( i > 0 )
        printf( "\ni > 0" );
    else
@@@@@@@@@@ BRANCH NOT EXECUTED @@@@@@@@@@
        printf( "\ni <= 0" );
    while ( i > 0 )
    {
        printf( "\ni = %d", i );
        printf( "\nEnter the value of i: " );
        scanf( "%d", &i );
        fflush( stdin );
    }
    printf( "\nEnter the value of i: " );
    scanf( "%d", &i );
    switch ( i )
    {
        case 1:
@@@@@@@@@@ BRANCH NOT EXECUTED @@@@@@@@@@
            printf( "\ni is equal to 1\n" );
            break;
        case 2:
@@@@@@@@@@ BRANCH NOT EXECUTED @@@@@@@@@@
            printf( "\ni is equal to 2\n" );
            break;
        case 3: printf( "\n is equal to 3\n" );
            break;
        default:
@@@@@@@@@@ BRANCH NOT EXECUTED @@@@@@@@@@
            printf( "\ni has some value\n" );
    }
    fflush( stdin );
    printf( "\n\nDo you wish to invoke the function test? (y/n)? " );
    scanf( "%c", &ch );
    fflush( stdin );
    if ( ch == 'y' )
        test();
}
```

View File file2.bpv *After Running Software System*

```
void test()
{
    printf( "\nIn function test.\n" );
}
```

The software system is to be modified as part of a maintenance update. This change requires modifications to the component file1. It is desired to modify this software component by removing the branches labeled 5 and 8 (along with its associated prompt to the user) and by adding an additional branch with a for loop. The modified file file1.bps is shown next. After modification, file1.bps is renamed file1.c. The new branch with a for loop is shown in boldface.

Maintenance: Modified file1.bps

```
#include <stdio.h>

extern test();

main()
{ /*@0*/
    int i;
    char ch;

    printf( "\nEnter the value of i: " );
    scanf( "%d", &i );
    fflush( stdin );
    if ( i > 0 ) /*@1*/
        printf( "\ni > 0" );
    else /*@2*/
    printf( "\ni <= 0" );
    while ( i > 0 )
    { /*@3*/
        printf( "\ni = %d", i );
        printf( "\nEnter the value of i: " );
        scanf( "%d", &i );
        fflush( stdin );
    }
    printf( "\nEnter the value of i: " );
    scanf( "%d", &i );
    switch ( i )
    {
        case 1: /*@4*/ printf( "\ni is equal to 1\n" );
            break;
        case 3: /*@6*/ printf( "\n is equal to 3\n" );
            break;
        default: /*@7*/ printf( "\ni has some value\n" );
    }
    for ( i = 1; i < 6; i++ ) printf( "\n For loop i = %d", i );
}
```

After the modified file is renamed file1.c and instrumented again, the newly generated file1.bps identifies all current branch numbers and is given in the following listing. Note that the new branch (shown in **boldface**) is given the identification number 9 and not 5 or 8. Deleted branches 5 and 8 are no longer present, and their branch numbers will not be reused.

Modified Source File file1.bps *Before Running Software System*

```
#include <stdio.h>

extern test();

main()
{ /*@0*/

    int i;
    char ch;

    printf( "\nEnter the value of i: " );
    scanf( "%d", &i );
    fflush( stdin );
    if ( i > 0 ) /*@1*/

        printf( "\ni > 0" );
    else /*@2*/

        printf( "\ni <= 0" );
    while ( i > 0 )
    { /*@3*/

        printf( "\ni = %d", i );
        printf( "\nEnter the value of i: " );
        scanf( "%d", &i );
        fflush( stdin );
    }
    printf( "\nEnter the value of i: " );
    scanf( "%d", &i );
    switch ( i )
    {
        case 1: /*@4*/
    printf( "\ni is equal to 1\n" );
            break;
        case 3: /*@6*/
    printf( "\n is equal to 3\n" );
            break;
        default: /*@7*/
    printf( "\ni has some value\n" );
    }
    for ( i = 1; i < 6; i++ ) /*@9*/ printf( "\n For loop i = %d", i );
}
```

Exercising the view option on the newly instrumented and modified file1 before any further execution of the software system indicates that previous testing data are preserved and that the new branch is not yet executed. The following listing shows file1.bpv under these conditions.

Modified View File file1.bpv *Before Running Software System*

```
#include <stdio.h>

extern test();

main()
{
    int i;
    char ch;

    printf( "\nEnter the value of i: " );
    scanf( "%d", &i );
    fflush( stdin );
    if ( i > 0 )
        printf( "\ni > 0" );
    else
@@@@@@@@@@ BRANCH NOT EXECUTED @@@@@@@@@@

        printf( "\ni <= 0" );
    while ( i > 0 )
    {

        printf( "\ni = %d", i );
        printf( "\nEnter the value of i: " );
        scanf( "%d", &i );
        fflush( stdin );
    }
    printf( "\nEnter the value of i: " );
    scanf( "%d", &i );
    switch ( i )
    {
        case 1:
@@@@@@@@@@ BRANCH NOT EXECUTED @@@@@@@@@@

    printf( "\ni is equal to 1\n" );
            break;
        case 3: printf( "\n is equal to 3\n" );
            break;
        default:
@@@@@@@@@@ BRANCH NOT EXECUTED @@@@@@@@@@

    printf( "\ni has some value\n" );
    }
    for ( i = 1; i < 6; i++ )
@@@@@@@@@@ BRANCH NOT EXECUTED @@@@@@@@@@
printf( "\n For loop i = %d", i );
}
```

Exercising the view option on the newly instrumented and modified file1 after recompiling of file1.c, and relinking and execution of the software system indicate that the new branch has been executed as expected. The following listing shows file1.bpv under these conditions.

Modified View File file1.bpv *After Running Software System*

```
#include <stdio.h>

extern test();

main()
{
    int i;
    char ch;
    printf( "\nEnter the value of i: " );
    scanf( "%d", &i );
    fflush( stdin );
    if ( i > 0 )

        printf( "\ni > 0" );
    else

        printf( "\ni <= 0" );
    while ( i > 0 )
    {
        printf( "\ni = %d", i );
        printf( "\nEnter the value of i: " );
        scanf( "%d", &i );
        fflush( stdin );
    }
    printf( "\nEnter the value of i: " );
    scanf( "%d", &i );
    switch ( i )
    {
        case 1:
@@@@@@@@@@ BRANCH NOT EXECUTED @@@@@@@@@@
    printf( "\ni is equal to 1\n" );
            break;
        case 3: printf( "\n is equal to 3\n" );
            break;
        default: printf( "\ni has some value\n" );
    }
    for ( i = 1; i < 6; i++ ) printf( "\n For loop i = %d", i );
}
```

6.2 OBJECT-ORIENTED DESIGN

6.2.1 Design Objective

An object-oriented design is to be accomplished for the C-language branch path analyzer. The design is to use the principles of object-oriented design and is to be independent of the choice of implementation language. The design is to be developed using a class hierarchy that promotes reusability.

The approach used in this design is given by the following steps. The steps are chronological; however, the actual design process usually requires considerable refinement and iteration of these steps.

1. Develop logic and pseudocode for performing the major functions of the software system. For the C-language branch path analyzer this means development of pseudocode for the instrument, strip, and view options.
2. Define the major objects that are part of a solution to the problem. Describe the private data that these objects will need.
3. Define the supporting objects that are part of a solution to the problem. They include the private data of the objects identified in step 2 and other fundamental objects that are part of most problem solutions (for example, strings, numbers, characters, and streams).
4. Define actions to be taken on or by the objects to effect a solution to the problem. The approach is to begin with high-level messages and refine the actions to lower levels. For example, the message instrument sent to object aCBPA suggests the instrumenting option is being performed. This is a high-level message whose intent is clear and without cumbersome details.
5. Develop a hierarchy of new classes required for a solution. Show the hierarchy of any existing or new supporting classes. Indicate supporting objects that are to be included as private data for each new class.
6. Verify the design using a prototyping object-oriented language (Smalltalk is by far the best for this activity). This step will produce a working software system in the prototyping language. At a minimum it should verify the primary logic of the pseudocode. Cosmetic details should be left for the final implementation phase of the software development.

In the following sections, we will describe these steps by example.

6.2.2 Design Logic

This section presents the logic for the object-oriented design. Specifically, it gives pseudocode logic for the three major options of the branch path analysis: intrument, view, and strip. The pseudocode is a mixture of terms found in elementary programming texts and of Smalltalk syntax.

Instrumenting a Source File. The first step in the branch path analysis for a C-language software system is to identify and calibrate the branch paths in specified source files. This is referred to as the instrument option. Its logic is based on recognizing key tokens in the C-language source file that begin and end branch paths.

The instrument option consists of the following operations.

1. Scan the C-language source file for key tokens until an end of file is reached. Use the key tokens to identify branches.
2. Create a .bps file with all branches identified by a special comment block.
3. Create a new source file (filename.c) that has inserted calibration code. This new file must be compiled and linked with the software system for branch path analysis to be performed on the software component represented by the file.

4. Update an existing .bpd file or create a new .bpd file for storing information on which branch paths have been executed.

The following listings give the top-level algorithm for the instrument option and supporting algorithms for encoding, marking branches, and scanning the source code file. The scanning algorithm produces a .bps file, an updated or new .bpd file, and a calibrated source file for insertion into the new encoded source file. It is based on ten key tokens for identifying branch paths. The outer loop seeks these key tokens and takes appropriate action. They are if, while, for, else, }, switch, case, default, {, and #define. The instrumented file contains a beginning block of code, BeginCode, followed by the instrumented source code, followed by an ending block of code, EndCode.

Instrumenting C-Language Source Files for BPA

```
for eachComponentToInstrument
    encode: aComponent
endFor.
```

Encoding a C-Language Software Component for BPA; Pseudocode for Method encode: aComponent

```
newSourceFile ← openNewFileForWriting.
encodeResult ← scanAndMarkBranchesFor: aComponent.
    "encodeResult is an association with
        key = number of branches and
        value = the encoded source as a string."
newSourceFile
    addModifiedBeginCodeUsing: encodeResult key;
    addCalibratedSourceFrom: encodeResult value;
    addEndCode.
```

Marking Branches for a Software Component for BPA; Pseudocode for scanAndMark-BranchesFor: aComponent

```
scanner ← CScanner on: aComponent using: dataDirectory.
scanner scan. "Does the actual encoding"
return
    key: scanner branchNumber
    value: scanner contents.
```

Scanning a C-Language Source File for BPA; Pseudocode for scan

"There are 6 major loops labeled as L1 through L6. Loop L1 has three minor loops, labeled La through Lc. These loops are referenced in the appropriate messages in Section 2.4.1." Most of the complexity for the software system lies in this algorithm.

```
    create bpsFile.
    create codeStream.
    newPos ← 0.
```

```
              bpdFile exists
                 ifTrue: [ branchNumber ← numberOfExistingBranches ]
                 ifFalse: [ branchNumber ← 0.
                          create bpdFile ].
          inFile ← C-component source file.
          loop "major loop"
              oldPos ← newPos.
              tc ← getNextNonStringNonCommentToken.
              copy.
              whileFlag ← false.
"L1"      if ( tc = if or tc = while
                   or tc = for or tc = else )
              if ( tc = while )
                  whileFlag ← true
              endif.
              if ( tc ~= else )
                  skipPastExpression
              endif.
              commentFlag ← lookAheadForOldBranch.
              commentFlag
                  ifTrue: [ number ← getOldBranchNumber ].
              tc ← getNextNonStringNonCommentToken.
"La"      if ( tc = ; )        "do-while"
                  if ( whileFlag )
                      commentFlag
                          ifFalse: [ number ← branchNumber increment ].
                      calibrate: number adding: ".
                  endif.
"Lb"      elsif ( tc = { )
                  copy.
                  commentFlag ← lookAheadForOldBranch.
                  commentFlag
                      ifTrue: [ number ← getOldBranchNumber ]
                      ifFalse:[ number ← branchNumber incremented ].
                  calibrate: number adding: ';\n{' .
"Lc"      else
                  if ( tc ~= while and tc ~= do and tc ~= if
                      and tc ~= for and tc ~= switch )
                  add: '\n{' to: codeStream.
                  commentFlag
                      ifFalse: [ number ← branchNumber incremented ].
                  calibrate: number adding: ';' .
                      loop "get past next ; "
                          tc ← getNextNonStringNonCommentToken
                      while ( tc ~= ; ).
                      copy.
                      add: '\n}' to: codeStream.
```

```
                      else
                          newPos ← oldPos.
                      end if else.
                  end if elsif else. "end L1"
"L2"   elsif ( tc = } )
           add: '\n}' to: codeStream.     "end L2"
"L3"   elsif ( tc = switch )
           loop "get past first { "
               tc ← getNextNonStringNonCommentToken
           while ( tc ~= { ).
           copy.
           add: '\n{' to: codeStream.     "end L3"
"L4"   elsif ( tc = case or tc = default )
           loop "get past the : "
               tc ← getNextNonStringNonCommentToken
           while ( tc ~= : ).
           copy.
           commentFlag ← lookAheadForOldBranch.
           commentFlag
               ifTrue: [ number ← getOldBranchNumber ]
               ifFalse:[ number ← branchNumber increment ].
           calibrate: number adding: ';\n'. "end L4"
"L5"   elsif ( tc = { )
           findMatchingBrace.
           isStructOrUnion
               ifTrue: [ copy ]
               ifFalse: [
                   commentFlag ← lookAheadForOldBranch.
                   commentFlag
                       ifTrue: [ number ← getOldBranchNumber ]
                       ifFalse:[ number ← branchNumber increment ].
                   calibrate: number adding: ';\n{'. ]   "end L5"
"L6"   elsif ( tc = # )
           tc ← getNextNonStringNonCommentToken.
           tc = define
               ifTrue: [ skipEntireMacro ].
           copy. "end L6"
       while (inFile not atEnd). "end major loop"
```

Viewing a Source File. The view option reads the .bps file to identify branches and then reads the .bpd file to determine which branches have been exercised. It creates a new .bpv file containing source code and inserts a message as a comment into branches that have not been executed. The following listings give the high-level pseudocode for the view option and the details for viewing a single component of the software system.

High-Level Pseudocode for the view *Option; Pseudocode for* runViewUsing: driverFile

```
for eachComponentToView
    view: aComponent
endFor.
```

Pseudocode for Viewing a single Component File; Pseudocode for view: aComponent

```
(CScanner view: aComponent using: dataDirectory) createView.
"Details of createView"
inStream ← readStreamOn: 'aComponent.bps' .
outStream ← writeStreamOn: 'aComponent.bpv' .
loop
    findNextBranchComment.
    copyUpToCommentInto: outStream.
    branchIsExecuted ifFalse: [ copyNotExecCommentInto: outStream ].
    skipOverBranchComment.
while ( inStream not eof ).
copyToEOFInto: outStream.
```

Stripping a Source File. The strip option reads the .bps file as input and creates a new .bps file with all branch comments removed. It produces a C-language source file that retains all formatting of the original source file before instrumentation.

Pseudocode for the strip *Option; Pseudocode for* strip

```
inStream ← readStreamOn: 'aComponent.bps' .
outString ← inStream contentsOfEntireFile.
outString containsBranchComment
    whileTrue: [ replace: branchComment with: nullString ].
inStream close.
outStream ← writeStreamOn: 'aComponent.bps'. "Overwrites existing file"
outStream nextPutAll: outString.
outStream close.
```

6.2.3 Object-Oriented Design Details

This design is based on the statement of the problem and the list of specifications as given in the requirements and specifications in Section 6.1. A number of objects can be identified that are part of an object-oriented solution to the C-language branch path analyzer. These are listed and described next in two categories.

The first category represents major objects that are part of the solution. These objects will be instances of new classes. The second category represents objects that serve a supporting role to the solution. They will typically be private data to the major objects. Supporting objects will be instances of existing classes or of new classes. This approach represents a topdown design.

Primary Objects. The following major objects are identified as being part of the solution to a C-language branch path analyzer. Each one represents an instance of a new class. The hierarchy for these new classes is presented in Section 6.2.4.

1. objectSoftwareTesting. This object is an abstract object that represents test software systems. It provides an umbrella for different kinds of software testing. This object is an instance of an abstract superclass (SoftwareTesting) for software testing. Its private data include an object, softwareSystem, representing the software system that is to be tested.

2. aBranchPathAnalyzer. This object is an abstract object representing branch path analysis test software systems. Its private data include objects instrumentedSoftware and dataDirectory, representing instrumented software components and a directory for saving test results, respectively. Protocol for this object includes operations common to branch path analysis for software systems implemented in any appropriate language. The class of this object (BranchPathAnalyzer) will be a subclass of the class SoftwareTesting.

3. aCBPA. This object is a test software system for branch path analysis of C-language software systems. Protocol for this object includes operations specific to branch path analysis for software systems implemented in the C language. The class of this object (CBPA) will be a subclass of class BranchPathAnalyzer.

4. aSoftwareSystem. This object defines the components of a software system or of a subset of a software system. Its private data include an object, components, that is the list of components in a software system. This object is used as private data for the software testing object (objectSoftwareTesting) described in object 1. It has application to other problem solutions that reference software systems. It will be an instance of a new class (Software-System).

5. aCSoftwareSystem. This object defines the components or a subset of a C-language software system. The class of this object (CSoftwareSystem) is a subclass of the class SoftwareSystem.

6. aTestScanner. This object is an abstract object, with class (TestScanner), that provides the protocol for scanning source code of a specific software system for the purposes of testing. In the process of scanning the source code, modifications are made to the code for test purposes. Details of the modifications are dependent on the language and the specific test. Private data of this object include an input stream, inStream, on the source code and an output stream, outStream, on the modified source code.

7. aCScanner. This object scans C-language source code for the purpose of testing. In the process of scanning the source code, modifications are made to the code for branch path analysis. A number of private data objects are used to facilitate the scanning and encoding process. The class of this object (CScanner) is a subclass of the class TestScanner.

Supporting Objects. Supporting objects for each of the major objects given in the previous section are described here. These supporting objects are private data for the major objects. In addition there are other supporting objects required in the design that are not private data of one of the primary objects. These are described in paragraph 8.

1. *Supporting objects for major object* objectSoftwareTesting. One object, aSoftwareSystem, which is also a major object, defines the components of a software system that is to be tested. Details of aSoftwareSystem are dependent on the specific language being tested.

2. *Supporting objects for major object* aBranchPathAnalyzer. One supporting object (aSoftwareSystem) is inherited from objectSoftwareTesting. Three new objects support branch path analysis as private data: (a) instrumentedSoftware is also a major object

(aCSoftwareSystem) that defines the components of the system that are to be instrumented for branch path analysis, (b) dataDirectory is a String defining the directory path for saving test results, and (c) fileToStripOrView is a String that is the filename for a file to be stripped or viewed.

3. *Supporting objects for major object* aCBPA. One object (aSoftwareSystem) is inherited from objectSoftwareTesting. Three objects (instrumentedSoftware, dataDirectory, and fileToStripOrView) are inherited from aBranchPathAnalyzer. Three new objects support the object aCBPA: (a) BeginCode is a String that includes the C-language calibration code inserted at the beginning of all instrumented files, (b) EndCode is a String that is the C-language calibration code inserted at the end of all instrumented files, and (c) NotExecuted is a String containing the not executed message inserted by the view option into branches that have not been executed.

4. *Supporting objects for major object* aSoftwareSystem. One supporting object, components, is a Set of filename strings defining the components of aSoftwareSystem.

5. *Supporting objects for major object* aCSoftwareSystem. None other than object components, inherited from aSoftwareSystem.

6. *Supporting objects for major object* aTestScanner. Two new objects as private data support this object: (a) inStream is an instance of FileStream, which is a file stream on the source code to be scanned for testing, and (b) outStream is a WriteStream on the modified source code.

7. *Supporting objects for major object* aCScanner. Two objects (inStream and outStream) are inherited from superclass object aTestScanner. Thirteen new objects support aCScanner as private data: (a) char is a Character object, (b) position is an Integer representing the offset into inStream, (c) tokenType is a Symbol that defines the type of char, (d) whileFlag is a Boolean, (e) commentFlag is a Boolean set to true when a branch comment is encountered, (f) number is an Integer that is either an old or new branch number, (g) branchNumber is an Integer that is the running count of new branches, (h) bpsStream is a FileStream on the .bps file, (i) executedBranches is a Set representing the executed branch numbers of a software component, (j) TypeTable is an Array of 256 symbols that define types for the 256 characters, (k) KeyTokens is a Set of symbols defining the key token types for char, and (l) CR is a String containing the Character for carriage return.

8. *Other supporting objects*. In addition to the supporting instance variables in items 1 to 7, there is need for the following supporting object types as well: (a) String literals are required for equality testing, (b) Character literals are required for equality testing, (c) objects representing true and false are required to support class Boolean, (d) Association objects that pair keys and values are useful but not essential, (e) a FileDirectory object or its equivalent is required for checking the existence of files on the current directory, (f) an iteration object is required for most problem solutions (may be a BlockContext as used in Smalltalk or its equivalent), and (g) Number literals are required for tracking branch numbers (bit manipulation on integers is required for optimum representation of a Set).

Actions to Be Taken on or by Objects. This section defines the key messages to which the objects just described must respond. These key messages form the basis for an initial design of the software system. Building from these key messages and the already described objects, a design is prototyped using Smalltalk. During the process of prototyping and testing, a refined design is accomplished. Each message is identified as either a class method or an instance method.

1. *Messages to create and use objects in class* SoftwareTesting. This is an abstract superclass for all software testing objects. There are no key methods in this class.

2. *Messages to create and use objects in class* BranchPathAnalyzer. A branch path analyzer is a specific kind of test object that must provide methods for creating instances for instrumentation, viewing, and stripping. Specific details are subclass responsibility and depend on the native language of the software system to be tested. The following key methods are identified.

— instrumentUsing: aFile—Class method. Create an instance of BranchPath-Analyzer for instrumenting a source file. Parameter aFile is a String that is the full name of the driver file.
— viewUsing: fileToView with: driverFile—Class method. Create an instance of BranchPathAnalyzer for viewing the test results of fileToView (a String) using driverFile (a String).
— stripUsing: aFile. Class method. Create an instance of BranchPathAnalyzer for stripping all instrumentation from aFile (a String).
— instrument—Instance method. Initiate the instrument option. Implement as subclass responsibility.
— runViewUsing: driverFile—Instance method. Initiate the view option. Implement as subclass responsibility.
— strip—Instance method. Initiate the strip option. Implement as subclass responsibility.

3. *Messages to create and use objects in class* CBPA. An instance of CBPA is a C-language branch path analyzer. It must implement key methods inherited from its superclass that were implemented as subclass responsibility. In addition, it must initialize values for its own and inherited class variables or instance variables. The following key methods are identified.

— initialize—Class method. Establish values for class variables BeginCode, EndCode, and NotExecuted.
— initialize: fromFile—Instance method. Initialize instance variables for a new instance of CBPA using information in the driver file fromFile.
— instrument—Instance method. Instrument all specified components of a C-language software system. Inherited from BranchPathAnalyzer as subclass responsibility.

— runViewUsing: driverFile—Instance method. Create a view file for a specified component using driverFile. Inherited from BranchPathAnalyzer as subclass responsibility.

— strip—Instance method. Strip all instrumentation from a specified file. Inherited from BranchPathAnalyzer as subclass responsibility.

— encode: aComponent—Instance method. Create an encoded source file that consists of the BeginCode, instrumented source file, and EndCode. Use method scanAndMarkBranchesFor: to create the instrumented source file.

— scanAndMarkBranchesFor: aComponent—Instance method. Create a CScanner, have it scan and mark all branches in source file aComponent.

4. *Messages to create and use objects in class* SoftwareSystem. This is an abstract superclass for all software system objects. There are no key methods in this class.

5. *Messages to create and use objects in class* CSoftwareSystem. Instances of this class represent C-language software systems. Typically a C-language software system is defined by a list of file names. Key methods for this class include the following.

— new: fromFile—Class method. Create an instance of CSoftwareSystem using file names contained in the driver file fromFile. Send message for establishing instance variable components.

— setComponents: fromFile—Instance method. Create a Set as components that contains filename strings for the software components of a C-language software system.

— getComponents—Instance method. Answer the Set that is components.

6. *Messages to create and use objects in class* TestScanner. This is an abstract superclass for all software testing scanner objects. There are no key methods in this class.

7. *Messages to create and use objects in class* CScanner. The purpose of an instance of CScanner is to scan a source file, identify all branches, create an instrumented source file, create a .bps file with all branches marked by comments, and create or update a .bpd file. The key methods in this class include the following.

— initialize—Class method. Initialize values of CR, TypeTable, and KeyTokens.

— on: aComponent using: dataDirectory—Class method. Create an instance for instrumentation of aComponent with data file to be stored in directory dataDirectory.

— view: aComponent using: dataDirectory—Class method. Create an instance for viewing the test results of aComponent based on the data file in dataDirectory.

— initFor: aComponent and: dataDirectory—Instance method. Initialize instance variables for a new instance created for instrumentation.

— initViewFor: aComponent and: dataDirectory—Instance method. Initialize instance variables for a new instance created for viewing.

— scan—Instance method. Scan inStream, create an instrumented source file, a .bps file, and a new or updated .bpd file. This is the primary instrumentation method in this class.

— findBranches—Instance method. A method called by scan that finds tokens and executes the appropriate tokenLoop method.

— creatOrUpdateBPD—Instance method. Creates a new .bpd file or updates an existing .bpd file to represent all branches in a software component.

— createView—Instance method. Create a view file, .bpv, using the .bps and .bpd files for a specified software component.

— calibrateAndAdd: aString—Instance method. Add calibration to the .c source file and add comment branch identifiers to the .bps file for a specified component.

— copy—Instance method. Copy text from the original source file into both the .c encoded source file and the .bps file.

— tokenLoop methods—Instance methods for processing key tokens. There will be one method for each type of token that must be processed.

— testing methods—Instance methods for testing token types. There will be one method for testing the occurrence of each token type.

6.2.4 An Initial Hierarchy of Classes

The hierarchy of classes presented in Fig. 6.1 is a part of the design for the C-language branch path analyzer. New classes specific to the solution are given in boldface. Instance variables are listed in parentheses for each new class. Supporting classes required by the solution that are not specific to this problem solution are also shown in bold typeface. Connecting classes are shown in regular typeface. The illustrated hierarchy for supporting classes is consistent with the Smalltalk class hierarchy (as distributed by ParcPlace Systems).

New Classes Specific to This Design. This section presents a more detailed design of the new classes developed to support solution of the C-language branch path analyzer. The design is prototyped, tested, and refined in Smalltalk. The following class descriptions are a result of the Smalltalk rapid prototyping.

SoftwareTesting

Hierarchy: Object—SoftwareTesting

Comment: This is an abstract superclass for a number of testing related subclasses. It has no instances.

Shared Data: None

Private Data: softwareSystem, an instance of SoftwareSystem or one of its subclasses that identifies the components of a software system. Implementation is subclass responsibility. Default is an empty software system.

Class Methods: None

Instance Methods: None

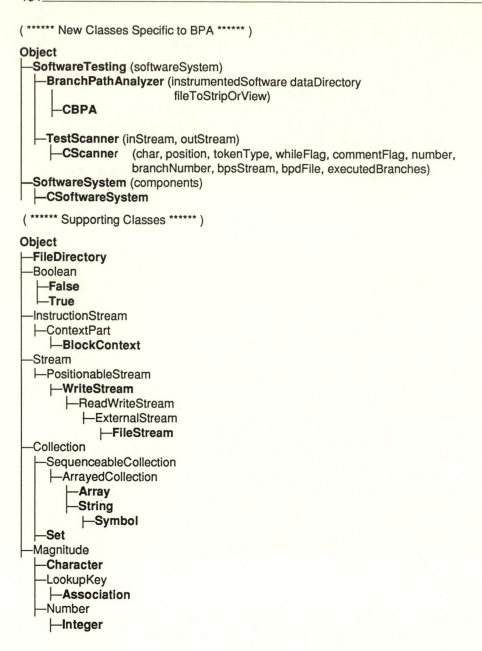

(****** New Classes Specific to BPA ******)

Object
—**SoftwareTesting** (softwareSystem)
  —**BranchPathAnalyzer** (instrumentedSoftware dataDirectory
                fileToStripOrView)
    —**CBPA**

  —**TestScanner** (inStream, outStream)
    —**CScanner**   (char, position, tokenType, whileFlag, commentFlag, number,
                branchNumber, bpsStream, bpdFile, executedBranches)
—**SoftwareSystem** (components)
  —**CSoftwareSystem**

(****** Supporting Classes ******)

Object
—**FileDirectory**
—Boolean
  —**False**
  —**True**
—InstructionStream
  —ContextPart
    —**BlockContext**
—Stream
  —PositionableStream
    —**WriteStream**
      —ReadWriteStream
        —ExternalStream
          —**FileStream**
—Collection
  —SequenceableCollection
    —ArrayedCollection
      —**Array**
      —**String**
        —**Symbol**
  —**Set**
—Magnitude
  —**Character**
  —LookupKey
    —**Association**
  —Number
    —**Integer**

Figure 6.1 _____

Hierarchy of Classes for C-Language Branch Path Analyzer.

BranchPathAnalyzer
 Hierarchy: Object—SoftwareTesting—BranchPathAnalyzer
 Comment: This is an abstract superclass of all classes that perform branch path analysis
   on the software components in a specific language.
 Shared Data: None
 Private Data: instrumentedSoftware, an instance of SoftwareSystem or one of its
   subclasses. Default is an empty software system. Each subclass has
   responsibility for identifying the components to be instrumented. Instrumented components are those that are to be included in a branch path
   analysis. This instance variable must be a subset of instance variable
   softwareSystem inherited from class SoftwareTesting.

   dataDirectory, an instance of String that is the complete directory path
   for storing data files with results of branch path analysis testing.

   fileToStripOrView, an instance of String that is the filename of a file
   to be stripped or viewed.
 Class Methods: Three methods in one category.
  BranchPathAnalyzer class methodsFor: 'instance creation'
  instrumentUsing: aFile
   "Create an instance of me for instrumentation using aFile as the driver"
  stripUsing: aFile
   "Create an instance of me for stripping aFile"
  viewUsing: fileToView with: driverFile
   "Create an instance of me for viewing"
 Instance Methods: Seven methods in three categories.
  BranchPathAnalyzer methodsFor: 'execution'
  instrument
   "Subclass should implement"
  run: mode
   "Initiate an instance of me as an instrumentation or stripping version"
  runViewUsing: driverFile
   "Mark the indicated file for viewing"
  strip
   "Subclass should implement"
  BranchPathAnalyzer methodsFor: 'accessing'
  getFileToStripOrView
   "Answer fileToStripOrView"
  setFileToStripOrView: aFile
   "Set fileToStripOrView = aFile"
  BranchPathAnalyzer methodsFor: 'initialize'
  initialize: fromFile
   "Subclass should implement"

CBPA
 Hierarchy: Object—SoftwareTesting—BranchPathAnalyzer—CBPA
 Comment: Instances of this class represent objects that perform branch path

analysis on C-language source files. The minimal software component is a separate C-source file.

Shared Data: Three class variables.

BeginCode—an instance of String that is C-source code to be inserted at the beginning of instrumented source files.

EndCode—an instance of String that is C-source code to be inserted at the end of instrumented source files.

NotExecuted—an instance of String that is inserted into nonexecuted branches under the view option.

Private Data: None.

Class Methods: Four methods in two categories.

CBPA class methodsFor: 'class initialization'
initialize
   " Set values for BeginCode, EndCode, and NotExecuted "
CBPA class methodsFor: 'general inquiries'
beginCode
   "Answer BeginCode"
endCode
   "Answer EndCode"
notExecuted
   "Answer NotExecuted"

Instance Methods: Eight methods in two categories.

CBPA methodsFor: 'initialize'
initialize: fromFile
   "Initialize instance variables using fromFile"
CBPA methodsFor: 'execution'
encode: aComponent
   "Instrument the file represented by aComponent"
instrument
   "Instrument all the source files given in the instrumentedSoftware"
modify: aComponent using: aNumber
   "Modify the BeginCode to reflect number of branches"
runViewUsing: driverFile
   "Run cbpa in view mode for fileToStripOrView using the appropriate driver file"
scanAndMarkBranchesFor: aComponent
   "Read the input source file and append marked source to outFileStream"   "Answer an Association with key = number of branches and with value = a String containing the marked source code"
strip
   "Strip all branch path encoding from the .bps file"
view: aComponent
   "Create a view of an instrumented and tested component"

TestScanner
> *Hierarchy*: Object—SoftwareTesting—TestScanner
>
> *Comment*: This is an abstract superclass of scanners for identifying specific constructs in a software component that are important for a particular kind of testing. This class has no instances. Its purpose is dependent on the kind of testing being performed, and details are subclass responsibility.
>
> *Shared Data*: None.
>
> *Private Data*: inStream, an instance of FileStream that streams over an input source file for any given language.
>
> outStream, an instance of FileStream that streams over an output source file with parsing information included.
>
> *Class Methods*: None.
>
> *Instance Methods*: None.

CScanner
> *Hierarchy*: Object—SoftwareTesting—TestScanner—CScanner
>
> *Comment*: This class represents objects whose purpose is to scan C-language source code to identify branch paths for branch path testing.
>
> *Shared Data*: Three class variables.
>
> CR, an instance of String containing a single character for carriage return.
>
> KeyTokens, an instance of Set containing symbols representing the key tokens in the scanner logic.
>
> TypeTable, an instance of Array containing 256 symbols representing character ASCII values.
>
> *Private Data*: Thirteen instance variables.
>
> char, an instance of Character used to access the next character in the source code.
>
> position, an instance of Integer that is a reference position in File-Stream inStream. Its actual value may be different from the offset in inStream.
>
> tokenType, an instance of Symbol that characterizes the type of char.
>
> whileFlag, an instance of Boolean for tracking while logic.
>
> commentFlag, an instance of Boolean that is true when an existing branch comment is encountered.
>
> number, an instance of Integer that is the current branch number to be instrumented.
>
> branchNumber, an instance of Integer that is a running count of the highest branch number in an instrumented software component.
>
> bpsStream, an instance of FileStream on the .bps file.
>
> executedBranches, an instance of Set that contains numbers representing the executed branches of an instrumented software component.

Class Methods: Three methods in two categories.

CScanner class methodsFor: 'instance creation'

on: aComponent using: dataDirectory

"Create an instance of me on file aComponent.c for instrumenting"

view: aComponent using: dataDirectory

"Create an instance of me on file aComponent.bps for viewing "

CScanner class methodsFor: 'class initialization'

initialize

"Establish values for CR, TypeTable, and KeyTokens"

Instance Methods: Fifty-six methods in seven categories.

CScanner methodsFor: 'testing'

isCase

"Answer if next token is case"

isCharProhibited

"Answer true if character begins a set of special tokens"

isDefault

"Answer if next token is default"

isDefine

"Answer if next token is #define"

isDo

"Answer if next token is do"

isElse

"Answer if next token is else"

isFor

"Answer if next token is for"

isIf

"Answer if next token is if"

isSwitch

"Answer if next token is switch"

isWhile

"Answer if next token is while"

CScanner methodsFor: 'accessing'

addBranches: intOffset from: integer

"Extract one-bits from intOffset'th integer in bpdFile"

branchNumber

"Answer branchNumber"

outStream

"Answer outStream"

setExecutedBranches

"Read the .bpd file and determine which branches have been executed"

CScanner methodsFor: 'calibration'

calibrateAndAdd: aString

"Calibrate using old or new branch number. Add aString as suffix"

checkForStructOrUnion

"Answer true if a struct or union follows, else false"

checkMarker
   "Peek for /*@ in inStream"
copy
   "Copy from position to inStream position into outStream and bpsStream;
   Move position to inStream position"
createBPD: fileStream
   "Create and initialize a .bpd file"
createOrUpdateBPD
   "Create a new .bpd file or update existing one"
innerCalibrate
   "Calibration from pseudocode inner loop Lc"
updateBPD: fileStream
   "Create and initialize a .bpd file"
CScanner methodsFor: 'tokenLoops'
case
   "Loop 4 for CASE in pseudocode"
closeBrace
   "Loop 2 in pseudocode"
default
   "Loop 4 for DEFAULT in pseudocode"
define
   "Loop 6 for # in pseudocode"
doWhile
   "Calibrate a do—while loop under loop La of pseudocode"
else
   "Loop 1 for ELSE in pseudocode"
eof
for
   "Loop 1 for FOR in pseudocode"
genericLoop
   "Sub-loop under loop 1 in pseudocode"   " Process (IF, WHILE, FOR,
   ELSE)--> generic conditional loop abc in pseudocode"
if
   "Loop 1 for IF in pseudocode"
nestedBrace
   "Nested open brace in pseudocode loop Lb"
openBrace
   "Loop 5 for { in pseudocode"
switch
   "Loop 3 in pseudocode"
while
   "Loop 1 for WHILE in pseudocode"
CScanner methodsFor: 'viewing'
addComment
   "Add the non-executed comment to the .bpv fileStream"

copyView

"Copy from position to inStream position into outStream on .bpv file; Advance the value of position"

createView

"Scan the .bps file using the .bpd file to create a .bpv file"

isExecuted

"Check to see if branch has been executed and write outStream accordingly"

lineContainsToken

"Answer true if a token appears prior to CR"

offsetSpaces

"Answer number of spaces to maintain token offset"

CScanner methodsFor: 'scanning'

clearStringOrComment

"Current character is doubleQuote or slash" "Move inStream pointer beyond string or comment"

currentCharEndsStructOrUnion

"Return true if next char is $; or $, or begins an identifier followed by ; or = "

findBranches

"Find all branches and make entry into outStream"

getCharOfType: aType

"Find next occurrence of a character of type aType; Moves pointer in inStream"

getMatchingBrace

"Move inStream pointer to character beyond matching brace" "Skip over strings and comments"

getNextNonSeparator

"Find the next non-separator in inStream"

getOldBranchNumber

"Extract existing branch number; skip past the marker comment in inStream"

ourGetCharOfType: aType

"Find next occurrence of a character of type aType. Moves pointer in inStream" "Skip over strings and comments"

scan

"Scan inStream and create an instrumented source stream, a .bps file, and a new or updated .bpd file for a given component"

skipPastExpression

"Move inStream pointer to matching parenthesis" "Skip over strings and comments"

step: aNumber

"Advance the pointer in inStream by aNumber"

CScanner methodsFor: 'initialize'

getBranchNumber

"Answer the number of branches in existing data file as a 16-bit integer"

      initFor: aComponent and: dataDirectory
        "Initialize instance variables for instrumentation"
      initViewFor: aComponent and: dataDirectory
        "Initialize instance variables for creating view file"

SoftwareSystem

Hierarchy: Object—SoftwareSystem.

Comment: An abstract superclass of software systems in different languages. This class provides protocol common to all software systems. It has no instances. Definition of the private datum, components, is subclass responsibility.

Shared Data: None

Private Data: components, an instance of Collection or one of its subclasses that is a list of the software components for a specific software system.

Class Methods: None

Instance Methods: None

CSoftwareSystem

Hierarchy: Object—SoftwareSystems—CSoftwareSystem

Comment: This class represents instances of complete C-language software systems. Its inherited private data is a list of all the C-source files comprising the system.

Shared Data: None.

Private Data: None.

Class Methods: One method in one category.

    CSoftwareSystem class methodsFor: 'instance creation'
    new: fromFile
      "Create an instance whose components are defined in fromFile"

Instance Methods: Two methods in one category.

    CSoftwareSystem methodsFor: 'accessing'
    getComponents
      "Answer components"
    setComponents: fromFile
      "Build a set of software components using fromFile"

Supporting Classes. The following descriptive summaries of supporting classes include only those messages required in the design for the C-language branch path analyzer.

WriteStream

Hierarchy: Object—Stream—PositionableStream—WriteStream

Class Methods Used: One instance creation method is used.

    on: aCollection
      "Create a new instance streaming over aCollection"

Instance Methods Used: Three accessing methods are used.

    nextPutAll: aCollection
      "Add aCollection to the stream"
    nextPut: aCharacter
      "Add aCharacter to the stream"

contents
"Answer the collection over which the stream streams"

FileStream
Hierarchy: Object—Stream—PositionableStream—WriteStream—
ReadWriteStream—ExternalStream—FileStream
Class Methods Used: Two instance creation methods are used.
oldFileNamed: aFile
"Answer a fileStream on an existing file; Report an error if aFile does not exist"
newFileNamed: aFile
"Answer a fileStream on a new file; If aFile exists delete it and create a new version"
Instance Methods Used: Nineteen instance methods in four categories are used.
FileStream methodsFor: 'mode setting'
binary
"Set file mode to binary"
readOnly
"Set mode to read only"
readWrite
"Set mode to allow reading and writing"
FileStream methodsFor: 'accessing'
getString
"Answer the next string in a file. Strings are terminated by separators"
peek
"Answer what the next character in a file would be without moving the file pointer"
next
"Answer the next character in a file"
next: anInteger
"Answer the next anInteger characters in a file"
nextWord
"Answer the next two bytes in a file as an Integer"
contentsOfEntireFile
"Answer the complete string of characters in a file"
cr
"Append a carriage return to a file"
nextPutAll: aString
"Append aString to the fileStream beginning at the current pointer position"
nextWordPut: anInteger
"Append anInteger to a file using the next two bytes"
nextNumber: num1 put: aByte
"Append aByte into the next num1 bytes of a file"
FileStream methodsFor: 'positioning'
atEnd
"Answer true if file pointer is at end of file"

reset
>"Move the file pointer to the beginning of a file"

setToEnd
>"Move the file pointer to the end of a file"

position
>"Answer the current file pointer position"

position: anInteger
>"Set the file pointer position to anInteger"

FileStream methodsFor: 'file manipulation'

close
>"Close the fileStream"

FileDirectory

Hierarchy: Object—FileDirectory

Class Methods Used: One method is used.

> includesKey: aString
>>"Answer true if filename aString exists in the current directory"

Instance Methods Used: None.

Character

Hierarchy: Object—Magnitude—Character

Class Methods Used: One method is used for nonprintable characters.

> cr
>>"Answer the ASCII code for carriage return as a character"

Instance Methods Used: The primary use of characters is as literals and for testing equality.

> == aChar
>>"Answer true if receiver and aChar are the same object"

> asciiValue
>>"Answer the ascii code for the receiver"

String

Hierarchy: Object—Collection—SequenceableCollection—ArrayedCollection—String

Class Methods Used: One instance creation method is used.

> new
>>"Answer a new String"

Instance Methods Used: The following five methods for manipulating String objects and literals are used.

> , aString
>>"Answer a new string that is the concatenation of the receiver with aString"

> findString: aString startingAt: location
>>"Return the offset of aString in the receiver. Start searching at location"

> copyReplaceFrom: start to: stop with: aString
>>"Replace contents of receiver from start to stop with aString"

= aString
"Answer true if the receiver and aString have the same contents"
← aStringLiteral
"Set the contents of the receiver to aStringLiteral"

Symbol

Hierarchy: Object—Collection—SequenceableCollection—ArrayedCollection—String—Symbol
Class Methods Used: Symbols are used as literals.
Instance Methods Used: Symbols are unique. Their primary usage is in equality testing.
== aSymbol
"Answer true if the receiver and aSymbol are the same object"

Array

Hierarchy: Object—Collection—SequenceableCollection—ArrayedCollection—Array
Class Methods Used: One instance creation method is used.
new: size withAll: anObject
"Answer an array of size elements, all equal to anObject"
Instance Methods Used: Two accessing methods are used.
at: location put: anObject
"Place anObject in the array at location"
at: location
"Answer the object at location in the array"

Integer

Hierarchy: Object—Magnitude—Number—Integer
Class Methods Used: None are required unless literal support is not provided.
Instance Methods Used: Methods for arithmetic, comparison, and iteration are required.
+ aNumber
"Answer the sum of the receiver and aNumber"
- aNumber
"Answer the receiver minus aNumber"
// aNumber
"Answer the integer dviision of the receiver by aNumber"
= aNumber
"Answer true if the values of the receiver and aNumber are equal"
~= aNumber
"Answer true if the values of the receiver and aNumber are not equal"
> aNumber
"Answer true if the receiver is greater than aNumber"
to: stop do: aBlock
"Execute aBlock once for parameter between receiver and stop"

BlockContext

Hierarchy: Object—InstructionStream—ContextPart—BlockContext

Class Methods Used: Instance creation or literal support is required.

Instance Methods Used: Deferred or conditional execution methods are required for blocks.

whileFalse: aBlock
   "Execute aBlock until the receiver block evaluates to true"
value: paramValue
   "Evaluate receiver block with one parameter whose value is paramValue"

True

Hierarchy: Object—Boolean—True

Class Methods Used: Instance creation or literal support is required.

Instance Methods Used: Testing methods are required.

ifTrue: aBlock
   "Execute aBlock since the receiver is true"
ifFalse: aBlock
   "Do nothing since the receiver is true"

False

Hierarchy: Object—Boolean—False

Class Methods Used: Instance creation or literal support is required.

Instance Methods Used: Testing methods are required.

ifTrue: aBlock
   "Do nothing since receiver is false"
ifFalse: aBlock
   "Execute aBlock since receiver is false"

Set

Hierarchy: Object—Collection—Set

Class Methods Used: Instance creation is required.

new
   "Answer an empty set"

Instance Methods Used: Methods for adding and testing set membership are required. A method for iterating across all members of a set is also required.

add: anObject
   "Add anObject to the set"
includes: anObject
   "Answer true if anObject is a member of the receiver set"
do: aBlock
   "Execute aBlock one time for each member of the receiver set"

Association

Hierarchy: Object—Magnitude—LookupKey—Association

Class Methods Used: An instance creation method is required.

key: key value: value
   "Answer a new association with key = key and value = value"

Instance Methods Used: Two accessing methods are required.
key
    "Answer the key of the receiver"
value
    "Answer the value of the receiver"

6.3 SUCCESSES, FAILURES, AND AN EVALUATION OF THE OBJECT-ORIENTED DESIGN

6.3.1 Successes

This project was, in general, very successful. The following specific successes are presented as primary goals along with discussion.

* *Produce a successfully operating software system that meets the stated objectives of the C-language branch path analyzer*. This goal was achieved, and the software system has been verified as working correctly for all test cases examined to date. This includes a number of maintenance cycles on several C-language software systems.
* *Develop the software system using the object-oriented paradigm*. This goal has been achieved in three separate object-oriented languages. The initial design and prototyping were accomplished in Smalltalk-80. Since then, solutions have been implemented in C++ and in Objective-C. The Smalltalk system is best for prototyping an initial design because of the extensive support environment and instant verification of code using the interpretive properties of Smalltalk. The C-based versions are faster.
* *Evaluate a specific methodology for development of an object-oriented design and implementation*. The steps in this methodology were given earlier in this chapter. The method worked quite well for this software system.
* *Develop a software solution that lends itself to later expansion with reusable components*. This goal was achieved in the sense that abstract superclasses for software testing, for a software system, and for a source code scanner were developed. These classes provide an umbrella for new subclasses dealing with other languages and other testing methods. The bulk of the software system is, however, specific to the C-language branch path analyzer. In fact, over half of the code is contained in the protocol for the class, CScanner.

6.3.2 Failures

There were no actual failures in developing of the software system if one ignores the inevitable occurrence of implementation errors. The period of time for debugging the software system after its attainment of "run" status was relatively short. Partial credit goes to the use of an object-oriented design and partial credit goes to the powerful Smalltalk environment with its debugger, inspectors, and instant gratification for changes.

6.3.3 Evaluation of the Object-Oriented Design

An object-oriented design was achieved for the C-language branch path analyzer software system. It is difficult to place a quantitative measure on how "object-oriented" the design is. In terms of the primary objects, it is clear that the object aCScanner is a complicated object. Its list of protocol includes all the required variations on logic for identifying branch paths and inserting instrumentation coding.

A qualitative comparison of the object-oriented design and an earlier design done in C indicates that the object-oriented solution is much easier to explain to someone unfamiliar with the solution and is much easier to modify. For these reasons, we give the object-oriented design a very positive evaluation.

6.4 SUMMARY AND CONCLUSIONS

The C-language branch path analyzer was designed, developed, and implemented using an object-oriented methodology. The design consisted of several distinct steps as follows.

- State the problem and develop algorithms for accomplishing the primary task of identifying the branch paths in a C-language software system.
- Develop an algorithm and methods for marking branches in a C-language software system. Develop a function based on branch numbers that updates a data file containing a list of all branches in a C-language software system.
- Develop an algorithm for inserting a function call in each branch of the C-language software system that automatically updates a data file whenever the branch is entered.
- Develop an algorithm and methodology for accepting maintenance changes to the software system that automatically updates the list of branches, eliminates consideration for removed branches, and maintains results of any previous testing.
- Develop an algorithm for viewing the state of branch path execution that is simple, user-friendly, and difficult to misinterpret.
- Develop an algorithm and methodology for removing all instrumentation code from a software system that has undergone complete testing.
- Define the major objects in an object-oriented solution to the problem.
- Define properties of the major objects (as instance variables).
- Define secondary supporting objects that are essential to a solution
- Develop an initial hierarchy of classes representing all objects that are part of a solution.
- Identify key messages to which the primary and supporting objects must respond.
- Develop a high-level sequence of object-message expressions that solve the problem.
- Refine the high-level design until all functions are implemented. This includes addition of new lower-level messages and algorithm implementation.

The objectives for the software system were all achieved using the outlined object-oriented design methodology. The system has been tested using several C-language software systems with ongoing maintenance and has been successful.

It has been our experience that an object-oriented approach to software development fits some problems naturally and must be forced to fit other problems. Still other problems fall somewhere between a natural and a difficult fit. Even with this variation, we have found an object-oriented solution to always provide advantages.

The completed Smalltalk implementation has been used as a template for implementations in C++ and Objective-C of the C-language branch path analyzer. These implementations are similar to the Smalltalk design (with minor modifications to take advantage of the efficiency of C) and are considerably faster.

DoubleVision—A Foundation for Scientific Visualization

DoubleVision is a scientific application for the Apple® Macintosh®, written in Object Pascal using MacApp™, a class library for the Macintosh. DoubleVision provides the scientist with a facade of direct data manipulation, where the data is in the form of two parametric values that are associated with each point in a two-dimensional domain. DoubleVision is discussed in Chapter 5.

Color Plate 5.1 DoubleVision's Two Main Windows when the Application is Launched.

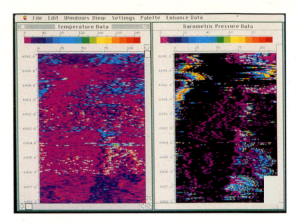

Color Plate 5.1

Color Plate 5.2 A DoubleVision Main Window as a Column Selection is Formed. The gray cursor indicates the mouse position when the mouse button was pressed. As the mouse is dragged, columns between that point and the current cursor position are highlighted. The black cursor indicates the mouse position when the mouse button is released, forming the selection.

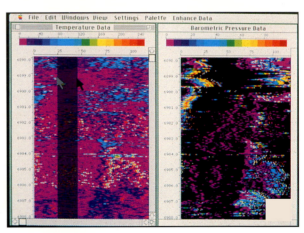

Color Plate 5.2

Color Plate 5.3 Column Selection Extension. Holding down the shift key when the mouse button is pressed adjusts whichever side of an existing column selection is closer to the right side. Thus the right side of the column selection will be adjusted. The new position for the adjusted side is determined by the mouse position when the mouse button is released. The position can be anywhere within the width of the main view, even to the left of the fixed side. The adjusted column is shown in the right window.

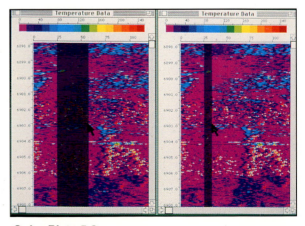

Color Plate 5.3